Investment
Psychology
Explained

Investment Psychology Explained

Classic Strategies to Beat the Markets

Martin J. Pring

John Wiley & Sons, Inc.

New York • Chichester • Brisbane • Toronto • Singapore

Copyright © 1993 by Martin J. Pring.
Published by John Wiley & Sons, Inc.

Library of Congress Cataloging-in-Publication Data

Pring, Martin J.
    Investment psychology explained : classic strategies
  to beat the markets / Martin J. Pring.
        p.   cm.
    Includes bibliographical references and index.
    ISBN 0-471-55721-8 (alk. paper)
    1. Investments.   2. Stocks.   3. Investment analysis.   I. Title.
HG4521.P836   1993
332.678—dc20   92-15914

Printed in the United States of America

10 9 8 7 6 5 4 3 2

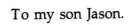
To my son Jason.

Acknowledgments

*T*his book represents a distillation of the knowledge contained in the sources listed in the bibliography so the wisdom and experience of these authors should be acknowledged at the outset.

Many others have helped me both directly and indirectly with the preparation of the material that follows. Robert Meier introduced me to a number of sources from his extensive library on the subject and was directly responsible for the inclusion of the chapters on Brokers and Money Managers; any omissions or mistakes that may have crept in are entirely my own responsibility. My editor at John Wiley, Karl Weber, also deserves mention for his very helpful suggestions concerning the structure and outline of the book.

Special thanks goes to John Conroy for his help in translating the book into readable English, to my son Jason for his helpful suggestions on several of the chapters, and to Sheila Silvernail for her usual excellent job of preparing the manuscript and charts.

Finally, I would like to thank my partners in the Pring Turner Capital Group, Joe Turner and Bruce Fraser, for their constant encouragement and constructive suggestions.

Preface

Over the last hundred years, countless books have been written on the psychological aspects of markets and market participants. My objective in writing this one, therefore, is not to break new ground. Most of what you will read has been said before, but in different places, spread over a long expanse of time. My reason for writing a book of this nature is to bring together in one volume a distillation of the soundest wisdom and most basic common sense on the subject of market psychology, offering the market wisdom of the ages in a complete, easy-to-read, and clearly organized format. Anyone wishing to pursue the subject further is encouraged to refer to the bibliography at the end of the book.

As you read the book, it will become apparent that the road to success is not an easy one. Financial well-being has to be earned in incremental steps and built on a solid psychological base.

MARTIN J. PRING

Contents

Investment
Psychology
Explained

Introduction

◆

*F*or most of us, the task of beating the market is not difficult, it is the job of beating ourselves that proves to be overwhelming. In this sense, "beating ourselves" means mastering our emotions and attempting to think independently, as well as not being swayed by those around us. Decisions based on our natural instincts invariably turn out to be the wrong course of action. All of us are comfortable buying stocks when prices are high and rising and selling when they are declining, but we need to develop an attitude that encourages us to do the opposite.

Success based on an emotional response to market conditions is the result of chance, and chance does not help us attain consistent results. Objectivity is not easy to achieve because all humans are subject to the vagaries of fear, greed, pride of opinion, and all the other excitable states that prevent rational judgment. We can read books on various approaches to the market until our eyes are red and we can attend seminars given by experts, gurus, or anyone else who might promise us instant gratification, but all the market knowledge in the world will be useless without the ability to put this knowledge into action by mastering our emotions. We spend too much time trying to beat the market and too little time trying to overcome our frailties.

One reason you're reading this book is that you recognize this imbalance, but even a complete mastery of the material in these pages will not guarantee success. For that, you will need experience in the marketplace, especially the experience of losing.

The principal difference between considering an investment or trading approach and actually entering the market is the commitment of money. When that occurs, objectivity falls by the wayside, emotion takes over, and losses mount. Adversity is to be welcomed because it teaches us much more than success. The world's best traders and investors know that to be successful they must also be humble. Markets have their own ways of seeking out human weaknesses. Such crises typically occur just at the crucial moment when we are unprepared, and they eventually cause us financial and emotional pain. If you are not prepared to admit mistakes and take remedial action quickly, you will certainly compound your losses. The process does not end even when you feel you have learned to be objective, patient, humble, and disciplined, for you can still fall into the trap of complacency. It is therefore vitally important to review both your progress and your mistakes on a continuous basis because no two market situations are ever the same.

Some of the brightest minds in the country are devoted to making profits in the markets, yet many newcomers to the financial scene naively believe that with minimal knowledge and experience, they too can make a quick killing. Markets are a zero-sum game: For every item bought, one is sold. If newcomers as a group expect to profit, it follows that they must battle successfully against these same people with decades of experience. We would not expect to be appointed as a university professor after one year of undergraduate work, to be a star football player straight out of high school, or to run a major corporation after six months of employment. Therefore, is it reasonable to expect success in the investment game without thorough study and training? The reason many of us are unrealistic is that we have been brainwashed into thinking that trading and investing are easy and do not require much thought or attention. We hear through the media that others have made quick and easy gains and conclude incorrectly that we can participate with little preparation and forethought. Nothing could be further from the truth.

Many legendary investment role models have likened trading and investing in the markets to other forms of business endeavor. As such, it should be treated as an enterprise that is slowly and steadily built up through hard work and careful planning and not as a rapid road to easy riches.

People make investment decisions involving thousands of dollars on a whim or on a simple comment from a friend, associate, or broker. Yet, when choosing an item for the house, where far less money is at stake, the same people may reach a decision only after great deliberation and consideration. This fact, as much as any, suggests that market prices are determined more by emotion than reasoned judgment. You can help an emotionally disturbed person only if you yourself are relatively stable, and dealing with an emotionally driven market is no different. If you react to news in the same way as everyone else, you are doomed to fall into the same traps, but if you can rise above the crowd, suppressing your own emotional instincts by following a carefully laid out investment plan, you are much more likely to succeed. In that respect, this book can point you in the right direction. Your own performance, however, will depend on the degree of commitment you bring to applying the principles you find here.

At this point, clarification of some important matters seems appropriate. Throughout the book, I have referred to traders and investors with the male pronoun. This is not in any way intended to disparage the valuable and expanding contribution of women to the investment community but merely to avoid "he or she" constructions and other clumsy references.

In the following chapters, the terms "market" or "markets" refer to any market in which the price is determined by freely motivated buyers and sellers. Most of the time, my comments refer to individual stocks and the stock market itself. However, the principles apply equally, regardless of whether the product or specific market is bonds, commodities, or stocks.

All markets essentially reflect the attitude and expectations of market participants in response to the emerging financial and economic environment. People tend to be universally greedy when they think the price will rise, whether they are buying gold, cotton, deutsche marks, stocks, or bonds. Conversely, their mood can easily swing to fear or panic if they are sufficiently persuaded that prices will decline. Human nature is the same in all markets the world over.

I will also be referring to traders and investors and, to some extent, speculators. Traders focus their attention on intraday and intraweek market activity. Their time horizon is rarely longer than a couple of weeks. They tend to work on margin in the futures and options markets, so their equity is highly leveraged. As a result, they must be highly disciplined and quick to recognize a mistake, or they will soon be wiped out financially. The vast majority of traders use technical analysis as a basis for making decisions.

Speculators have a longer time horizon that can stretch up to six months. In his classic book, *The ABC of Stock Speculation,* Samuel Nelson defined speculation as "a venture based on calculation." This definition could just as easily apply to traders. He distinguished between speculation and gambling by concluding that gambling is a venture that is not based on calculation.

While traders and speculators are solely interested in capital gain, the investor also considers current and future income streams when making a decision. The time horizon of investors is much longer, usually spanning at least two years, often much longer. As a rule, investors do not use margin trading and take fewer risks than traders or speculators.

Even though the risks that each type of participant is willing to take, as well as the relevant time horizons, are different, the principles of market psychology are essentially the same. All market participants must be ready to take a contrary position when the crowd moves the market to an extreme. Similarly, each participant must strive to keep a clear and impartial mind, limiting emotional responses to an absolute minimum.

The techniques practiced by traders and speculators are as different from investors' techniques as a sprinter's training is different from that of a marathon runner. Both need to be disciplined and fit, but each has a different goal demanding a different regimen. There are many different approaches to the business of trading and investing. Two basic approaches, fundamental and technical, have their own branches and schools of thought. Fundamental analysis is concerned with the goods in which the market deals: profit-and-loss statements, balance sheets, prospects for a specific stock commodity or currency, for example. This type of analysis determines what the market outlook is likely to be in relation to current values. If a stock is cheap, for example, and the outlook is favorable, then it should be bought (and vice versa).

Technical analysis, on the other hand, is concerned with the price action of a specific market or stock. Technicians assume that the price reflects all the knowledge of all participants, both actual and potential, and that prices move in trends. Their objective is to try to spot these trend reversals at an early stage and to profit from that trend until the reversal becomes reality.

It makes no difference what approach a trader or investor takes or, for that matter, what method of analysis he chooses. The most important tool required by anyone approaching the markets is a methodology on which to base rational judgments.

No methodology is perfect, but it is necessary first, to satisfy yourself that it works, and second, to feel totally comfortable using it. It's no good adopting a chartist approach, for instance, if you hate the sight of graphs. And a final thought on methodology: Even when you possess a good one, you still need to master your emotions. Without the ability to do this, you are doomed.

Trading, speculating, or investing in the markets, then, is not a science, but an art that is carefully learned, nurtured, and practiced over a long period of time.

Part I of this book is concerned with personal psychology; learning to master and control our natural, but financially destructive, emotional tendencies. It discusses why decision making based on sentiment leads to ruin, and it makes constructive suggestions for overcoming this problem.

An understanding of the psychology of markets would not be complete without a discussion of crowd psychology and contrary opinion; Part II provides this perspective. Most of us know that when an idea becomes too popular, everyone has latched onto it and is positioned accordingly in the market. We know that we should go against the crowd and take the opposite stance, but we also know that this is far easier said than done. We will examine why this is so, and we will learn when contrary opinion can be profitable and how to recognize when to "go contrary."

Part III examines the attributes of successful traders and investors, the super money-makers—what sets them apart from the rest of us and what rules they follow. This Part also incorporates many of the points made earlier to help you set up a plan and follow it successfully. To solidify and emphasize the key rules and principles followed by leading speculators and traders in the past hundred years or so, I have compiled those guidelines followed by eminent individuals. While each set of rules is unique, you will see that a common thread runs through all of them. This theme may be summarized as follows: Adopt a methodology, master your emotions, think independently, establish and follow a plan, and continually review your progress.

This recurring pattern did not occur by chance but emerged because these individuals discovered that it works. I hope that it can work for you as well. All that is needed is your commitment to carry it out.

Part I

KNOWING
YOURSELF

1

There Is No Holy Grail

Nothing is more frequently overlooked than the obvious.

—*Thomas Temple Hoyne*

You probably bought this book hoping that it would provide some easy answers in your quest to get rich quickly in the financial markets. If you did, you will be disappointed. There is no such Holy Grail. On the other hand, this book can certainly point you in the right direction if you are willing to recognize that hard work, common sense, patience, and discipline are valuable attributes to take with you on the road to smart investing.

There is no Holy Grail principally because market prices are determined by the attitude of investors and speculators to the changing economic and financial background. These attitudes tend to be consistent but occasionally are irrational, thereby defying even the most logical of analyses from time to time. Garfield Drew, the noted market commentator and technician, wrote in the 1940s, "Stocks do not sell for what they are worth but for what people *think* they are worth." How else can we explain that any market, stock, commodity, or currency can fluctuate a great deal in terms of its underlying value from one day to the next? Market prices are essentially a reflection of the hopes, fears, and expectations of the various participants. History tells us that human nature is more or less constant, but it also tells us that each situation is unique.

Let us assume, for example, that three people own 100% of a particular security we will call ABC Company. Shareholder A is investing for the long term and is not influenced by day-to-day news. Shareholder B has bought the stock because he thinks the company's prospects are quite promising over the next six months. Shareholder C has purchased the stock because it is temporarily depressed due to some bad news. Shareholder C plans to hold it for only a couple of weeks at most. He is a trader and can change his mind at a moment's notice.

A given news event such as the resignation of the company's president or a better-than-anticipated profit report will affect each shareholder in a different way. Shareholder A is unlikely to be influenced by either good or bad news, because he is taking the long view. Shareholder B could go either way, but shareholder C is almost bound to react, since he has a very short-term time horizon.

From this example, we can see that while their needs are different, each player is likely to act in a fairly predictable way. Moreover, because the makeup of the company's holdings will change over time, perhaps the short-term trader will sell to another person with a long-term outlook. Conversely, the long-term shareholder may decide to take a bigger stake in the company, since he can buy at depressed prices. Although human nature is reasonably constant, its effect on the market price will fluctuate because people of different personality types will own different proportions of the company at various times. Even though the personalities of the players may remain about the same, the external pressures they undergo will almost certainly vary. Thus, the long-term investor may be forced to sell part of his position because of an unforeseen financial problem. The news event is therefore of sufficient importance to tip his decision-making process at the margin. Since the actual makeup of the market changes over time, it follows that the psychological responses to any given set of events also will be diverse. Because of this, it is very difficult to see how anyone could create a system or develop a philosophy or approach that would call every market turning point in a perfect manner. This is not to say that you can't develop an approach that consistently delivers more profits than losses. It means merely that there is no perfect system or Holy Grail. We shall learn that forecasting market trends is an art and not a science. As such, it cannot be reduced to a convenient formula.

Having the perfect indicator would be one thing, but putting it into practice would be another. Even if you are able to "beat the market" the greater battle of "beating yourself," that is, mastering your emotions, still lies ahead. Every great market operator, whether a trader or an investor, knows that the analytical aspect of playing the market represents only a small segment compared with its psychological aspect. In this respect, history's great traders or investors—to one degree or another—have followed various rules. However, these successful individuals would be the first to admit that they have no convenient magic formula to pass on as a testament to their triumphs.

The false "Holy Grail" concept appears in many forms; we will consider two: the expert and the fail-safe system, or perfect indicator.

◆ The Myth of the Expert

All of us gain some degree of comfort from knowing that we are getting expert advice whenever we undertake a new task. This is because we feel somewhat insecure and need the reassurances that an expert—with his undoubted talents and years of experience—can provide. However, it is not generally recognized that experts, despite their training and knowledge, can be as wrong as the rest of us.

It is always necessary to analyze the motives of experts. Britain's Prime Minister Neville Chamberlain, having returned from Hitler's Germany with a piece of paper promising "peace in our time," no doubt believed wholeheartedly the truth of his grand statement. The fact was, he was an expert, and he got it wrong. President John Kennedy also had his problems with experts. "How could I have been so far off base? All my life I've known better than to depend on the experts," he said shortly after the Bay of Pigs fiasco.

Classic errors abound in military, philosophical, and scientific areas. In the investment field, the record is perhaps even more dismal. One of the differences that sets aside market forecasters from other experts is that market prices are a totally accurate and impartial umpire. If you, as a financial expert, say that the Dow-Jones average will reach 3,500 by the end of the month and it goes to 2,500, there can be little argument that you were wrong. In other fields, there is always the possibility of hedging your bets or making a prognostication that can't be questioned until new evidence comes along. Those experts who for centuries argued that the world was flat had a heyday until Columbus came along. It didn't matter to the earlier sages; their reputations remained intact until well after their deaths. However, conventional thinkers after 1493 did have a problem when faced with impeachable proof.

Experts in financial markets do not enjoy the luxury of such a long delay. Let's take a look at a few forecasts. Just before the 1929 stock market crash, Yale economist Irving Fischer, the leading proponent of the quantity theory of money, said, "Stocks are now at what looks like a permanently high plateau." We could argue that he was an economist and was therefore commenting on events outside his chosen field of expertise. In the previous year, however, he also reportedly said, "Mr. Hoover knows as few men do the terrible evils of inflation and deflation, and the need of avoiding both if business and agriculture are to be stabilized." Up to the end of 1929, both were avoided, yet the market still crashed.

When we turn to stock market experts, there is even less to cheer about. Jesse Livermore was an extremely successful stock operator. In late 1929, he said, "To my mind this situation should go no further," meaning, of course, that the market had hit bottom. Inaccurate calls were not limited to traders. U.S.

industrialist John D. Rockefeller put his money where his mouth was: "In the past week (mid-October 1929) my son and I have been purchasing sound common stocks." Other famous industrialists of the day agreed with him. One month later, in November 1929, Henry Ford is quoted as saying, "Things are better today than they were yesterday."

Roger Babson, one of the most successful money managers of the time, had in 1929 correctly called for a 60 to 80 point dip in the Dow. Yet, even he failed to anticipate how serious the situation would become by 1930, for he opined early in that year, "I certainly am optimistic regarding this fall. . . . There may soon be a stampede of orders and congestion of freight in certain lines and sections." Unfortunately, the Depression lasted for several more years. Perhaps the most astonishing quote comes from Reed Smoot, the chairman of the Senate Finance Committee. Commenting on the Smoot–Hawley Tariff Act, generally believed to be one of the principal catalysts of the Great Depression, he said, "One of the most powerful influences working toward business recovery is the tariff act which Congress passed in 1930." Figure 1–1 depicts market action between 1929 and 1932, thereby putting these experts' opinions into perspective.

The testimony of these so-called experts shows that some of the greatest and most successful industrialists and stock operators are by no means immune from making erroneous statements and unprofitable decisions. Common sense would have told most people that the stock market was due for some major corrective action in 1929. It was overvalued by historical benchmarks, speculation was rampant, and the nation's debt structure was top-heavy by any standard. The problem was that most people were unable to relate emotionally to this stark reality. When stock prices are rising rapidly and everyone is making money, it is easy to be lulled into a sense of false security by such "expert" testimony.

Of course, some individual commentators, analysts, and money managers are correct most of the time. We could, for instance, put Livermore and Babson into such a class. However, if

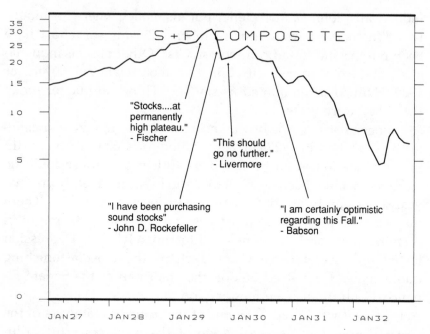

Figure 1–1 U.S. Stock Market 1927–1932. Source: *Pring Market Review.*

you find yourself blindly following the views of a particular individual as a proxy for the Holy Grail, you will inevitably find yourself in trouble—probably at the most inconvenient moment.

An alternative to using a single guide is to follow a number of different experts simultaneously. This solution is even worse because experts as a group are almost always wrong. Figure 1–2 compares Standard and Poor's (S&P) Composite Index with the percentage of those writers of market letters who are bullish. The data were collected by Investor's Intelligence* and have been adjusted to iron out week-to-week fluctuations. (A more up-to-date version appears in Chapter 8.) Even a cursory glance at the chart demonstrates quite clearly that most advisors are bullish at major market peaks and bearish at troughs. If this exercise were conducted for other investments such as bonds, currencies, or commodities, the results would be similar. At first glance, it may

---

Investor's Intelligence, Chartcraft, Inc., New Rochelle, NY 10801.

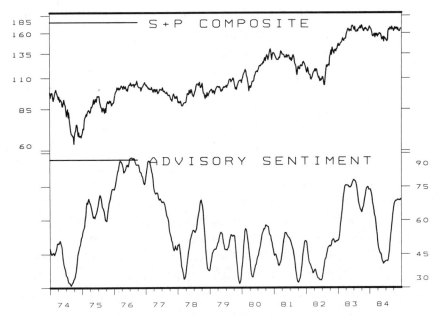

Figure 1–2 S&P Composite versus Advisory Service Sentiment 1974–1984. Source: *Pring Market Review.*

appear that you could use these data from a contrary point of view, buying when the experts are bearish and selling when they are bullish. Unfortunately, even this approach fails to deliver the Holy Grail, because the data do not always reach an extreme at all market turning points. At a major peak in 1980, for example, the Index couldn't even rally above 60%. In late 1981, on the other hand, the Index did reach an extreme, but this was well before the final low in prices in the summer of 1982. While the Advisory Sentiment Indicator does forecast some major peaks and troughs, it is by no means perfect and certainly lacks the consistency needed to qualify as the Holy Grail.

◆ *The Myth of the Perfect Indicator*

It is almost impossible to flip through the financial pages of any magazine or newspaper without coming across an advertisement promising instant wealth. This publicity typically features a computerized system or an investment advisor hotline that claims to have achieved spectacular results over the past few months or even years. Normally, such services specialize in the futures or options markets because these highly leveraged areas are in a more obvious position to offer instant financial gratification. The huge leverage available to traders in the futures markets significantly reduces the time horizons available to customers. Consequently, the number of transactions, (i.e., revenue for the brokers) is that much greater.

As a rule of thumb, the more money the advertisement promises, the more you should question its veracity. History tells us that it is not possible to accumulate a significant amount of money in a brief time unless you are extremely lucky. Moreover, if you are fortunate enough to fall into a situation where the markets act in perfect harmony with the system or approach that you have adopted, you are likely to attribute your success to hidden talents just discovered. Instead of walking away from the table, you will continue to be lulled back into the market, not realizing the true reason for your good fortune. You will inevitably fritter away your winnings trying to regain those lost profits.

Consider the advertisement's promises from another angle. If the system is so profitable, why are its proponents going to the trouble of taking you on as a client and servicing your needs? Surely, it would be less bothersome to execute a few orders each day than to go to the trouble, expense, and risk of advertising the service. The answer is either that the system doesn't work or, more likely, that it has been tested only for a specific period in the most recent past. You, as a prospective user, should focus on the likelihood of the method's operating profitably in the future and not on some hypothetical profits of recent history.

Most systems base their claims of success on back-tested data in which buy-and-sell signals are generated by specific price actions, for example, when the price moves above or below a specific moving average. It seems natural to assume that past successes can forecast future profits, but the results of back-tested data are not as trustworthy as they appear. First, the conditions in which the data are tested are not the same as a real market situation. For example, the system may call for the sale of two contracts of December gold because the price closed below $400. On the surface, this may seem reasonable, but in reality it may not have been possible to execute the order at that price. Quite often, discouraging news will break overnight causing the market to open much lower the next day. Consequently, the sale would have been executed well below the previous $400 close. Even during the course of the day, unexpected news can cause markets to fluctuate abnormally. Under such conditions, systems tested statistically under one-day price movements will not reflect a reasonable order execution. An example of this situation arises when market participants are waiting for the Commerce Department to release a specific economic indicator. Occasionally when the announcement falls wide of expectations, a market will react almost instantly, often rising or falling 1% or 2%. The time frame is so short that it is physically impossible for many transactions to take place. As a result, the system does not truly indicate a realistic order execution.

Another example is the violent reaction of the market to some unexpected news. On the evening of January 15, 1990 (Eastern Standard Time), U.S. and allied troops began the invasion of Kuwait. The next day the market, as measured by the Dow-Jones average, rose well over 75 points at the start of trading. In effect, there was no opportunity to get in (or out if you were short) anywhere near to the previous night's close. This is an exceptional example, but it is remarkable how many "exceptions" occur as soon as you try to adapt one of these methods to the actual marketplace.

Another flaw with these systems is that data are usually back tested for a specific time, and special rules are introduced so that the method fits the data retroactively solely to demonstrate huge paper profits. If you invent enough rules, it is relatively easy to show that a system has worked in the past. However, if rules are developed purely to justify profits in these specific periods, the chances are that these same rules will impede future success.

To ensure that a system is likely to work in the future, when it counts, the rules should be simple and kept to a minimum, and the testing period should cover many markets over many years. The problem with most of these advertised ventures is that they give you the results of only the most successful markets. If you ask the advocates of these schemes to report their findings for other time periods or other markets, you will be greeted with blank stares.

A final drawback of systems is that they usually fail when rolled out into the real world. The reason? Market conditions change. Figure 1–3 shows a system based on a simple moving average crossover. This method works well when the market shows a clear-cut trend of the kind seen between January and March 1991. However, the same system could hand you your head on a platter when price action is more volatile, as it was between mid-March and May 1991.

Figure 1–3 S&P versus a Twenty-Five-Day Moving Average. Source: *Pring Market Review.*

Changes in the character of a market are not just limited to changes in trend volatility. Any method that uses the past to forecast the future assumes that past behavior will repeat.

Systems constructed from assumptions concerning basic economic fundamentals are also subject to failure. For example, it has been established that, in almost all cases, stock prices sooner or later rally in the face of falling interest rates and begin to fall sometime after rates have begun to rise. The lags fall into a fairly predictable range most of the time but on occasion can be unduly long. These exceptions can result in missed opportunities or devastating losses. This problem occurred at the beginning of the Depression. Interest rates peaked in the fall of 1929, yet the stock market declined by about 75% over the next three years. In this instance, the knowledge that rates lead equity prices could have led to devastating losses. Timing is everything. In a similar vein, short-term interest rates bottomed out in December 1976 at 4.74% and almost quadrupled to a cyclical peak of 16.5% in March 1980. Yet stock prices in the same period as measured by the S&P Composite were unchanged.

While the inverse relationship of interest rates to equity prices works well as an indicator of market direction most of the time, these examples show that it is far from perfect and certainly no Holy Grail. The reason for this is that once a certain indicator or investment approach works for a while, word of its money-making capabilities spreads like wildfire. Then, when everyone is aware of its potential, it becomes factored into the price and the relationship breaks down.

This concept works just as well in reverse, where fear rather than greed is the motivator. People, it seems, tend to repeat past mistakes but not those of the most recent past. Once-bitten-twice-shy applies as much to trading and investing as to any other form of human activity. In the 1973–1974 bear market, for example, equity investors were clobbered principally due to rising interest rates. In virtually every business cycle throughout history, investors have waited to sell stocks *after* interest rates started to rise. In the cycle that followed the 1973–1974 market debacle, however, investors sold stocks *in anticipation* of rising rates. Since rising interest rates were already factored into equity prices, the stock market actually rallied along with rates in the 1978–1979 period.

In *New Methods for Profit in the Stock Market,* Garfield Drew tells us that the mind generally harks back to its last experience in the market and judges the market by that encounter. He shows that stung investors hold postmortems after each unforeseen collapse in prices to get a better grip on the warning signals that preceded the collapse. People then concentrate on these factors to prepare themselves for the next failure. Drew points out that this is seldom a smart idea, because the dangers have shifted to another sector of the economy by the time the next decline begins.

An excellent example of this tendency occurred in the 1920s. In 1921, the U.S. economy suffered a short depression stemming from a rampant commodity inflation. As a result, most people felt that the situation in 1929 was sound because commodity prices were subdued. What they did not realize was that the problem of inflation had moved from commodities to broker loans, that is, margin accounts. When these unsound debts were involuntarily unwound due to weak market conditions, they acted as a catalyst for the downward spiral in stock prices in late 1929.

At the peak of the next cycle in 1937, investors were again complacent, because the amount of margin debt was low compared with 1929. The problem had moved once again. This time the cause of the subsequent recession and bear market in equities was inflated inventories in the face of a declining demand.

Drew goes on to describe the popularity of business barometers designed to identify turning points in the business cycle and the stock market. For the most part, these models had worked extremely well, but they were based on historical data. However, they failed completely in the late 1920s and early part of the 1930s, because that experience defied any historical norm. Almost without exception, these barometers indicated that stocks were cheap in 1930 and should be bought. This advice preceded the final low by about two years, when prices had yet to undergo a decline of 50%. Drew continues: "But 'normal' at any given time merely means an average of the past. It does not allow for changed conditions, whereas the current or future 'normal' may be something quite different."

Traditional relationships may break down in other ways because of institutional or technological changes. For many years, technical analysts used to track the number of shares sold short (a bearish maneuver made by speculators who believe they could profit from lower stock prices). A bullish reading occurs when the volume of the total short position on the New York Stock Exchange is greater than twice the average daily trading volume. This high ratio implies that the public is bearish, because it is shorting heavily. Also, because every share sold short has to be repurchased, a high ratio also indicates a huge potential demand for stock.

The short interest ratio worked beautifully, signaling nearly all the major bottoms between the 1930s and the early 1970s. At that time, stock options and stock index futures were introduced and much of the subsequent short selling represented hedge positions against these derivative products. These transactions have had the effect of distorting the short-interest data so that a high short-interest ratio no longer reflects pessimism or potential demand to the extent that it had done previously.

Almost every student of the market would love to get his hands on the perfect indicator. For the preceding reasons, it is extremely unlikely that this creation ever has been or ever will be developed. The perfect indicator would have to anticipate changes in economic conditions, markets, and institutions. Moreover, word of this prognosticating marvel would gradually leak out, and in brief order it would be widely followed. In 1976 and 1977, stock market participants discounted the rise in rates during the 1978–1980 period, and they would just as easily anticipate the perfect indicator. In the end, market tops would occur when the indicator gave a buy signal and market bottoms would happen on sell signals. Later, the anticipators would anticipate the anticipators. The perfect indicator would be a joke.

In his book *Money and Investment Profits*, Hamilton Bolton, the founder of the Bank Credit Analyst, a monthly newsletter, commented, "It is perhaps ironic that to be of value an indicator must be far from ideal, subject to considerable controversy, and subject also to considerable vagaries in timing. The perfect indicator would be useless; the imperfect one may be of investment value" (p. 201). Until his untimely death in the late 1960s, he probably worked on more indicators in his investment career than any other person. Thus, a creative genius such as Bolton, who was a master at developing indicators and at forecasting markets, came to the conclusion that imperfection was an achievable and profitable goal, whereas perfection was an impossible objective and would be unprofitable anyway.

Many traders and investors spend their entire investment lives looking for the Holy Grail without realizing it. For example, a person may first get involved in the market through an appealing advertisement that promises investment success based on a particular approach or a wonderful track record. After a while, reality sets in and the investor sees that the approach has little or no merit. It is then discarded, and a new one is adopted. This process can continue ad infinitum.

This book, for example, may have been purchased as part of a search for the Holy Grail of investment. What often happens is that people become so engrossed in their search for quick profits that they rarely stand back and review their situation from a wider perspective. If they did, they would understand that these various approaches and systems in effect represent small psychological circles.

Each circle begins with the adoption of the new approach, indicator, expert, or system. Enthusiasm and confidence probably result in some initial profits as the user conveniently overlooks many of the new game's drawbacks. Gradually, losses begin to mount. This crumbling state of affairs eventually leads to dejection and the final jettisoning of the system, accompanied by firm resolutions "never to enter the market again." The passage of time is a great healer, and sooner or later another cycle in the search for the Holy Grail gets underway.

After a while, the thoughtful person will question this self-perpetuating cycle. One major plus is that the chastened investor has gained some experience along with the realization that investing and trading represent more an art than a precise science. Once market participants understand that the Holy Grail does not exist, they will have learned a valuable lesson. To paraphrase Bolton, the goal of imperfection in the investment world is likely to lead to greater profits than the pursuit of perfection.

2
How to Be Objective

There are no certainties in this investment world, and where there are no certainties, you should begin by understanding yourself.

—*James L. Fraser*

As soon as money is committed to a financial asset, so too is emotion. Any biases that were present before the money was placed on the table are greatly increased once the investment has actually been made. If none were present before, they certainly will appear now. However hard we may try, certain prejudices are bound to creep in. A successful investor realizes this and knows that he must try to maintain psychological balance through self-control.

Even if perfect objectivity is an unrealistic goal, we must still take steps to increase our impartiality as much as possible. Both internal and external forces can upset mental balance. By "internal," I am referring to the psychological makeup of an individual. Obtaining objectivity then becomes a matter of assessing mental vulnerabilities and determining how best to overcome them; this process is the subject of Chapter 2. External forces, which emanate from elements such as colleagues, the media, and events going on around us, will be covered in Chapter 3.

An investor or trader faces a constant bombardment of emotional stimuli. News, gossip, and sharp changes in prices can set the nerves quivering like the filament in an incandescent lamp unless properly controlled. These outside influences cause the emotions to shift between the two extremes of fear and greed. Once you lose your mental balance, even for an instant, your will and reasoning will be swept away, and you will find yourself acting as the vast majority of market participants act—on impulse.

To counteract this tendency, you must be as objective as possible. Remember: Prices in financial markets are determined by the *attitude* of investors to the emerging economic and financial environment rather than by the environment itself. This means that price fluctuations will be determined by the hopes, fears, and expectations of the crowd as they attempt to downplay future events and their biases toward them. Your job is to try as much as possible to ignore those around you and form an independent opinion while making a genuine attempt to overcome your own prejudices.

The markets themselves are driven by crowd emotions. Nothing you can do will change that; it is a fact that you have to accept. Despite this, becoming a successful investor demands that you overcome your mental deficiencies and rise above the crowd. As a natural result, you will find yourself outside the consensus.

◆ Learning to Act on Well-Founded Beliefs, Not Prejudices

The character and psychological makeup of each individual is unique. This means that some of us come to the marketplace with more biases than others. In this respect, it is important to note that many of our prejudices are shaped and influenced by our experiences. Someone who has suffered a great deal from financial insecurity through bankruptcy or a recent job loss, for example, is much less likely to take risks when investing. A given piece of bad news will send this person scurrying to his broker to sell. On the other hand, another investor may have had the opposite, pleasant experience of receiving a raise or an unexpected inheritance. Such an individual would come to the marketplace with a completely different outlook and would be much more likely to weather any storms. By the same token, this more fortunate person would be more likely to approach the markets with an overconfident swagger. Since such an attitude results in muddled thinking and careless decision making, this individual also would come to the marketplace with a disadvantage.

So we see that neither person is objective, because his actions are based on his experiences rather than on his beliefs. In the preceding example, both investors acted on impulse, not logical thought. The confident investor made the right decision, but he was lucky. If the price had dropped, the fearful investor would have come out in a relatively better position than his self-assured counterpart. Thus, for any of us, achieving objectivity involves different challenges based on our own characteristics—whether they be bullish, bearish, daring, or cautious—and shaped by our unique experiences.

This discussion will set out the major pitfalls that prevent us from reaching objectivity and establish some broad principles for avoiding these hazards. You are the only person who can appraise your experiences and the type of biases that you may bring to the marketplace. Only you can measure the nature and degree of your own preconceived ideas. Once you have assessed them, you will be in a far stronger position to take the appropriate action to offset them.

A doctor examines a patient for symptoms and prescribes the appropriate remedy. Treating a bad case of the "subjectives" is no different. Pain is the symptom of a headache; a string of losses is the symptom of poor investment and trading decisions. The treatment is to reexamine the events and decisions that led up to those losses using some of the concepts discussed in this chapter, and then to follow up by using the remedies suggested later in this book.

◆ *Mastering Fear and Greed*

Figure 2–1 shows that the target of objectivity or mental balance lies approximately in the middle between the two destructive mental forces of fear and greed. Fear is a complex emotion taking many forms such as worry, fright, alarm, and panic. When fear is given free rein, it typically combines with other negative emotions such as hatred, hostility, anger, and revenge, thereby attaining even greater destructive power.

Aspects of Fear

In the final analysis, fear among investors shows itself in two forms: fear of losing and fear of missing out. In his book *How I Helped More Than 10,000 Investors to Profit in Stocks*, George Schaefer, the great Dow theorist, describes several aspects of fear and the varying effects they have on the psyche of investors:

A Threat to National Security Triggers Fear. Any threat of war, declared or rumored, dampens stock prices. The outbreak of war is

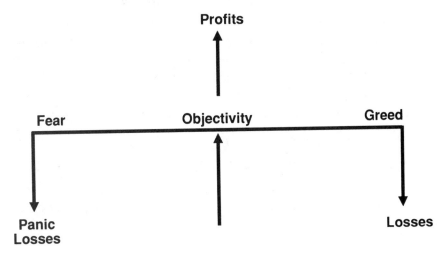

Figure 2–1 Fear–Greed Balance. Source: *Pring Market Review.*

usually treated as an excuse for a rally, hence the expression: "Buy on the sound of cannon, sell on the sound of trumpets." This maxim is derived from the fact that the outbreak of war can usually be anticipated. Consequently, the possibility is quickly discounted by the stock market, and, therefore, the market, with a sigh of relief, begins to rally when hostilities begin. As it becomes more and more obvious that victory is assured, the event is factored into the price structure and is fully discounted by the time victory is finally achieved. "The sound of trumpets" becomes, therefore, a signal to sell. Only if the war goes badly are prices pushed lower as more fear grips investors.

All People Fear Losing Money. This form of fear affects rich and poor alike. The more you have the more you can lose, and therefore the greater the potential for fear in any given individual.

Worrisome News Stimulates Fear. Any news that threatens our economic well-being will bring on fear. The more serious the situation, the more pronounced is the potential for a selling panic.

A Fearful Mass Psychology Is Contagious. Fear breeds more fear. The more people around us who are selling in response to bad news, the more believable the story becomes, and the more realistic the situation appears. As a result, it becomes very difficult to distance ourselves from the beliefs and fears of the crowd, so we also are motivated to sell. By contrast, if the same breaking news story received less prominence, we would not be drawn into this mass psychological trap and would be less likely to make the wrong decision.

Fear of a Never-Ending Bear Market Is a Persistent Myth. Once a sizable downtrend has gotten underway, the dread that it will never end becomes deeply entrenched in the minds of investors. Almost all equity bull markets are preceded by declining interest rates and an easy-money policy that sow the seeds for the next recovery. This trend would be obvious to any rational person who is able to think independently. However, the sight of sharply declining prices in the face of such an improving background reinforces the fear that "this time it will be different" and that the decline will never end.

Individuals Retain All Their Past Fears.   Once you have had a bad experience in the market, you will always fear a similar recurrence, whether consciously or subconsciously, or both. If you have made an investment that resulted in devastating losses, you will be much more nervous the next time you venture into the market. As a result, your judgment will be adversely affected by even the slightest, often imagined, hint of trouble. That intimation will encourage you to sell so that you can avoid the psychological pain of losing yet again.

This phenomenon also affects the investment community as a whole. Prior to 1929, the collective psyche lived in dread of another "Black Friday." In 1869, a group of speculators tried to corner the gold market. When the gold price plummeted, they were forced to liquidate. This resulted in margin calls, the effect of which also spilled over into the stock market causing a terrible crash. Even though few of today's investors experienced the "Black Thursday" crash of 1929, this event still casts a shadow over the minds of most investors. As a consequence, even the mere hint of such a recurrence is enough to send investors scurrying.

The Fear of Losing Out.   This was not one of Schaefer's classifications of fear, but it is a very powerful one, nonetheless. This phenomenon often occurs after a sharp price rise. Portfolio managers are often measured on a relative basis either against the market itself or against a universe of their peers. If they are underinvested as a sharp rally begins, the perception of missing out on a price move and of subsequent underperformance is so great that the fear of missing the boat forces them to get in.

This form of fear can also affect individuals. Often, an investor will judge, quite correctly, that a major bull market in a specific financial asset is about to get underway. Then when the big move develops, he does not participate for some reason. It might be because he was waiting for lower prices, or more likely because he had already got in but had then been psyched out due to some unexpected bad news. Regardless of the reason, such "sold out bulls" suddenly feel left out and feel compelled to get back into the market. Ironically, this usually occurs somewhere close to the top. Consequently, the strong belief in the bull market case coupled with the contagion of seeing prices explode results in the feeling of being left out.

I have found personally that this fear of missing the boat is frequently coupled with anger, which may be triggered by a minor mishap that compounds my frustration. These mistakes typically take the form of an unfortunate execution, a bad fill, a lost order, and so on. Inevitably, I have found this burst of emotion to be associated with a major, often dramatic turning point in the market. This experience tells me two things. First, I have obviously lost my sense of objectivity as the need to participate at all costs overrides every other emotion. My decision is therefore likely to be wrong. Second, the very nature of the situation—a lengthy period of rising prices culminating in total frustration—symbolizes an overextended market. It is reasonable to expect that others are also affected by the same sense of frustration, which implies that all the buying potential has already been realized.

When you find yourself in this kind of situation it is almost always wise to stand aside. A client once said to me, "There is always another train." By this, he meant that even if you do miss the current opportunity, however wonderful it may appear, patience and discipline will always reward you with another. If you ever find yourself in this predicament, overcome the fear of missing out and look for the next "train."

Fear, in effect, causes us to act in a vacuum. It is such an overpowering emotion that we forget about the alternatives, temporarily losing the perception that we do have other choices.

Fear of losing can also take other forms. For instance, occasionally we play mental games by refusing to acknowledge the existence of ominous developments. This could take the form of concentrating on the good news, because we want the market to rally, and downplaying the bad news, although the latter may be more significant. Needless to say, this kind of denial can lead to some devastating losses.

Alternately, an investor may get into the market in the belief that prices are headed significantly higher, say by 30%, over the course of the next year. After a couple of weeks, the stock may have already advanced 15%. It then undergoes a minor correction that has absolutely no relevance so far as the long-term potential is concerned. Nevertheless, the investor's fear of losing comes to the surface as he mentally relives experiences of previous set-backs. The reasoning may be, "Why don't I get out now? The short-term correction that is likely to take place may well push the price below my entry point and I will be forced to take another loss. Far better if I liquidate and get back in when it goes lower." He has diverted his focus from what the market can give him to what it can take away. Getting out would be quite in order if his assessment of conditions had changed, but if the appraisal is based purely on a change in perceptions unaccompanied by an alteration in the external environment, liquidation would not make sense. One way of solving this dilemma would be to take profits on part of the position. This would relieve some of the pressure but would also leave him free to participate in the next stage of the rally.

A more permanent and viable solution is first to recognize that you have a problem in this area. Next, establish a plan that sets realistic goals *ahead of time* and also permits the taking of partial profits under certain predetermined conditions. This approach would stand a far greater chance of being successful than knee-jerk trading or investment decisions caused by character weakness. If this type of planning went into every trading or investment decision it would eventually become a habit. The *fear of losing* would then be replaced by a far more healthy *fear of not following the plan.*

Greed

Greed is at the other extreme of our emotional makeup. It results from the combination of overconfidence and a desire to achieve profitable results in the shortest amount of time. In this age of leveraged markets, be they futures or options, the temptation to go for the quick home run is very strong. The problem is that this quick-grab approach is bound to lead to greater stress and subjectivity.

Let's consider the case of a trader, Rex, who decides that gold is in the early stages of a dynamic rally. He concludes from his fundamental and technical research that the bull market is more or less the proverbial "sure thing." There are a number of ways in which to participate. One would be to invest in the metal or in gold shares by paying for either in full. An alternative and far more tempting possibility would be to take a significant portion of available capital and speculate in the futures or options markets. In this way, his capital will be highly leveraged, and if he is right, the gains will be many times those of a simple cash investment.

Options are instruments that allow you to purchase a financial asset or futures contract at a given price for a specific period of time. Their primary advantage is that you cannot lose more than 100% of your money and yet you gain from the tremendous leverage that options offer. The disadvantage is that if the price does not rally by the time the option expires you stand to lose everything. With options it is possible to be dead right on the market and yet lose everything because the price did not meet your objective by the time the option expired.

The other leveraged alternative—the purchase of futures—does not suffer from this drawback because the contract can always be "rolled over," or refinanced, when it expires. The problem with futures is that markets rarely move in a straight line. Let's say that Rex has a capital investment of $25,000, and expects the price of gold to advance by $150. Margins vary with volatility in the market, but let's suppose that the current margin or deposit requirement is $2,000 per contract. This means that Rex could buy twelve contracts. Every $1 movement in the gold price changes the value of each contract by $100, so a dollar movement for an account holding 12 contracts would be $1,200. If the price moves up by $150, his account will profit to the tune of $180,000. If he deducts $10,000 for commissions and carrying charges, that's still a very healthy profit on a $24,000 investment.

The problem is that leverage can work both ways. Let's say, for example, that the price of gold does eventually go up by $150, but it goes down $15 first. This means that Rex's account initially loses $18,000. You might think that the $7,000 balance would be sufficient to enable him to ride out the storm. However, his broker will be quite concerned at this point and will issue a margin call. Either he must come up with the $17,000 or he will be forced to liquidate the position. Here is an example where the analysis is absolutely correct but the extreme leveraging of the position, that is, the greed factor, results in disaster. How much more sensible it would have been just to purchase two contracts, ride out the storm, and take profits when the price rallied to $150.

Another way in which people succumb to the greed factor is through pyramiding. Let's say Rex takes our advice and buys 2 gold contracts. He sees the price rise by $25 and has a comfortable feeling when he looks at his account to see that it has now increased from $25,000 to $30,000. Rex is quite happy because the market is telling him that his assessment of the conditions is absolutely right. "What's wrong with adding a couple of contracts?" he asks himself. After all, his account has grown by $5,000 and the addition of 2 more contracts will only increase his margin requirement by $4,000, so his excess equity over margin will still be $1,000 more than when he started. He then suffers a $10 setback in the price, which pushes his total equity position back to $26,000. This troubles him a little, but soon the price takes off again, and it's not long before the price has advanced another $15 above where he bought his second tranche. His equity now stands at $36,000, and his confidence is higher than ever. Having fought one battle successfully and seen his view once again confirmed by the market, he calculates that if he buys another 5 contracts and the market fulfills the last $110 of potential, he will end up with his current $37,000 plus another $110,0000. At this point, his original investment has already grown by about 50%, a very good rate of return. Unfortunately, Rex has become the victim of his own success and finds the temptation of the extra $110,000 to be irresistible, so he plunges in with the 5 contracts.

Then the price rallies another $10, but instead of buying more, he decides to stay with his position. The next thing he knows the price suffers a setback to the place where he added the 5 contracts. The mood of most market participants is quite upbeat at this time and many are accounting for the decline as "healthy" profit-taking. Having resisted the opportunity to add at higher prices, Rex is quite proud of himself and looks on the setback as a good place to augment to his position "on weakness," so he buys 3 more contracts for a total of 12. Remember his equity is still at a healthy $37,000. What often happens at this stage is that the price fluctuates within a narrow trading range. After all, it has rallied by $45 without much of a correction. The price erodes a further $5 in a quiet fashion and then experiences a sharp $17 selloff. This means that it has retraced about 50% of the advance since Rex entered the market. Rex still has a profit in his original purchase, but the problem is that he pyramided his position at higher prices and is now under water. The price has dropped by $22, which means the equity in his account has fallen from $37,000 to $10,600 (i.e., twelve contracts × $2,200).

Rex now has three choices: Meet the inevitable margin call by injecting more money in the account, liquidate the position, or sell enough contracts to meet the margin call. All three alternatives are unpleasant but would have been unnecessary if he had stuck to his original plan. If he had, his equity would currently be at $29,400, and he would be $4,400 to the good.

As we know, his original prediction was correct, and the price eventually did reach his price objective. If he had decided at that point to consolidate his position and hold, he would still have come out with a profit. However, he didn't realize his strong position at that point. All he could see is that his account had fallen from a very healthy $37,000 to a very worrying $10,600—a loss of over 50%. The temptation for most people in this type of situation is to run for cover, as fear quickly overtakes greed as the motivating force. Moreover, when prices decline, there is usually a rationale trotted out by experts and the media. This justification may or may not hold water, but it is amazing how its credibility appears to move proportionately with the amount the account has been margined.

The odds are therefore very high that our friend Rex will decide to liquidate his entire position. A devastating loss of this nature is a very worrying experience, but most traders will tell you that once the position has been liquidated, most people feel a sense of relief that the ordeal is over. The last thing Rex wants to do at this point is speculate in the futures markets. However, it is only a matter of time before his psychological wounds heal and he ventures back into the market. Like most people, he will vow that he has learned from his mistake, but it is not until those prices go up and his equity grows that he will find out whether or not he has really learned his lesson.

This example shows that success, if not properly controlled, can sow the seeds of failure. Anyone who has encountered a long string of profitable trades or investments without any meaningful setbacks is *bound* to experience a feeling of well-being and a sense of invincibility. This in turn results in more risk taking and careless decision making. Markets are constantly probing for the vulnerabilities and weaknesses that we all possess, so this reckless activity presents a golden opportunity for them to sow the seeds of destruction. In this respect, remember that *no one*, however talented, can succeed always. Every trader and investor goes through a cycle that alternates between success and failure. Successful traders and investors are fully aware of their feelings of invincibility and often make a deliberate effort to *stay out of the market* after they have experienced a profitable campaign. This "vacation" enables them to recharge their emotional batteries and subsequently return to the market in a much more objective state of mind.

Investors who have had a run of success, whether from short-term trading or long-term investment, have a tendency to relax and lower their guard, because they have not recently been tested by the market. When profits have been earned with very little effort, they are not appreciated as much as when you have to sweat out painful corrections and similar market contortions. Part of this phenomenon arises because a successful campaign reinforces our convictions that we are on the right path. Consequently, we are less likely to question our investment or trading position even when new evidence to the contrary comes to the fore. We need to recognize that *confidence moves proportionately with prices.*

As our confidence improves, we should take countermeasures to keep our feet on the ground so that we maintain our sense of equilibrium. At the beginning of an investment campaign, this is not as much a requirement as it is as the campaign progresses, because fear and caution help rein in our tendency to make rash decisions. As prices move in our favor, the solid anchor of caution gradually disappears. This means that sharp market movements that go against our position hit us by surprise. It is much better to be continually running scared and looking over our shoulder for developments that are likely to reverse the prevailing trend. Such unexpected shocks will be far less frequent because we will have learned to anticipate them. When events can be anticipated, it is much easier to put them in perspective. Otherwise, their true significance may be exaggerated. The idea is to try to maintain a sense of mental balance so that these psychological disruptions can be more easily deflected when they occur.

Think of how a practitioner of karate maintains the poise that enables him to deflect physical blows. The same should be true for the investor or trader. Try to maintain your mental balance by taking steps to be as objective as possible. Succumbing to the emotional extremes of fear and greed will make you far more vulnerable to unexpected outside forces. Unless you can assess their true importance and then take the appropriate action by using your head, you are more likely to respond emotionally to such stimuli, just like everyone else.

Many other emotions lie between the destructive polar extremes of fear and greed. These traps, which also have the potential to divert us from maintaining an objective stance, are discussed in the following sections.

◆ *Overtrading, or "Marketitis"*

Many traders feel they need to play the market all the time. Reasons vary. Some crave the excitement. Others see it as a crutch to prop up their hopes. If you are out of the market, you cannot look forward to its providing financial gain. When everything else in your life results in disappointment, the trade or investment serves as something on which you can pin your hopes. In such situations, the trader or investor is using the market to compensate for his frustrations. For others, the motivation of constantly being in the market is nothing less than pure greed. In all these cases, the motivations are flawed so it is not surprising that the results are also.

H. J. Wolf, in his 1926 book *Studies in Stock Speculation*, calls this phenomenon "marketitis." He likens it to the same kind of impulse that makes a man board a train before he knows in which direction it is headed. The disease leads the trader to believe that he is using his judgment when in fact he is only guessing, and it makes him think he is speculating when he is in fact gambling. Wolfe viewed this subject to be of such importance that he made it the "burden" of his ninth cardinal principle of trading, "Avoid Uncertainty." (See Chapter 14.)

He is telling us that everyone should stay out of the market when conditions are so uncertain that it is impossible to judge its future course with accuracy. This conclusion makes a lot of sense when we consider that one of the requirements of obtaining mental balance and staying objective is to have confidence in our position. If we make a decision on which we are not totally convinced, we will easily be knocked off course by the slightest piece of bad news or an unexpected price setback.

Another consequence of overtrading is loss of perspective. Bull markets carry most stocks up just as a rising tide lifts all boats. In a bear market, most stocks fall most of the time. This means that the purchase of a perfectly good stock is likely to go against you when the primary or main trend is down. If you are constantly in the market, your time horizon will be much shorter, so much so that you will unlikely recognize the direction of the prevailing primary trend. Only after a string of painful losses will you come to the conclusion that the tide has turned.

When business conditions deteriorate, manufacturers cut back on production because there is less chance of making a sale. Traders and investors should regard their market operations in a similar businesslike approach by curtailing activity when the market environment is not conducive to making profits.

◆ The Curse of the Quote Machine, or "Tickeritis"

A constant resort to price quotations clouds judgment. Uncontrolled tape watching or quote gathering is a sure way of losing perspective. Just after I began trading futures in 1980, I remember renting a very expensive quote machine that also plotted real-time charts. At the beginning of the trading day, the screen was blank. As the day wore on, it gradually filled up as each tick or trade was plotted on the screen. This seemed to be a good idea at the time, because my approach to speculation had a technical, or chart-watching, bent. What better way to trade than to have the most up-to-date information.

Unfortunately, the task of actually following these charts and trading from them was emotionally draining. At the end of the day, it seemed as though I had endured several complete bull and bear cycles. As a result, my perspective changed from a long-term to an extremely short-term outlook. To make matters worse, the market had usually moved a great deal by the time my orders reached the floor of the exchange. Consequently, the executions were not what I had expected.

This point is not meant to reflect badly on the brokers concerned but merely to indicate that the time lags involved in such transactions were not conducive to trading successfully on such a short-term horizon. I am not suggesting that one should never trade on an intraday basis. Very few people, however, have the aptitude and quick access to the floor of the exchange to make such an approach profitable. You really need to be a professional, devoting a full-time effort into such a project to have even a small chance of success.

In 1926, Henry Howard Harper wrote an excellent book called *The Psychology of Speculation*. He describes this constant need to watch the market as "tickeritis." A sufferer of tickeritis, he reasoned, "is no more capable of reasonable and self-composed action than one who is in the delirium of typhoid fever." He justified this comment by explaining that the volatile action of prices on a ticker tape produces a sort of mental intoxication that "foreshortens the vision by involuntary submissiveness to momentary influences." Just as an object seems distorted when looked at too closely through the camera's lens, so does close, constant study of the ticker tape or quote machine distort your view of market conditions and values.

If you are in the quiet of your own home, it is possible to conduct a careful and reasoned analysis of what investment or trading decisions you would make the next day or next week based on certain predetermined triggering points. In the quickly shifting sands of rumor, manipulation, and unexpected news, however, it becomes very easy to lose your reasoning powers. Occasionally, you will find yourself subject to the hysteria of the crowd, frequently doing the exact opposite of what you may have been planned in the quiet solitude of the living room last night. This does not mean that everyone who turns off the TV or quote machine will be successful, merely that such a person will have greater perspective and a more open mind than one who submits to the lure of ticker or quote.

Some traders and investors have an ability to sense important reversals in price trends based on their experience, observation, and interpretation of price quotes or ticker action. In this case, they are using the price action solely as a basis for making decisions. But this ability takes a great deal of expertise. Successful practitioners of this method live and breathe markets and are extremely self-controlled. The main difference between these individuals and the vast majority of us is that they become *buyers* after prices have reacted adversely to bad news and *sellers* when prices respond upward to good news. They do not react to news in a knee-jerk fashion but use their experience to move in the *opposite* direction of the crowd.

◆ Hope, the Most Subtle of Mind Traps

After prices have experienced a significant advance and then undergo a selling frenzy, the activity often leaves the unwary investor with a substantial loss. It is natural to hope that prices will return to their former levels, thereby presenting him with the opportunity to "get out." This redeeming concept of hope is one of the greatest obstacles to clear thinking and maintenance of objectivity.

Hope often becomes the primary influence in determining a future investment stance. Unfortunately, it can only warp or obscure sound judgment and will undoubtedly contribute to greater losses. In a sense, the victim of hope is mentally trying to make the market do something that he *desires* rather than make an objective projection based on a *solid appraisal of conditions.*

Hope is defined as the "expectation of something desired." Sound investment and trading approaches are based, not on desire, but on a rational assessment of how future conditions will affect prices. Whenever your position is under water, you should step back and ask yourself whether the reason for the original purchase is still valid or not. Ask these questions: If all my money were in cash right now, would this investment or trade still make sense? Are the original reasons for making the purchase still valid? If the answers are positive, then stay with the position; if not, then the only justification is one based on hope.

Whenever you can identify hope as the primary justification for holding a position, close it out immediately. This action will achieve two things. First, it will protect you from a potentially serious loss. If your exposure is being rationalized on hope alone, you will be ignorant of any lurking dangers and will be that much more vulnerable to further price declines. Second, it is vital for you to regain some objectivity and free yourself from as many biases as possible. This can be achieved only by selling your position and making an attempt at a balanced assessment of your situation.

◆ *Sentimentality*

Everyone involved in markets sooner or later discovers an area for which they have a special liking. It may be a specific commodity, stock, or industry group. It could be the company you work for or an old inherited stock that has consistently grown and grown. So-called "gold bugs" feel that way about the price of gold, for example. There is certainly nothing wrong in developing a philosophy or expertise that empathizes with a particular asset class or individual entity provided you hold it for sound reasons. On the other hand, if you become married to a particular stock, for example, never questioning its justification in your portfolio, you are really holding it for sentimental and not rational reasons.

Companies go through life cycles and cannot be expected to grow at a consistently high rate forever. Figure 2–2 shows the life cycle of a typical company. First comes the dynamic stage of innovation. This is followed by consolidation and maturity. Finally, as new innovations and techniques come to the fore, the process of decay begins. This final stage usually occurs long after the original founders have left the scene. The current management essentially is resting on the reputation of a company that was built up by the nucleus of the original farsighted managers. Unmotivated by the same ideals and goals of its founders, the firm has become fat and lazy. At the same time, new dynamic competition has appeared on the scene, and the business environment

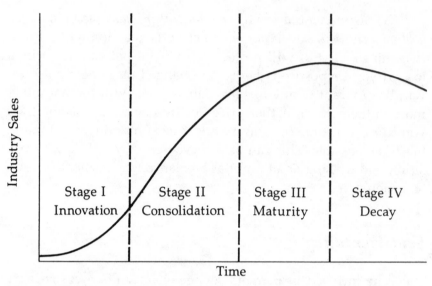

Figure 2–2 The Industrial Life Cycle. Source: Investment Information Services, Inc.

conspires against the company's maintenance of its number one position in the market.

This process is not immutable; many corporations that have successfully managed to rejuvenate and proceed to even greater heights. The point is that no one should ever be married to a particular company or market just because it has treated them well in the past. Here's a typical refrain: "I bought Consolidated at $10 years ago because of its prospects. It's now at $100 and owes me nothing." The reason you bought "Consolidated" stock in the first place is not a justification for owning it today. Anyone who makes such a statement or who feels that way is really taking the easy way out. Such a person is saying to himself, "I don't really want to take the time to look at alternatives. I don't want to have the worry of getting involved with something new." Being married to a particular area or stock avoids the important process of continuous objective analysis. If the situation is reviewed on a periodic basis and it still makes sense to own the stock that is fine, but conditions can and do change. What might have been a good situation for the past 10 years is not necessarily going to be a good one for the next 10.

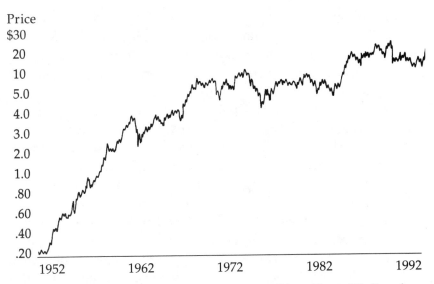

Figure 2–3   IBM 1931–1991. Source: Perrett, *Diversify*, p. 77, (London: Longman, 1990).

Figure 2–3 shows the long-term history of one of this century's premium growth stocks, IBM. In the 30 years prior to 1983, the price had risen from just over $1 to over $100, but something new happened in 1983. Prior to this date IBM had always been a bull-market leader, but the decade following 1983 saw the stock move sideways. Anyone "married" to IBM would not have lost much money, but they would have lost the opportunity to run with one of the strongest bull markets in history, since almost any other blue-chip company would have done much better than Big Blue.

◆ Projecting a Market Direction We'd Like to See, Instead of the Direction Indicated by the Facts

A principal obstacle to maintaining an objective stance occurs when we inflexibly adopt a preconceived idea of where the market is headed. This is quite different from postulating several scenarios of what might happen in a given set of circumstances because that practice implies a more open and flexible state of mind. The greatest danger occurs when we become quite dogmatic about our interpretation of where things are headed. The result is that we are more likely to blot out of our minds any evidence that might conflict with these preconceived notions. It is only after the market has moved against our position and is dealing out some financial pain that we begin to question our original belief. Consequently, anyone who holds a strong inflexible view is coming to the market with a tremendous bias that is inconsistent with the desired state of objectivity.

There is an old saying that the market abhors uncertainty. This adage makes sense, because the market is—as you now know—effectively the sum total of the attitudes, hopes, and fears of each participant. As individuals, we do not like uncertainty. The need to have a firm opinion of where prices are headed is therefore a mental trick that many of us use to eliminate this uncertainty. Removing this bias is difficult, because we are all influenced by events and news going on around us.

Let's take an example of an economy coming out of a recession. The news is usually quite bad as unemployment, which is a lagging indicator of economic health, gets prominent play in the media. However, leading indicators of the economy such as money supply and the stock market do not have the same human interest aspects as mass layoffs and similar stories. You don't sell a lot of newspapers or increase your TV ratings if you tell people that overtime hours, which are a reliable leading indicator of the labor market, are rebounding sharply. As a result, we experience a continual bombardment of bad news at the very moment that the economy is emerging from hard times. This media hype is bound to have a detrimental effect on our judgment, causing us to come up with unrealistically pessimistic scenarios. We find ourselves deciding that stocks will decline, and we execute our investment plans accordingly. When the market rallies, it catches us completely by surprise. We deny the reality, since it does not fit in with our preconceived notions of the direction that it "should" be taking.

One way of overcoming such biases is to study previous periods when the economy was emerging from recession and try to identify economic indicators that might have signaled such a development ahead of time (i.e., leading indicators). This exercise need not be that complicated. Some signs to look for would be a six-month or longer decline in interest rates, including a couple of cuts in the discount rate by the Federal Reserve, a four- to six-month pickup in housing starts, and an improvement in the average amount of overtime worked.

This exercise can provide a foundation for a sound view of the economy's future course. If we rely on a consensus of a number of indicators such as the preceding ones, we will be alerted to any important change that may take place in the direction of the economy.

Economic indicators move in trends lasting a year or more. If you base a long-term scenario on one month's data, the chances are that it will give you a misleading portrait of the economy, especially as this interpretation is most likely to be similar to that held by other market participants and the media. In effect, it will be highly believable to the unwary.

An investment approach based on solid indicators that reacts in a cautious manner to highly publicized monthly readings of the market beats one that is based on a knee-jerk reaction to economic stories that the media have hyped or exaggerated way beyond the bounds of reality. Careful study of the economic indicators just cited and others that have a good forecasting track record help to establish a set of objective criteria that make it less likely an investor would try to make the market dance to his or her tune.

I have presented but one instance of a simple framework that could serve as such an unbiased foundation. Any proven investment philosophy or carefully designed system would serve the same function. For example, stock pickers may base their investment decisions on a specific set of fundamental criteria that over a long period of time have proved to be profitable. Others might use a technical system based on price action. The essential factor is that all these approaches give the practitioner an objective basis for making investments or trading decisions.

◆ Summary

A good starting point for self-examination is to review your own investment or trading record over the past few years. Even if you have made a profit, careful examination may reveal that the record owes a considerable debt to one particular investment whose success was due as much to chance as to any other positive factor.

Even successful investing, then, leaves room for improvement, and this can be achieved by anyone with determination. The improvement will not come overnight because it involves a change in habits, and this can occur only with constant repetition and reinforcement over a long period. Our habits are deeply ingrained emotional patterns that were established fairly early in our lives. Psychologists tell us that they are unlikely to change unless we make repeated and concentrated efforts to change them.

All our emotions lie ready to give or receive impulses based on external criteria. The direction of these impulses, or the manner in which we react to a given stimulus, is determined by our previous experiences and biases. The very fact that you are reading this book indicates that you have the desire to improve your thinking.

3

Independent Thinking

A man must think for himself; must follow his own convictions. Self-trust is the foundation of successful effort.

—*Dickson G. Watts*

*I*n the previous chapter, I established that one of the most important requirements for successful investing is the ability to achieve total objectivity. This is far easier said than done because however hard we try to achieve mental balance, biases from our experiences or outside influences are bound to color our judgment. Despite the difficulty, however, we must try to increase our impartiality as much as possible.

Forces both internal and external can upset our mental equilibrium. To attain objectivity, we must assess the internal forces—our psychological vulnerabilities—and determine how best to overcome them. This process was covered in Chapter 2. External forces emanate from colleagues, the media, and events going on around us. These factors will be discussed in this chapter.

For the most part, exogenous factors have an unhealthy effect on our emotions, distracting us from clear and independent thinking. As such, they represent a major obstacle to achieving our investment goals. It is difficult for people operating in a highly technological society to insulate themselves from all these destructive tendencies. The obvious solution would be to move to an isolated part of the world, turn off all communications, and never read a newspaper. In this way, we would never have our views distorted by events and outside opinions. Such a solution is, of course, totally impractical. Moreover, as we shall learn later, these negative outside influences in the form of group-think or crowd behavior can actually be used in a positive way. Media hype, broker talk, tips, and idle gossip can themselves become invaluable analytical tools for making wise investment decisions when used as a basis for contrary investment thinking.

Once we accept that random opinion creates a certain level of mental "noise," then achieving the goal of maximum objectivity requires us consciously to filter out as many of these unhealthy influences as possible. Jesse Livermore, acknowledged by many as one of history's greatest speculators, tried to insulate himself from external influences that might affect his ability to make money in the markets. In his book *Jesse Livermore's Methods of Trading Stocks,* author Richard D. Wyckoff describes the steps taken by Livermore to avoid such influences.

> For a long while he did not enjoy the advantages of silence and seclusion but many years since, he has made a practice of trading from his own private offices where he is not disturbed by the demoralizing hubbub of a customer's room. The morning journey from his town house . . . is made by automobile; he does not use the railroad trains or subways. Many wealthy and prominent financiers do so, but *they have no special reason for avoiding contact with other people.* [author's italics] Livermore has; he knows that if he mixes during the trip to his offices, the subject is bound to turn to the stock market, and he will be obliged to listen to a lot of *tips and gossip which interfere with the formation of his own judgment.* [author's italics] Playing a lone hand, he does his own thinking and does not wish to have his mental processes interfered with morning, noon or night. (p. 12)

Wyckoff later describes Livermore's office setup. Essentially, it was very simple, consisting of a stock tape and quotations of some leading stocks and commodities. (This indicates that the interconnections among the various markets being popularized today were already known and practiced more than half a century ago.)

Jesse Livermore spent his day closely watching the tape and seeing how the ticker responded to news stories. His interest in monitoring the news flashes was based not on emotion (i.e., buying on good news and selling on bad), but on careful reflection of how those news stories affected the market or a particular stock. Livermore was a great believer in the theory that *the real news is not in the headlines but behind them*. He believed that the only way to succeed in the market was through careful studying and understanding the economic conditions that underlay the financial and fundamental situation of specific companies. Livermore had a particular affinity for studying and interpreting the action on the tape. Other successful people have taken different approaches. In this respect, each of us must search out investment philosophies and decide which one suits us best. Some may choose value investing; others might specialize in growth stocks, asset allocation, or the execution of some simple but effective technical system. As long as it works reasonably well, the nature of the approach is unimportant. What is essential, though, is an ability to execute a chosen technique in a way that does not become sidetracked by unhealthy outside influences.

Although he was not an extremist, Livermore did believe that a sound body helps to create a sound mind. This idea of clearheadedness growing out of good physical condition is reflected in the fact that he was almost always on his feet and standing erect during the trading day. This posture, he asserted, enabled him to breathe properly and ensured unimpeded circulation. Wyckoff also tells us that another Wall Street legend, James R. Keene practiced a similar standing routine.

This brief look at Livermore's operations shows us that he was prepared to make important changes in his habits and lifestyle to accommodate his ambitions. He understood early on that it was important to learn as much as he could about the subject of investing. Livermore also knew that market prices are very much influenced by psychological factors, and so he undertook the formal study of psychology as well. When Wyckoff asked him to identify the two most important attributes of a successful investor, Livermore said patience and knowledge. He insisted that to do well, a market operator must in some way isolate himself to control the debilitating psychological effects of outside influences because they can easily divert the unwary from executing an otherwise perfectly conceived plan of action.

Having established the importance of maintaining an objective stance, we can now turn our attention to some of the more common ways in which our judgment may be distorted. At the same time, we can consider some techniques to help us overcome these seductive influences. The influences that we will examine fall under these headings: The Price–News Drug Effect; Gossip, Opinion Experts, and Gurus; and what I shall call "The Greener Pastures Effect."

◆ The Price–News Drug Effect

Years ago, the only way investors and traders could obtain continuous, up-to-the minute price quotes was to visit a broker's boardroom. These rooms featured a ticker tape set aside for the firm's customers. The boardrooms enabled them to obtain up-to-date information on the performance of their favorite stocks. This was not, of course, an exercise in philanthropy by the sponsoring broker, because the firm knew quite well that exposure to tape action would stimulate trades, thereby lining the firm's pockets with commissions.

Today, the situation is far different, since traders and investors have access to a tremendous selection of inexpensive on-line data, stock-quotation news, and charting services. It is now possible to get instant access to every trade and emerging news event in the comfort of your own home or office. Financial news channels featuring every conceivable analyst with his or her "expert" opinion on the latest developments also are available. The value of such instant and hardly thoughtful analysis is questionable. Moreover, the prognosticators typically appear free of charge, so they are motivated invariably by self-promotion and ego enhancement.

In essence, any investor or trader now has extremely easy access to prices, news, and analyses that tend to stimulate emotions and override the intellect. Last night, for example, you might have done some pretty thorough research on the bond market and concluded that interest rates were about to decline and bond prices would rally over the next few months. This morning you call your broker and purchase some bonds. Even though you have bought them for their long-term potential, you are so excited about their prospects that you can't avoid the temptation to check in with your broker, a financial channel, or an on-line quote service to see how they are doing. As it turns out, they are rallying. This makes you feel good, so later on in the day you check in again. This process has stimulated your emotions to the extent that you are already "booking" the paper profits on the way home from the office and wondering about buying some more tomorrow. The following morning you can't wait for the market to open because you are really anxious to buy more bonds.

Even though the extra purchase goes against your game plan, you feel that this rally is "for real." You just *have* to get some more. As it turns out, other people have the same idea. Bond prices open higher. This just serves to increase your confidence, for you think, "I'm on the right track." During the day, prices continue to rally. You are fully informed of this because the frequency of calls to your broker has now increased substantially. Even though bond prices actually close lower on the day, you regard this to be of little significance, because your confidence level is very high.

Let's analyze what happened. You have made a perfectly good investment based on sound judgment. However, frequent calls to your broker have heightened your emotional involvement. As a result, you have purchased far more bonds than you intended to originally and have greatly shortened your time horizon. Remember that the bonds were initially bought with a holding period of 3 to 4 months in mind. Now you are watching *and being influenced by* every twist and turn in the price, and so you find it difficult to see the forest for the trees.

It's not all that surprising then that you decide to sell the bonds when your broker calls the next day with the news that the securities have sold off sharply and are now at a value below the price you paid for them. From the point of view of your original analysis, the *reason* for the decline is immaterial. You have liquidated your long-term position because you have lost your sense of perspective and ability to think independently.

This is just one example of what can happen in an actual trading situation. Usually this process will be much more subtle and will play itself out over a much longer period. In effect, the desire for news and price quotes becomes a kind of drug on which your emotional psyche needs to feed. As with all drugs, it takes ever greater amounts to maintain the same level of "high." In this case, the dose takes the form of more and more calls to your friendly broker, more often than not resulting in the pyramiding of positions to a very unhealthy level. All addictions are unpleasant to kick, and this type of predicament is no different. In this case, the withdrawal symptoms typically assume the form of devastating losses, as the market slowly but surely assaults every badly conceived position that you have taken.

The obvious way to overcome this problem is to take a leaf from Livermore's book and try to stop such frequent contacts. I am not suggesting that you should never look at price quotes or read the news, because everyone needs to do that from time to time. However, if you keep these contacts to a minimum, your investment results are bound to improve.

One way of lowering exposure to unwanted clutter is to deliberately structure your decision-making process so that purchase and sell decisions are made only when the markets are closed. A particularly busy person may decide to do this over the weekend when there is more likely to be adequate time for contemplation and reflection. You should also do your research when the markets are inactive. In this way, news events will have a less impulsive influence on your decisions. If you are an active trader, it makes sense to use technical analysis to make trading decisions. Leave orders ahead of time with your broker based on the probable action of certain stocks. Your decisions about when to enter and exit the market will then be based on cold, predetermined criteria and not on hot impulses and you will get in and out because of predetermined market action not on an impulse.

◆ Gossip, Opinion Experts, and Gurus

Virtually every book on market psychology warns us against paying undue attention to gossip and rumors. In the old days, this used to take the form of one-on-one contact between brokers and clients, for example. Today, gossip takes other forms. Newspaper and TV reporting may be viewed as a form of institutionalized gossip. A recent variation of this phenomenon is the growing popularity of gurus, who, in many instances are a human substitute for the financial Holy Grail. Let us look at each of these in turn, starting with the general gossip and rumor mill.

Broker, There's a Loss in My Account

The information lifeline of the vast majority of investors is their broker. In most instances, however, people are far better off thinking for themselves than taking the advice of a broker. There are exceptions, of course, and most brokers when asked will count themselves in this category. Never forget, though, that almost all brokers obtain their income from commissions, which naturally sets up a conflict of interest. Experience tells us that the most successful investors are those who hang in for the long term, rarely selling their holdings. This policy contrasts with the objective of the broker and his management. Their idea of success is to maximize commissions.

In reality, a good and successful broker, who looks after his customers' long-term financial well-being, will find that the commissions take care of themselves through referrals from happy customers, growing accounts, and so forth. The unsuccessful broker will be the one who churns the account through constant switching of positions. His clients will invariably lose money, and he will lose their accounts. He will gain over the short run but lose over the long one.

Even if you are lucky enough to run into one of the select few brokers with a mature attitude, there is still no substitute for thinking through each situation for yourself. If you are unable to set realistic profit objectives and decide ahead of time the kinds of conditions or events that will justify the liquidation of a position, you will certainly be more susceptible to news stories or other digressions that even the most enlightened broker will put in your way.

Do not be fooled by luxury sedans and smart clothes, they reflect merchandising ability, not market acumen and success. Brokers also deal in fashion when recommending financial assets. Most sell the merchandise that is sent out from the head office. This could take the form of research on a stock, a "hot" new issue or a "can't-lose" tax shelter. Some brokers will sell their clients anything that has a large commission attached to it. This is hardly different from a car salesperson who receives an extra commission for selling a particularly slow-selling but heavily stocked car. Brokers in large offices often get carried away by particularly aggressive colleagues. In such a competitive environment, it is easy for your broker to recommend individual issues without a careful examination of its underlying value and prospects. The attitude is: "After all, if Charlie is selling it to his clients, then it must be all right."

Never forget that it is *your* money and that *you* are the boss. Consequently, *you* must do the thinking and are the only one who should make the decisions. Use the broker as a source of information to help you to arrive at more enlightened conclusions than you could have arrived at on your own. Use the tremendous research resources to which most brokers have access. After all, your commission dollars are indirectly paying for this information. You might as well take advantage of it.

Differentiate Between Facts and Opinions

When considering a particular piece of news or the news background, it is important to differentiate between facts and opinion. In almost all instances, it is the news and the stories behind the news that merit further study. Opinions do not. Moreover, general news rather than stock market news is usually more helpful in formulating a view on the future direction of prices. This is because the freshest market news, unless it is unexpected, has already been factored into the price structure. On the other hand, the general news reflects underlying economic and financial trends that unfold slowly. They are also more difficult to detect and are therefore not generally discounted by the market.

Beware of Experts!

When it comes to opinions, we must remember that the experts are no more immune from personal biases than we are. In almost all instances, they consciously or unconsciously color what they say or write. In *Speculation, Its Sound Principles,* author Thomas Hoyne warns us that we should never "accept as authoritative any explanation of any person for a past action of the market." Hoyne justifies this on the ground that we should think these things out for ourselves. This practice, he claims, gives us the best preparation for deciding what may happen in the future. We always feel more comfortable if we can come up with a rational justification for a specific price fluctuation. Just think how an "expert" feels when someone calls up from *The Wall Street Journal* to ask why the market fell today. The expert must either come up with a plausible explanation, or risk looking uninformed by replying, "I don't know." The same is true of your broker or anyone in the position of being paid to "know." In essence, long-term swings in the financial markets can be rationalized by the changing perceptions of investors toward basic changes in economic and financial conditions. Unfortunately, that sort of explanation does not sell papers or maintain viewers, so the media are forced to resort to the more rational price movement justification approach.

The problem of literal interpretation of news reporting is made even worse because financial reporters typically contact several analysts to get their views on the day's market action. From these reports, there emerges a sort of consensus from which the journalist can create a headline. A typical article appeared on September 25, 1990. The headline read "Bond Yields Hit March 1989 Levels." Anyone picking up the paper and reading the article would come away with the distinct impression that yields were headed much higher and prices much lower because of soaring oil prices, and so on. However, several days later, on the 28th of September, the same market advanced and the headline read "Treasury Bond Prices Jump After Nervous Investors Bail Out of Major Banking, Financial Issues." Anyone making a decision to sell based on the article would have been wrong, because the price then went back up again. (See Figure 3–1, points A and B.)

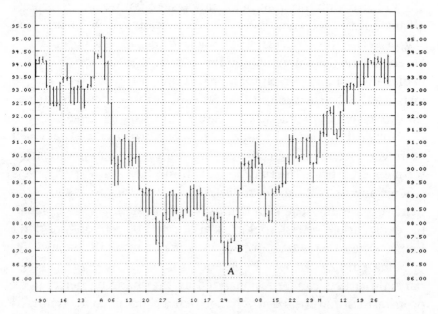

Figure 3–1 Government Bond Futures November 1990. Source: *Pring Market Review.*

This is a typical example of market-related news as it is presented in the financial press. I do not mean to criticize the *Wall Street Journal* specifically for it is arguably the world's premier financial newspaper. The journalists who write such articles are not paid to forecast but to report the news. That, of course, includes street gossip. I am merely stressing that you should not take these articles literally and use them as a basis for making investment decisions because the price movement has normally taken place by the time they are published. Think of it this way: There is no story until the price moves, but the price movement itself creates the need for a story because it has to be rationalized. When you think about it, newspaper reporting of this nature is really a sophisticated and widely disseminated form of gossip featuring off-the-cuff opinions and rumors. A principal difference between media-promulgated and regular gossip is that the former carries the aura of authority and is therefore more believable.

Don't Take Action Based on Tips or Rumors

One of the investor's most useful pieces of information is the certain knowledge that market prices are determined by the mental attitude of market participants to emerging underlying business conditions. In his excellent book *Psychology of the Stock Market* G. C. Selden devoted a whole chapter to the concept of "they." "They" are familiar to anyone who has talked to brokers or other people who earn their living from the financial markets. Typical comments are "They are going to take the stock up this week," or "They have sold off the bonds." It is clearly not possible to identify who "they" are because "they" effectively means all other market participants.

Most investors at one time or another have bought stocks or other financial assets on the basis of tips provided by brokers or other "informed" sources. The opportunity to purchase something based on "exclusive" information is always very appealing. Unfortunately, such transactions almost invariably end in disaster, although that is obviously never the expectation at the outset. For good reason, hot tips are rarely profitable. If you are the recipient of one, you buy the stock based on the assumption that this is a closely guarded secret. In most instances, however, you can be fairly certain that quite a few other people know about the impending development so it has probably been discounted already. Another reason may be that the information contained in the tip is erroneous. Finally, the information may be quite legitimate but not as significant as you might think. For example, you may learn that Company A has just developed a new device for making widgets. On the surface, this may sound like a breakthrough, in reality, however, the market may know of other companies in a similar stage of widget development making your tip somewhat less than exciting.

Another form of tip is the broker-sponsored advertisement for a company that, it is claimed, has a bright future. The copy may be very convincing, but you should consider that the broker typically has a vested interest in seeing the security rise in price. Perhaps the brokerage firm is making a market in the shares, in which case it will be carrying an inventory of the stock. If the price falls, the firm loses money, but if it rises, the inventory can be sold at a healthy profit.

Sometimes such advertisements take the form of promoting a particular asset category or specific commodity, such as gold or silver. In this instance, the broker gains from commissions generated through any resulting transactions. This type of advertising appears all the time, and it is not particularly helpful from an analytical point of view. However, it can be extremely instructive when the same item is advertised by several sources *at the same time*. Usually, the advertisement will make the basic argument claiming that there is a threat to the potential supply of the commodity and thus there is good reason to expect demand to increase. Precious metals are often advertised in this way. The point here is that if everyone is advertising the "story" on silver then the reason for buying it is well known. An old adage on Wall Street says, "A bull market argument that is known is understood." In other words, if all market participants are aware of the potentially good news, it has already been factored into the price. After all, if you know that the price will be influenced by some positive factors down the road, doesn't it make sense to buy *before* the news becomes reality? If you sit back and wait, someone else will learn the story and surely get there before you.

These advertised stories are usually believable because they typically occur over a background of rapidly rising prices. This euphoric market condition is, of course, a result of the rapid dissemination of the bullish news. Be wary of any broker advertisements that promote a specific market or financial asset, especially if the advertisement is sympathetic to the prevailing trend which has been underway for some time and is appearing from a number of different sources.

Having said all that, there are some examples of broker advertisements for issues that have ultimately proved to be profitable. For example, a Merrill-Lynch campaign promoted bonds in the dark days of 1981 (see Figure 3–2). The advice was a few

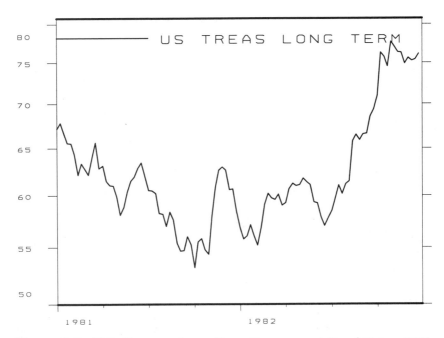

Figure 3–2 U.S. Treasury Long-Term Government Bond Prices 1981. Source: *Pring Market Review.*

weeks premature, but anyone purchasing bonds would have done very well over the next few years. The same effect occurred following a similar campaign by Shearson in early 1982. This was also premature since prices did not reach their lows until the summer (Figure 3–3). Even so, the long-term investor would have profited handsomely since the U.S. equity market was just about to begin one of the largest bull runs in history.

The concepts behind these campaigns and the one described earlier for the silver market are quite different. The first one is concerned with quick profits and catches the excitement of the moment. On the other hand, the bullish Merrill-Lynch and Shearson advertisements emerged when prices were falling and went against the prevailing trend. They reflect two bullish characteristics. First, it is a response by the marketing people who are trying desperately hard to generate more commissions, which have declined as a result of the bear market. Second, values have slipped to bargain basement levels, an important story that the research

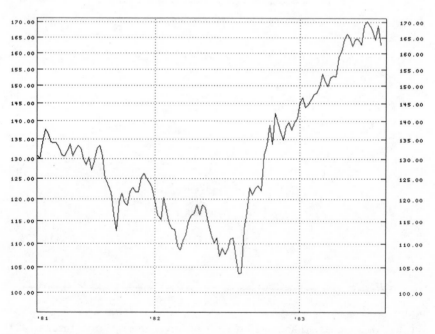

Figure 3–3 S&P Composite 1981–1982. Source: *Pring Market Review.*

departments want to broadcast. The research people are prepared to put their necks on the line because they believe strongly that the market in question is forming a major bottom. By definition, such a campaign must take place after a long price decline when the environment is one of doom and gloom. Disappointing and frustrating whipsaw rallies will have interrupted the bear-market period so that the last thing most investors want to do is buy the particular asset in question. Such advertisements therefore represent a good sign that the market is bottoming even though the timing might be out by a few months.

The Cult of the Guru*

A guru is a market prognosticator who has earned his fame by calling every important turn in a specific market. The reputation of a guru builds up after a number of years of market calls that the investment community perceives to be correct. Sometimes the track record is not all that is claimed; it is the perception of seeming invincibility that is important. During this period, the guru is building a base of followers who are anxious to spread the word. People love to relate tales of market success; setbacks, however, they keep to themselves. At some point, the reputation of the market expert really takes off, and he becomes famous throughout the financial community. This often occurs as a direct result of some article or unusual publicity of a timely market call. From this point on, all eyes are on the guru as market participants and the media wait for his every word. Even rumors of a change of opinion that are later denied can influence prices. The media always need to justify price movements with a logical reason so the guru presents them with a perfect rationale. The mutual respect of the guru and the media initially proceeds to a perfect honeymoon. For his part, the guru is hungry for publicity to promote his following and to perpetuate the myth. By the

---

*A number of these ideas are adapted from "The Life Cycle of Gurus" by Alexander Elder (*Futures and Options World*, Sept. 1990).

same token, the media are constantly searching for a story or a new angle to sell more copies or improve the Nielsen ratings. What better vehicle than a stock market guru who can tie in the human angle with the price-movement rationalization?

The fallacy of the whole guru concept is that it is not possible for one person to consistently call every important twist and turn in the market. Gurus are human like the rest of us. Their market-calling ability moves in cycles, just like the achievements of athletes. For a while they are very hot, but later their ability to call markets becomes questionable. Typically, when a person graduates to guru status, he has already experienced a long period of success. Consequently, the "spotlight" period is normally quite brief as the inevitable period of disastrous forecasting begins.

Another factor, overconfidence, is also at work. This is caused by a combination of "brilliant" market calls and the widespread publicity and adulation that the guru has received. The two feed on each other and give him a false sense of invincibility. Joe Granville, the stock market guru of the late 1970s, reportedly said, "I will never make another mistake again." Of course he did, and some of his mistakes were monumental. Unfortunately, gurus, however talented, become accustomed to their own success and get carried away by the adulation. The marriage between guru and follower then turns into a bitter relationship. The follower does not question the guru's prognostications, and the guru—believing himself to be infallible—is careless and arrogant. The follower loses money solely because he fails to think for himself, and the guru in his turn suffers a decline in reputation. Reputation is important in the financial community. It takes many years to build up, but it can be lost in the time it takes to make just one market call. Moreover, a sufficient number of insecure people in the investment business regard the rise of the guru with incredulity and jealousy. These people, who may well have been proved wrong by the guru in the recent past, now seize the moment to pounce, going for the jugular at the first hint of blood.

The media helped to build the guru's reputation during his climb to fame, but the symbiotic relationship can be equally destructive during his fall from grace. That an "infallible" guru is making mistakes is a newsworthy story in its own right.

Some gurus reach the public's attention through a series of lucky calls and a transitory knack for self-promotion. Such personalities rarely have the analytical staying power to remain successful and soon fade into oblivion. On the other hand, the true guru is usually quite talented. He often develops a new theory, indicator, or philosophical approach that he improves over a number of years. Occasionally, he grabs onto the theories or approaches of analysts who have long ago passed from the scene, taking them to a new level of refinement. The method gradually catches on with a small band of followers and word spreads. The emerging philosophy and its success have an intoxicating effect on the followers, especially as the theory grows bit by bit in popularity, adding even greater prestige to the whole approach.

Unfortunately, the markets are continually changing. What is popular in one cycle rarely works in the next. The legendary technician Edson Gould is a classic example. He had been in the analyst business for several decades, reaching the zenith of his popularity in the 1973–1974 bear market. The world at large first began to here about him through a famous interview in *Barron's*. I remember reading how he called the famous "last 100 points" as the Dow rallied from the low 900s to a new peak, at the time, of just over 1,000. Gould's predictions then called for equities to enter a devastating bear market that did in fact materialize. Gould's most famous indicator was the so-called three-step-and-stumble rule. He argued that once the Federal Reserve raised the discount rate for the third time it was time to begin worrying about a new bear market. He also used some other indicators such as the Sentimeter, which basically measured the cost of one dollar's worth of dividends on the Dow Jones Industrial Average. By his reckoning when the Sentimeter rallied to the 30 level— meaning investors were willing to pay $30 for $1 worth of dividends—the market was overvalued. This also was bearish for the market in 1973. Based on these and other analytical tools, Gould correctly predicted a low in the Dow of about 500. Bear markets, he argued, often cut prices in half. His original projection called for an August 1974 bottom, but the actual bottom in October was still pretty close to his projection.

There is no question that a substantial amount of Gould's forecasting power derived from his many decades of study and practice. But there was also a significant element of chance. Sometimes prices are cut in half, sometimes in quarters, and sometimes in thirds. In this example, Gould clearly got lucky. Unfortunately, Gould faded from the scene almost as fast as he arrived. His three-step-and-stumble rule failed to work on such a timely basis as in the past. The market actually peaked in 1976 as participants, remembering that rising rates had killed the market in the 1973–1974 period, discounted the next rise before it really got underway. As a result, Gould's three-step-and-stumble missed the top and only came into force in the early part of the 1978–1980 advance. By this time, Gould was well into retirement age and never recovered his former glory.

Joe Granville was a market guru of undoubted ability who combined his "revolutionary" theory of on balance volume with a tremendous talent for self-promotion. "Volume is the steam that makes the choo go" is how he described his approach. It is normal for volume to "go with the trend" (i.e., when prices are rallying, volume should be expanding and vice versa). The object of the on-balance volume indicator is to identify the subtle changes in the relationship that develops just before a market turning point.

During the mid-to-late 1970s the market followed Granville's script to a T. He toured the world and drew attention to himself and his methods. Playing the piano and singing and appearing on stage in a coffin were some of the many stunts that he pulled. In early 1981, he turned bearish and the market declined 40 points in one day. This was a huge drop when it is considered that the Dow was trading at less than 1000 at the time. Then, in September 1981 at around the historical high in U.S. interest rates, his grip on the market began to falter. He was abroad at the time and had projected a major decline in the stock market. On September 26, 1981, interest rates peaked and stocks rallied. Although the market eventually went a little lower, September

1981 represented the bottom for many stocks. In the early 1980s, Granville was totally discredited because he remained bearish in the face of one of the biggest bull markets in history. Later on in the decade, he was able to regain some of his credibility, but he never again rose to the level of recognition that he had achieved at the turn of the decade.

Both Granville and Gould were good analysts, but in the case of Granville, his ego undoubtedly got in his way. There is certainly an advantage in following a guru's advice in the early stages; but as his reputation develops, there is less and less chance that the advice will be profitable. The public will always have a certain fascination with the guru cult, but the lesson of history is that the guru is unlikely to make you rich unless you are clever enough to make opposite market decisions at the time when his personal grip on things is peaking.

◆ *The Greener Pastures Effect*

One of the psychological snares that entrap all of us from time to time is the false assumption that we are missing the boat because our investments are consistently underperforming. At the end of every quarter *Barron's*, *Money*, and other financial magazines and newspapers report the performance of the top mutual funds. Naturally, they place great emphasis on the top performers. Statistics show that very few individuals have the good fortune to have invested their money in these funds, yet this publicity often leads us to believe that our investments are performing poorly. Before we make any ill-considered changes, we should remember that such funds are rarely, if ever, consistently at the top of the league. Often the funds on the list have achieved their position purely because their investment philosophy is in vogue or because they represent a particular market sector such as biotechnology or gold shares. These funds do not normally remain on the best performers list for more than one or two quarters, because their style or the sector they reflect can only outperform the market for a limited period. They naturally get the attention of the media because success makes news. After all, does the public really want to read about the fund managers half way down the list?

If you get this "left-out" feeling, it is best to avoid the temptation of asking yourself, "Why didn't I invest in those funds?" If you do this when the funds are in the top-five performance list for the past quarter, the chances are good that they will underperform during the next quarter. This is not as true of funds that reach the top of the list based on five years of performance, because a long-term track record holds a greater likelihood that ability and not luck played the larger role in a good record of return.

Even so, it is worth your while to examine the reasons for good performance over a long period just to make sure that the results were not unduly inflated by one very strong period. Another point worth checking is the size of the fund. It is much easier to obtain high returns with a small asset base of $10 million to $50 million than with one of $500 million to $1 billion.

Part of the reason for this "greener pastures" attitude is that the financial community has recently become much more competitive with greater emphasis placed on performance. Rapid electronic communications have resulted in a corresponding telescoping of the time horizon for most investors. It is now much easier to dump a load of statistics into the computer and analyze the results in a flash. It is hardly surprising then that investors do not have the patience to stick with a nonperforming position when they can see all the fast-moving merchandise around them. Cocktail party chatter always revolves around the winners; losses and disappointments are forgotten.

Is it little wonder therefore that many investors develop a complex that they are missing out on the action? However, does it make more sense to invest in a stock or a fund because it represents sound value and has good prospects or just because it has already moved substantially in price? A far better strategy is to look at the poorest performing funds and industry groups, recognizing that the worst is probably factored into their prices. Then ask this question: What might go right for me in these areas that others have not yet seen?

4

Pride Goes Before a Loss

Pride of opinion has been responsible for the downfall of more men on Wall Street than any other factor.

—*Charles Dow*

There are no statistics to back up this claim by Charles Dow, who was the founder of *The Wall Street Journal.* Anyone who has studied traders and investors in action, however, will know that this statement has substantial merit. It is surprising, therefore, that when I started to do some research on this aspect of market psychology, I could not find one reference to the subject in the index of *any* of the 30 or so books that I examined.

Basically, pride of opinion means stubbornness and the inability to admit a mistake. In most of life's ventures, this attitude can temporarily obstruct relationships and the achievement of specific goals. In the investment world, such dogmatism is a recipe for disaster.

After a long winning streak, almost every investor and trader falls into the trap of thinking that he is infallible. Unfortunately, the market has a way of exposing this weakness, and quite often a long run of success is wiped out in a fraction of the time that it took to accumulate the profit. Overconfidence and enthusiasm breed carelessness leading to poor market judgment and an inappropriate amount of leverage, since it is a human tendency to take on more risk after a run of success.

Pride of opinion also can create problems when markets are falling, because dogmatic investors will often insist on maintaining their positions, even though the preponderance of the evidence shows that facts have changed. This haughtiness also contributes to the desire to break even.

In Chapter 3, we discussed the importance of maintaining an objective outlook. A person's ability to modify an opinion if the background factors or conditions altered was cited as a key determinant in whether he could be successful or unsuccessful in the marketplace. Anyone who holds on to strong views in total contradiction to what is actually going on around him will certainly run into trouble.

◆ Market Operations as a Business Endeavor

Every person engaged in market activity possesses a different psychological makeup, so pride of opinion as a potential weakness will appear in different forms and in differing degrees. Most people hold the view that it is relatively easy to make money when they initially get involved with markets. In the Introduction to this book, I emphasized that no reasonable person would expect to do well in any business or endeavor without first undergoing a substantial amount of training or gaining many years of experience. The same is true of the markets. Trading and investing in the marketplace should be viewed as any other business.

We do not view this field as another business endeavor for two principal reasons. First, the cost and effort required to begin a trading or investing program are relatively low. We need only a little capital and a phone to call a broker or mutual fund company. After answering a few questions and filling out a questionnaire, we are ready to begin.

That ease of entry is not the case in any other form of business activity. Usually, if we are applying for a job, we have to demonstrate that we have the requisite experience or qualifications. Starting a new business is also an involved process. There are government regulations to follow, credit checks to make, leases for equipment and office space to sign, employees to hire, and customers to attract. By comparison, entry into a financial market is a stroll in the park.

The second reason people think that playing the markets is easy is that on face value it does look uncomplicated. All we have to do is buy low and sell high. The media also give widespread attention to the best performing managers and assets, rarely focusing on the losers. This leaves the neophyte with the distinct feeling that trading and investing represent mostly reward and very little risk.

The notion that investing and trading are easy is inconsistent with reality. Successful practice of these arts requires a great deal of humility. Is it surprising that 90% of traders who open futures accounts are wiped out in the first year? If the average person knew ahead of time that the odds were very much against him, would he open up an account in the first place? If he were aware of this fact, surely he would conclude that a certain amount of study, reflection, and change in mental attitude were required to overcome these overwhelming odds.

Some of the sharpest minds in the world have spent huge amounts of time and money in an effort to beat the markets. In effect, these bright, experienced, and well-financed professionals are trying to take money away from you. Is it little wonder then that most individuals lose money when they first begin to trade? This fact in itself indicates that trading and investing are far more complicated than first appears to be the case. Is it really likely that someone with a lot of enthusiasm but little experience will be successful against such formidable opponents?

Not every market beginner is dogmatic, of course; nor is this rigidity the sole reason for the neophyte's lack of success. With your initial plunge into the stock market, however, you should be aware that pride of opinion is the first weakness that the market most likely will exploit. Consequently, it is the first one you must protect yourself against.

You may feel that pride of opinion is a fault that you do not possess. If that be the case, ask yourself whether you could have trimmed or even avoided that last losing trade had your attitude been less cocksure. The markets do not give something for nothing. As R. W. Schabacker wrote in *Stock Market Profits,* "They offer their chief rewards, both financial and psychic, to those who approach it with humility, with a desire for knowledge and with the will to work and study." The following example shows how pride of opinion can be an important obstacle to a successful trading or investment program.

◆ *Dogmatism in Action*

Some years ago a friend of mine was approached by a successful self-made businessman. This person—we'll call him Jack—had taken some large speculative positions in the commodities markets and was losing money at the time. He had known my friend, Bill, for several years and believed that he had a good feel for the market. Bill did not have a lot of experience in trading but had studied the markets for several years.

Jack proposed that they set up a joint account to be run and operated solely by Bill and financed primarily by Jack. Jack also made it quite clear to Bill that he wanted to maintain close contact so that he could stay in tune with Bill's assessment of the markets. This was not for philosophical or educational reasons but because Jack also wanted this information to help him trade his personal account, which was still underwater. Bill was happy to agree to this arrangement because it gave him the opportunity to put his ideas into practice using Jack's capital to help him build some wealth.

The arrangement got off to an excellent start, and the joint account made some substantial profits. Bill told me later that this was partly due to his own management of the account but that he probably owed more to the element of chance and the support and insight he was getting from Jack. They talked quite frequently, and over the short period in which they had been operating, Bill began to appreciate the astute thinking that had made Jack a successful businessman. Jack was also content because his personal account had also turned the corner and was now showing some substantial profits.

After a couple more months, they both saw even greater gains. They were both taking great risks, but fortunately market conditions were extremely favorable. Commodity prices were booming, the partners were bullish, and nothing seemed to stand in the way of higher prices and the ensuing profits. Naturally, both individuals were elated with their success since the markets were confirming beyond a doubt their view of the world. At its peak, the joint account increased by a factor of about 30 in the space of just under five months.

Bill tells me that, in retrospect, both he and Jack had been incredibly lucky to have begun their venture at a time when the markets were in an almost parabolic rise. Looking back on the whole venture, he also confesses that a substantial part of their success could be attributed to the fact that they took some unnecessarily large risks. Since their triumphs resulted far more from the element of chance than a disciplined psychological approach, it was not surprising that problems eventually occurred.

In the first place, they had both become overconfident, believing at the time that playing the markets was easy. In the partners' minds, all you had to do was take a "correct" line on the market's long-term trend, then go out and take chances. If the market turned against your position, you could ride it out, because the setback was only temporary and the market would eventually turn back in your favor.

They had already proved the validity of this course because when the Federal Reserve Board raised the discount rate early in their joint venture, their equity had declined substantially and then risen to a new high. Bill also had taken comfort in knowing from experience that traders who were undercapitalized were the ones who normally ran into trouble. If you took smaller positions and were well capitalized, you could ride out these countercyclical reactions. At the time, that's exactly what they did. As time elapsed, however, their opinion that commodity prices were headed significantly higher was reinforced by the markets' action and their own self-deception.

Bill still believed in the principle of small well-capitalized positions, but in practice he was not implementing such a policy. As so often happens in such cases, he decided to change tactics "temporarily" and take on some larger positions using the considerable equity that had built up in the account for margin deposit on which to leverage the account more heavily. In his mind, he had "resolved" to return to a more conservative approach, but right now he reasoned that this was the proverbial once-in-a-lifetime opportunity on which he should capitalize fully. Thus, not only was their success based on a false premise but also their euphoria caused them to toss out the rule book.

All trends come to an end, and this one was no exception. Because both Bill and Jack were so overconfident, they had become careless and lazy in their analysis. They had failed to look out for signs of a top. Interest rates, for one, were rising sharply. Margin requirements also were being raised for a substantial number of commodities on a regular basis because the authorities knew that a speculative bubble was in the making. Setbacks that would have sent both of them scurrying at the beginning of the venture now hardly fazed them. They had become used to dealing with big numbers and were immunized from the considerable volatility that had developed. They could "afford" to lose huge sums of money because they represented profits. Eventually, the surefire trend would bail them out, and they could sell during the next and final leg up.

That leg never came, and for the first time since the venture began, things started to go very badly. From our perspective, it would have been wise for them to have banked their profits and come back to the markets at a later time, but in their overconfident state they did not see the disaster awaiting them.

Even so, Bill began to show concern when they had lost about one third of their paper profits. Consequently, he suggested to

Jack that they begin to bail out. Jack had always given Bill complete control over their joint account but had constantly made disparaging remarks about how "they" (i.e., other, smarter investors) always drove the market down before it took off to wean out the weaker sisters. This scenario had certainly seemed to be the case on the way up, and it had largely been Jack's correctly proven cynicism that had convinced Bill to maintain positions he would otherwise have mistakenly jettisoned.

It was therefore with some degree of apprehension that Bill approached Jack with the liquidation suggestion. You have to remember, though, that Bill was not a wealthy person; he had a small amount of equity in his mortgaged house. But this equity now represented only about 5% of his total net worth. The balance of his wealth rested in the joint account. On the other hand, the bulk of Jack's net worth was still in his other business ventures, even though his stake in the joint venture and his personal commodity account represented a considerable sum. As a result, Bill now began to consider the implications of what might happen if things went wrong. If you're going to panic, panic early, he reasoned.

When Bill first had approached Jack about liquidating the account, Jack had agreed although Bill felt that his partner wasn't totally convinced. Events soon proved the wisdom of abandoning ship, however, because the markets continued their downward course. Bill recounts how one morning the two of them were up at 4 A.M. on a conference call to their London broker unloading their aluminum, copper, and gold positions. By the time Bill arrived at his office about four hours later the bottom had fallen out of the market as everyone else had the same idea and the speculative bubble had burst. By the time, the whole episode ended the joint account had declined 65% from its peak level. But this figure was still up considerably from the original investment. Bill had made many mistakes, but luck and a good dose of fear had enabled him to survive to invest another day.

Jack had not been so lucky. His own account was now in worse shape than when they first met. If Jack was trading off the joint account and had basically hired Bill to piggyback on their joint experience, how could this be so? The answer: pride of opinion.

Jack's experience is a graphic example of why so many talented and successful self-made businessmen have problems when they become involved in the markets. First, they would never dream of entering a new business without first gaining some experience or hiring some expert in the field. To some extent Jack did this by setting up the joint account, but by not following Bill completely, Jack, in his own account, was in effect saying to himself that he knew better than his partner. A little pride of opinion crept into his thinking.

Second, Jack had a tremendous knack for anticipating when a market was going to take off, and this astute thinking had undoubtedly been a major reason for the success of the joint account. On the other hand, Jack also had a stubborn streak. This character trait had been of great help in his other business ventures because, in buying and selling companies, it enabled him to negotiate a far better deal. He could easily walk away from a deal until the other party agreed to come to terms. In the marketplace, this trait worked to his disadvantage because it meant that he held on stubbornly to several positions long after the joint account was liquidated. Jack was very good at getting into a situation but totally lacked the flexibility to get out of it when the numbers went against him. Pride of opinion was the principal reason his personal account ended up with a loss and the joint account with a profit.

Jack and Bill eventually went their own ways. Jack gave up speculation, concentrated on his other business interests, and achieved even higher levels of success. Bill continued to manage money but never again repeated the kind of risk taking that he had undergone with Jack.

This true story demonstrates that it is not easy to transfer the skills and abilities that have been learned during a lifetime of business activity to the field of investing without modification. Jack's uncanny knack for searching out good business deals helped him to sense when a market was going to take off, but the same stubborn streak that had been so helpful in getting a good deal tripped him up when prices were falling. He was able to assess when a person might cave in and meet his price, but the psychology of the market is quite different. Markets are not interested in making deals. They are totally independent of the needs or desires of one individual. Consequently, when that person permits the stubborn part of his character to take over, the market sees an opening and pounces on the unsuspecting investor to deliver a financially debilitating blow.

Jack's attitude also demonstrates that someone coming to the market after a long and successful business career is initially at a greater disadvantage than someone like Bill, who had experienced few successes in his relatively short career. This is because someone who has been successful will generally be a lot more confident. Confidence, optimism, and enthusiasm are good qualities for investors and traders to possess but only if they are accompanied by an equal dose of flexibility and thoughtfulness. Given time, if the businessperson can learn from his errors in the marketplace, the chances are that the talents that enabled him to succeed in the business arena will also serve him well in the markets.

The principal lesson to learn is that good traders or investors are *always running scared*. By this, I mean that they are always looking over their shoulder to see what new development might be affecting the markets. This does not mean that they are constantly being whipped in and out of the market, nor does it mean that they must take a pessimistic view. What it does mean is that they have learned that the moment they relax and feel that they have got everything figured out they know very well that a new factor will come along to threaten their position. Their approach is not the hold-on-at-any-cost attitude engendered by pride of opinion. It is one of complete openness. The rationale is as follows, "Right now I think the market is going up, but if conditions unexpectedly change and I am lucky enough to spot it, I will change my view and liquidate."

Notice the contrasts between Jack's and Bill's attitudes. Jack's successful career had not conditioned him to run scared. He was in the business of buying failing enterprises and turning them around. Even if the economy deteriorated in a manner contrary to his beliefs, the cheap prices at which he was able to acquire the businesses combined with the productivity gains achieved through his management expertise more than offset a general reversal in business conditions. Dogmatism and pride of opinion therefore represented a small part of the equation.

◆ Ways of Fighting Pride of Opinion

Pride of opinion implies a dogmatic outlook. The result is a failure to take corrective action when you perceive that original conditions have changed. The first step in countering this obstacle is to recognize that you actually have a problem. You should review unprofitable transactions and analyze the thinking that got you to that point. That you are willing to undergo this procedure is in itself a step forward. It not only implies that you recognize that you are capable of making mistakes but it also demonstrates that you wish to correct the causes.

The next step is to set up some safeguards to minimize the chances of falling into the same trap again. When you set up a trade or investment, don't ask yourself how much money you expect to make. Presumably, you believe the reward outweighs the risk, otherwise you wouldn't enter the market at all. Instead, ask yourself, What is the worst that is likely to happen under normal conditions? In other words, consider the risk before the potential reward. This process achieves two objectives. First, it sets out the risk–reward relationship. Second, it helps put you in the state of mind that recognizes *ahead of time* that you can make mistakes.

Assuming that you still go ahead, next determine what conditions are likely to cause you to exit the position. This step will depend on your own philosophical approach to the markets. If your sympathy lies in the technical area, it will involve establishing a support level, the violation of which would trigger a sale. On the other hand, an investor who concentrates more on fundamentals may regard a reversal in the prevailing trend of interest as his trigger point. The device and methodology are unimportant as long as the practitioner has confidence in the chosen vehicle and the approach has been historically accurate. If the practitioner does not have confidence in his investment or trading philosophy and is just paying lip service to it, the chances are good that he will take no action when the condition is triggered. As a result, the whole exercise will turn out to be a waste of time. The final requirement is a commitment to follow through once a preestablished condition has been satisfied.

We have already seen that lucky investors and traders often develop a sense of overconfidence after a successful trading campaign so that clear signs of a pending market top are arrogantly ignored. This is pride of opinion in a more subtle form. We need to remember that it is highly unlikely that anyone will ever consistently turn in super performances year after year. The faster the gains, the more likely they have resulted from the element of chance. A safeguard to prevent that kind of arrogance is to decide ahead of time that once a certain percentage gain has been achieved, some positions should be liquidated and the proceeds taken out of the account and placed in a money market fund or other relatively safe vehicle. This is a typical technique employed by commodity money-management firms. They know full well that when their portfolio managers make huge gains they become careless and arrogant, and so the management of these firms removes the money from the account as a kind of institutionalized defense mechanism. Some firms require their managers to stop trading altogether once a certain amount of gain has been achieved. The manager is then given a "holiday" and asked to come back after several weeks to begin trading again. Because he has to begin all over again psychologically, he thus becomes much more careful.

These same firms have rules that also force managers to close the account down temporarily once they lose a certain amount of money. This also has a purpose because it gives their traders time to ponder their mistakes. Often a written report is required in which the money manager on the losing account reviews his poor performance and tries to identify where he went wrong. After a cooling-off period in which the manager is able to recharge his batteries and find his mental equilibrium, he is allowed to return and continue trading his firm's money. These are sound money-management practices. There is no reason individual investors and traders themselves should not follow them.

5

Patience Is a Profitable Virtue

Most investors and almost all traders and speculators enter the markets believing that they can accumulate profits very quickly. This expectation is fostered by prominent stories in the media featuring successful money managers and mutual funds or highlighting the riches awaiting us if we had only invested in a particular asset. Instant global communication and the rapid dissemination of news create the feeling that unless we act instantly we risk missing out on a major price move.

These attitudes mean that careful consideration and planning are shoved aside and replaced by impatience and impulsiveness. These temptations inevitably lead to situations where market participants attempt to run before they can walk. Under such circumstances, decisions are made in a manner that is the exact opposite of what was originally intended.

It is probably true that in no other business venture are the majority of participants so impatient for results as in the financial markets. Thoughts of individuals who struck it rich very quickly become the guiding force of many would-be investors who think that it will be quite simple for them to repeat the process. Thomas Gibson, who wrote *The Facts about Speculation* in 1923, had already considered this aspect of investing when he said, "The element of time can no more be eliminated from successful speculation than from any other business."

A major mistake made by most investors and traders is to try to call every market turn. This tactic has very little chance of success. Not only is there a tendency to lose perspective, but most of us operate in cycles, alternating between winning and losing streaks. In attempting to call every trend reversal, we invariably lose our objectivity and lose touch with the markets. It then becomes only a matter of time before we are pushed off balance psychologically. Trying to call every market turn also increases the temptation to act on impulse rather than fact. Decisions that are made infrequently are much more likely to be more thoughtful and reflective. Deliberation gives us a far greater chance of being successful than trying to call every twist and turn in the market.

Always remember: Even if a current opportunity is missed, there always will be another. The best investment decisions are made when the odds are in your favor. You increase those odds when you assess investment possibilities with a cold, indifferent eye and avoid the day-to-day clutter of the marketplace.

◆ Staking Out Your Claim

The daily financial press and electronic media brim with specialists who are willing to offer an opinion at any time on any of the markets or stocks that they cover. Sally from *Financial Daily* calls up Harry, a commodities analyst, and asks for his opinion on cocoa, for example. Harry may have no firm opinion one way or the other on the cocoa market, but he volunteers his view anyway purely because he will obtain some profitable exposure in the paper for both him and his firm. Since he has no strong facts to justify his opinion, the chances are good that his forecast will be inaccurate. Still, it will be held up as authoritative "expert opinion."

He would have served himself and everyone else much better had he politely declined the interview, adding that he would call Sally the next time he saw something of importance developing. Under these ground rules, Harry would choose the appropriate time to put forward an informed opinion rather than an off-the-cuff one. This is how guerrilla warfare is successfully carried out. Guerrillas by definition are always outnumbered by the army they are fighting, so they have to even the odds by getting the enemy to come to them. They are the ones who chose the time and the place for battle. If they decided to fight every time they came into contact with the enemy, they would run the risk of an open battle where the army would have an overwhelming advantage.

The same principle applies to people who comment on market activity or who are actively involved as traders or investors. Guerrillas have patience, and so should market participants. The degree of patience involved will depend on the time horizon over which the investment or trade is being made. For a futures trader, patience may demand a wait of one or two weeks; for the one-day trader, it could mean four or five hours, and for a long-term, conservative investor, the time horizon could extend beyond a year. The amount of time is immaterial. The guiding principle is that you should have the patience to wait until all your ducks are in a row. It is difficult making money in the markets at the best of times so make sure that *you*—not the markets—decide when the time has come for trading or investing.

Long-term investors who base their investment decisions on fundamental analyses need to wait for the market to become undervalued. One useful valuation measure is the dividend yield on the Standard & Poor Composite Index. In this respect, Figure 5–1 shows that a dividend yield of 6% or greater has traditionally been a good low-risk entry point. For individuals sympathetic to the technical approach, a reading in the 12-month rate of change indicator below -25% would represent a similar benchmark. These entry points are shown in Figure 5–2.

Neither of these indicators is infallible and that is why both the technically and value-oriented individuals in this example must also consider the position of several other indicators in their decision-making process. The approach or time frame makes no difference. The important thing is to make sure that you have the patience to wait for a low-risk entry point for your specific system

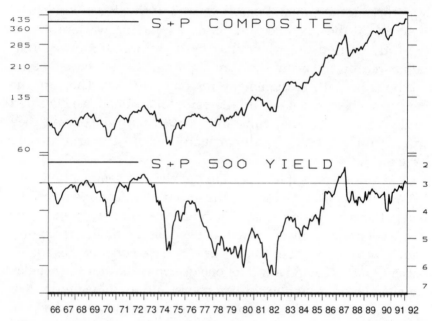

Figure 5–1 S&P Composite versus Its Dividend Yield 1966–1992. Source: *Pring Market Review.*

and time horizon. There is nothing in the rule book that says you *have* to invest. Your impulses may encourage you to get in. Disregard them. Let your head make the decisions.

The first principle in applying patience, then, is having the patience not to get in too soon. When you are in a position to conclude that most of the indicators or conditions that are associated with a major bottom are in place, this will give you a far higher degree of confidence to stay with the trade or investment when things get rough.

When I talk about a bottom, the term "major" in this context refers to a significant point in your own personal time frame. Thus, if you are a conservative, long-term investor, a major bottom in bonds or stocks may occur only every other year as the appropriate juncture in the four-year business cycle is reached. On the other hand, a major bottom for a short-term futures trader may appear once a month.

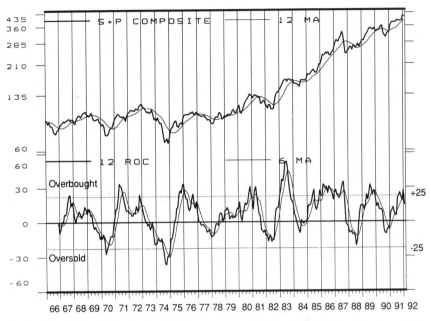

Figure 5–2 S&P Composite and a Twelve-Month Rate of Change. Source: *Pring Market Review.*

◆ Why Playing the Markets Is Different from Other Businesses

A portfolio or trading account at a broker should be run just as any other business. Operating principles should be established, goals should be set, plans should be followed, and the risks and rewards from potential transactions ascertained. We have already discussed that the perceived cost of entry into the investment business is far lower than any other business and that this encourages the inexperienced to try their hand. People who would never take a plunge in a business in the "real" economy are often willing to commit a large proportion of their net worth to the markets. This is due not only to the ease of entry and the view that playing the markets is relatively simple but also to the fact that markets are very liquid.

Let's compare the ease of buying and selling a stock or bond with that of buying and selling any other business. For example, you might purchase a small retail store and then find that running the business is not as easy as you had thought. Perhaps the hours are inconvenient, personnel problems are more difficult than you had originally estimated, and the tangle of government regulations becomes a burden. For whatever reason, getting out is not as easy as getting in. Retail stores are not that liquid, and no buyers are waiting with cash in hand. If there are, you may not like the bid and decide to wait for another one. You will probably have to pay a substantial commission to a business broker, normally 10% of the price. All these considerations add up to the fact that most businesses take time and money to liquidate.

On the other hand, in a financial market there is always a bid-and-ask, meaning that our asset can be readily priced. This liquidity is a powerful reason investing in the market is far more attractive than investing in any other business.

Unfortunately, this readily available pricing mechanism also has its downside. Every time you look at price quotes in the paper or call your broker, you know exactly how much your investment is worth. You can watch it when the price goes up, which will make you happy; and you can follow it when it goes down, which will depress you. This constant access to the pricing mechanism draws you into the market emotionally. Since it is very easy and relatively inexpensive to liquidate the position when your "business" temporarily hits the skids, the temptation is to do just that. So you sell. The odds are strong that you are responding emotionally to the fluctuation in the price rather than the change in the underlying market conditions.

On the other hand, consider the example of a person who buys a manufacturing business for which there is no easily available pricing mechanism. Initially, he may find that things go well. The cost-cutting measures that he takes immediately increase his cash flow. He uses the savings as capital to invest in more plant capacity and equipment to spur future growth. After awhile, though, he runs into problems; sales slow down and the economy looks weak. Our entrepreneur may decide to sell his business, but he is less likely to do so because he cannot find a suitable buyer. Eventually, he no longer experiences the urge to sell and hangs on until retirement several years later. When he finally liquidates the business after 15 years, he finds that it has appreciated in value to a considerable extent and he now has a wonderful nest egg. In this example, the business owner concentrated on running his business. He was not constantly looking to see how much it was worth each day for the principal reason that he couldn't. The nature of his business was such that it forced him to be patient. He could, of course, have sold it any time during those 15 years, but the costs and difficulties involved in selling were strong enough to keep him from taking that step.

Investing in the stock market, on the other hand, is much different. There, the constant price fluctuations, the market's addictive response to news, and its emphasis on short-term performance drag us in by our emotions, causing us to make hasty and ill-considered decisions. The liquidity and pricing mechanism that make it easy to enter the financial markets have their downside: They literally try our patience. We have a tendency to think that to be successful we need to have constant access to prices and other information. As we have seen in previous chapters, too much access actually works against our best interests.

◆ *Patient Investing Usually Means Profitable Investing*

In an article in the Burlington, Vermont, *Free Press* of March 5, 1991, Eric Hanson of Fraser Publishing quotes a study done by Jack Vander Vliet of Dean Witter, the brokerage house. The study assumed that a person put $2,000 into the stock market in each of the preceding 21 years, right at the market's yearly high. Each contribution was left to grow and was never sold. Even though each purchase was made at the worst possible time, the fictitious portfolio nevertheless appreciated at a compound average rate of 11.6%. The seed capital of $42,000 would have grown to $180,000. This strategy would have worked principally because the market advanced significantly during this 21-year period, according to the study. Even so, it is important to recognize that this time frame also embraced the devastating 1973–1974 bear market as well as the 1987 crash. Anyone buying bonds between 1960 and 1980 using the same methodology would not have fared so well, because bond prices were in a secular, or very long-term, decline.

The argument is not that you should blindly buy, hold for the long-term, and expect to prosper, because this just isn't the case. No, the real point of the example is that if you enter an investment with an optimistic and soundly reasoned view, the chances are that it will be profitable. If you respond to every news item and price setback you may or may not make money, but you will almost certainly fail to realize the profit potential of your idea. It is important to sit patiently with the investment—provided the underlying conditions have not changed—because then your odds of success will be that much greater.

To quote from Mr. Hanson's article, "The point is long-term planning. It's far more important to decide how much risk you want to take, how much money you are comfortable investing and how those assets should be divided among stocks, bonds, real estate, etc. than it is to worry about what is going to scare the market tomorrow." In other words if you do your homework properly, just relax and let the markets do the rest.

I can cite some personal experiences to back this up. In the early 1980s, I perceived, correctly as it turned out, that interest rates had reached a historical peak and that over the course of the next 10 years or so bond prices would rally. I also knew from studying markets that this huge rally was unlikely to be a straight-line affair but would be interrupted by some fairly important countersecular price moves lasting a year or more. Interest rates on government bonds were in the 11%–14% range at the time. Having done my homework, the next step was to purchase some bonds, which I did for both a personal account and a corporate pension fund that I was managing. Since the pension fund did not need the interest, was not subject to capital gains, and had a long-term profit objective, I purchased some zero coupon bonds. Regular government bonds were purchased for the personal account. Things began very well for both investments as interest rates did, in fact, decline.

After awhile, I began to study the economy and the technical position of the bond market a little closer and did not like what I saw based on a one-year outlook. This encouraged me to liquidate the bonds in the personal account. You can see that I had already broken one of the rules of investing, because I had originally estimated that some major corrections could be expected along the way. And, as it so often turns out, my short-sighted trading decision was wrong. Liquidation took place in the very early part of January 1986 at around a price of 87. By March, the market had reached 105. In the space of three months the bond gained as much as it had in the previous 16 months. You can imagine the exasperation and frustration I felt as a result of this foolish mistake. The psychology of the situation was that I was expecting yields to fall even further in this "once-in-a-lifetime" bond bull market. In 1984, I was very happy that I had indeed "locked in" historically high double-digit yields, even though the first part of the decline from 15% to 11.5% had been missed. But now I was actually out of a market that seemed destined to rally forever.

Frustration at this point drove me into the Australian bond market, where it was still possible to earn 13% on government-backed paper. Again my homework was quite accurate and over the next few years both the bonds and the currency rallied. It would have turned out to be an extremely profitable investment *if I had the patience to stay with it.* But, of course, I did not. Within a few weeks, both the bond price and the Australian dollar began to dip. I had also bought a substantial position and was not psychologically prepared for the twofold risk that was being undertaken. These were market and currency related. Australian bond prices declined and so did the Australian dollar—I lost heart and sold. During the ensuing five years I made various forays back into the U.S. bond market based on my expectation for the secular or very long-term trend. While each of these expeditions was profitable, none came anywhere near realizing the potential of the overall price move.

The lesson in patience comes from a comparison of my performance in the personal account as opposed to the pension account. You will remember that in 1984 the pension account purchased zero coupon bonds with the identical long-term objective as the personal one. The difference was that when I came to liquidate the pension account I found that the spread between the bid and ask price was considerable, because the bonds were illiquid. This meant that if I was going to repurchase the bonds at a later date and was wrong, the cost of doing so would have been prohibitive. Consequently, it was the expense of getting in and out that forced me to have the patience to stick with the position. If I had lost total faith in the secular interest rate decline thesis that would have been another matter, for then it would have paid to have liquidated regardless of the cost. But my fears were always of a short-term nature, and I could always justify getting out of a position in the personal account because of the ease and low cost of getting back in. What I did not realize was that the desire to reenter the market would fade rapidly once the price had moved above my point of liquidation.

I had read about the danger of losing your position in the middle of a trend in Edward LeFevre's *Reminiscences of a Stock Operator,* but it wasn't until I had gone through the process myself that the lesson *began* to sink in. The word "began" has been emphasized because it takes a long time for a learning experience to become a habit.

6

Staying the Course

One of the most difficult aspects of investing and trading is staying with your original investment philosophy. Quite often, you will find yourself reentering the market after a string of losses with the thought, "This time I will stick to my plan. I will *not* get sidetracked." It really doesn't matter whether you are a trader or an investor; you face the same problem. Only the time horizons or events may differ.

It sounds like a relatively simple proposition to make an investment or trading decision based on a particular approach and then to stick to that plan come what may. In practice, though, it is difficult. Many people, developments, and psychological hurdles are ready to trip us up at the very first opportunity. We begin with the very best of intentions; yet so often we find ourselves changing our plans in midcourse and losing out on what could have been a very profitable investment or trade.

While it is important to stay the course, it is also necessary to remain flexible enough to change direction if the need arises. This advice may sound contradictory. In fact, it makes eminent sense, but *only* if your shift in tactics or strategy is based on changes in the underlying economic conditions. Most of us face quite a different problem. We set off with a plan and, after awhile, get diverted by an unexpected news event, a comment by our broker, or a news story. We either totally forget or choose to ignore that nothing has basically changed. In fact, there *has* been a change. It is internal, however, and has taken place in our minds. It is not an external event that will affect the outlook for our investment. Something has happened to affect our *perception* of what is taking place rather than what is *actually* taking place. Let's examine a couple of examples. The first one involves an investment; the second, a trading approach.

◆ Sticking with the Plan

Investments

The business cycle lasts approximately four years from trough to trough. Equity prices are essentially determined by the attitude of investors to the outlook for corporate profits. Profits revolve around the business cycle, so bull markets for equities should last about half the length of the business cycle, a period of about two years. In fact, market history shows that cycles last a little longer, since it normally takes a longer time to build than to tear down. Price trends in financial markets are rarely straight-line affairs. They usually take the form of rallies interrupted by a retracing movement as shown in Figure 6–1. The overall trend is up but these corrections, known in the trade as secondary reactions, are usually of sufficient magnitude and suitably deceptive appearance to cause even the most stalwart bull to question the validity of the primary uptrend and vice versa in a bear market.

Secondary reactions typically retrace one third to two thirds of the previous rally and can last anywhere from six weeks to six months. Nothing is more likely to shake anyone out of an investment or trade than a market going against his position. The successful people are those who are able to ride out the storm psychologically because they refuse to abandon the underlying philosophy that originally led them to the market. The type of approach is not important, provided that it has a proven track record.

Let's suppose that you are lucky enough to recognize the start of a new bull market at a relatively early stage and that you

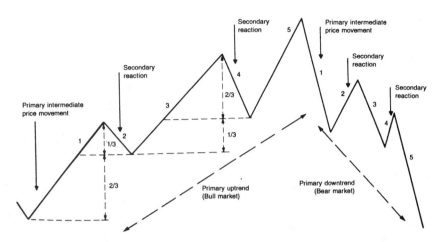

Figure 6–1 Secondary Corrections within a Primary Trend. Source: Pring, Martin J. (1991). *Technical Analysis Explained.* New York: McGraw-Hill. Used with permission.

are employing a very simple but tested investment plan. This approach recognizes that changes in financial conditions and Federal Reserve policy strongly influence equity prices. The method states that if the Fed lowers the discount rate following a series of hikes, equities are likely to experience a bull market.

Conversely, trouble is signaled after three successive hikes in the rate. The market, of course, is affected by many factors other than financial ones, but Table 6–1 shows that between 1956 and 1991 this simple approach worked reasonably well. There were periods such as 1958 when the third hike gave a premature sell signal and 1981 when the signal came early, but by and large this approach has proved to be a profitable method for long-term investing.

The rationale for its success is that easier money and lower interest rates sooner or later help stimulate the economy. Thus, expanding business means higher profits; greater profits imply higher dividends, which in turn mean higher stock prices. After a point, rising interest rates kill the economy. This in turn results in a bear market in equities.

Table 6–1   Discount Rate Principle Applied to the Stock Market

Bearish Periods

Date of Third Hike	S&P at Third Hike	Date of First Cut After Third Hike	S&P at First Cut After Third Hike	Gain or Loss (%)
Sept. 1955	44.34	Nov. 1957	40.35	−9.00
Mar. 1959	56.15	June 1960	57.26	1.98
Dec. 1965	91.73	Apr. 1967	90.96	−0.84
Apr. 1968	95.67	Nov. 1970	84.28	−11.91
May 1973	107.22	Dec. 1974	67.07	−37.45
Jan. 1978	90.25	May 1980	107.69	19.32
Dec. 1980	133.48	Dec. 1981	123.79	−7.26
Feb. 1989	293.40	Dec. 1990	328.33	11.91

Bullish Periods

Date of First Call	S&P at First Cut	Date of Third Hike After Cut	S&P at Third Hike After Cut	Gain or Loss (%)
Feb. 1954	26.02	Sept. 1955	44.34	70.41
Nov. 1957	40.35	Mar. 1959	56.15	39.16
June 1960	57.26	Dec. 1965	91.73	60.20
Apr. 1967	90.96	Apr. 1968	95.67	5.18
Nov. 1970	84.28	May 1973	107.22	27.22
Dec. 1974	67.07	Jan. 1978	90.25	34.56
May 1980	107.69	Dec. 1980	133.48	23.95
Dec. 1981	123.79	Feb. 1989	293.40	137.01
Dec. 1990	328.33			

Looking objectively at the table, it is difficult to see why someone who had adopted this approach would not or could not fail to follow it in view of its long history of profitability. The fact is that most people would not. A quick recount of the events and market action following one of the signals can help explain this apparent irrationality that lurks inside the psyche of most investors.

One of the best bull markets of all time occurred in the 1980s. Let's take a look at when the discount rate signal for this bull market was triggered and then at what followed. The rate was raised quite rapidly between the middle of 1980 and the beginning of 1981 and then was lowered in December 1981. This was the signal to enter the stock market. Figure 6–2 shows that the market rallied for a while and then sold off to a new bear market low. Almost immediately, the investment was under water. It also looked as if short-term interest rates had begun a new cyclical rise, because they rebounded from their December 1981 lows in January and early February. However, the discount rate did *not* change, so following the rule would have meant staying with the position.

During the next few months, there were plenty of reasons to bail out of stocks. In May 1982, for example, the market sold off substantially due to fears of some major bankruptcies. More bad news occurred in July 1982, as the headlines began to focus on

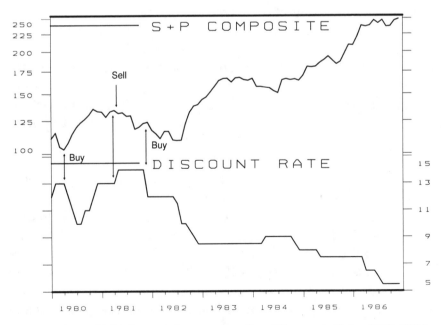

Figure 6–2 S&P Composite versus the Discount Rate 1980–1986. Source: *Pring Market Review.*

the debts of Mexico and other Third World countries. Most investors at the time feared an economic collapse triggered by an impending crisis due to overindebtedness.

It would certainly not be unreasonable for any investor to look at his losing position at this stage and, taking a cue from all the pessimistic news, liquidate his position. He could rationalize this hasty action by concluding that the discount rate approach was normally a good one but would not work this time "because conditions had changed." What we see here, though, is an investor letting events, rather than a thoughtfully considered investment philosophy, dictate his investment decision.

The investor entered the market on the basis that the Fed was easing the discount rate and that sooner or later this would favorably affect the economy and the stock market. In that respect, nothing had really changed. If anything, monetary conditions actually improved, because the discount rate was lowered again in July 1982. This indicated that the authorities in the Federal Reserve System were well aware of the weakening economy and the probable impending crisis. To the investor, it *appeared as if the financial picture was deteriorating*. The news was bad, and stocks were much lower than when he had entered the market. If the position had been liquidated in June or July 1982, it is unlikely that an investor in such a state of mind would have been able to get back into the market because of the speed of the subsequent advance. A great profit opportunity would have been lost. On the other hand, anyone who had faithfully followed the discount rate rule would not have had to worry about missing out because he would already have been positioned.

What often seems to happen is that people enter a market with the very best of intentions of following a system. They have proved to their own satisfaction that the approach has stood the test of time, and they begin the campaign with a great deal of enthusiasm. Unfortunately, they conveniently remember only the periods of good performance when they should be asking themselves how much they stand to lose if this current signal turns out to equal the worst one since the 1920s.

Failure to prepare for the worst raises expectations and leads to unnecessary frustration. When some bad news pushes prices lower, it is a natural instinct to head for the exits at precisely the wrong time. This is why it is so very important to stick to the rules for the approach that has been originally chosen. If it is a proven one, the chances are that the negative consequences of such a decision will be more than eclipsed by the benefits of staying the course.

We return to our example in the spring of 1984. At this time, the market was substantially higher than it was in 1982, but short-term interest rates had begun to rise. Dire predictions about the economy were being made at the time. In April 1984, the discount rate was actually raised from 8.5% to 9% after almost a year of rising short-term interest rates. It would have been quite easy to conclude that a second or even third discount rate hike was around the corner. The sensible thing appeared to be to liquidate stocks *before* the third hike. After all it was becoming fairly obvious that equities were in a bear market. Such anticipatory action would have been counterproductive because the market took off once again in the late summer. As it turned out, there were no more increases in the discount rate; indeed, several cuts took place before the rate was raised again.

By the summer of 1987, the discount rate had been raised twice, and the next major test occurred in October 1987 (Figure 6–3). This was the month of the stock crash in which prices declined by 25% in a matter of a few days. It would take tremendous will power for anyone to maintain an equity position after such devastation and in an environment of considerable uncertainty. The news background was extremely bearish, but interestingly the crash never spread from Wall Street to Main Street because the economy continued to expand. More to the point, the third discount rate hike did not come, and therefore the method called for a fully invested position. Ironically, the crash effectively extended the recovery as well as the bull market in equities, because the authorities lowered interest rates a little to maintain confidence. The third hike did not come until February 1989 when the Standard & Poor Composite Index stood at 290–300, slightly

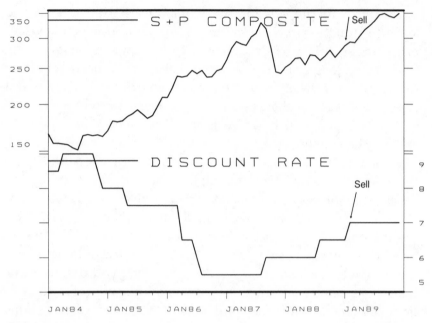

Figure 6–3 S&P Composite versus the Discount Rate 1984–1990. Source: *Pring Market Review*.

above its 1987 peak. Staying the course over the 1981–1989 period would have enabled an investor to ride the advance in the S&P Composite from 123 to 290.

Clearly, this approach to investing is not a perfect one. In the example shown, the method did not get the investor in at the bottom of the market and out at the top. But, as we discovered in Chapter 1, there is no such Holy Grail promising quick riches. The discount rate indicator system is one of many approaches to investing that over time keep you in the game for the big "up" movements, yet help you to avoid the worst aspects of a prolonged bear market. The chosen methodology could be something quite different. As long as it has a proven long-term track record and the practitioner feels comfortable with the approach, your chosen methodology will provide an invaluable form of discipline—provided, of course, that you follow the rules fairly rigorously.

An investment method's principal function, therefore, is to keep its adherent from becoming prey for the many traps and delusions that hinder sound decision making. Our example showed that the investor could have almost tripled his money using the discount rate indicator, but he would also have needed tremendous patience and discipline. If he had kept his eye on the ball, it would have worked very well, but just one incorrect move at the wrong time would have caused him to miss out on some spectacular opportunities.

Traders

The same principles apply to short-term traders in the futures markets. In this case the leverage is much greater and time horizons substantially shorter. With $1,500, it is possible for example, to "control" $35,000 worth of gold or $100,000 worth of bonds, and so forth. If the price of these contracts rises, correctly positioned traders can make a killing. Unfortunately, leverage works both ways so if the bet is placed in the wrong direction, in the absence of sound money management, it is just as easy for the equity in the account to be wiped out. For this reason, traders in the futures markets cannot afford to let the market go too far against their position.

Again, let's consider a mechanical indicator that might be employed in the bond market. Let's say that as a trader you are not interested in making a killing or getting in at the bottom and out at the top. You would be quite happy if you could adopt some kind of approach that can give you a satisfactory profit. One possibility might involve a simple 25-day moving-average crossover. The moving-average crossover works this way: You calculate a 25-day moving average of bond futures, buying when the price crosses above the average and selling when it moves below it. This approach does not consistently return profits. We are using it as a vehicle to explain a point, *not* as a recommended system. For the purposes of the example, it is assumed that this crossover method has been successfully back tested with historical data.

Figure 6–4 shows that a "buy" signal was generated in April of 1991 at Point A. Our hypothetical trader would have entered the market with great hopes for a profitable trade, but he would have soon been disappointed because it quickly turned into a loss. Undaunted, he reentered the market once again, only to be rebuffed by a further loss, Point B. It is only natural that he now begins to doubt the system. Even though he knows that it has turned in an overall profitable performance during the previous three years, and he recognizes that there have been some unprofitable periods, doubts still creep in. Nevertheless, he decides to enter the market once again when the next buy signal is generated, Point C. For a few days, his expectations rise as the market moves in the right direction. Then, some unexpectedly bad news occurs, pushing the price down once again and further compounding his losses. Now he is totally dejected, his system

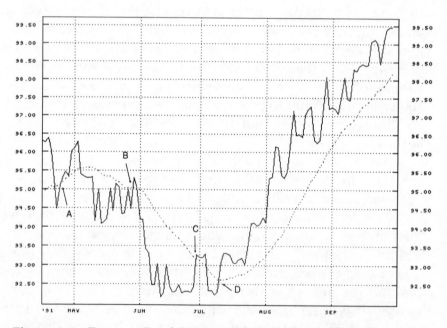

Figure 6–4 Treasury Bond Futures (3-Month Perpetual Contract) versus a Twenty-Five Day Moving Average 1990–1991. Source: *Pring Market Review*.

no longer seems to operate, and the news background is so terrible that he cannot face the prospect of getting back in when the next buy signal comes along, Point D. Figure 6–4 shows that this is precisely when he should have reentered the market, because the price subsequently experiences a very worthwhile rally. It is a fact of investment life that some of the best price moves are often preceded by a period of confusing price action in which markets fluctuate within a frustratingly narrow band. The failure of the moving-average crossover system to operate profitably is a symptom of this characteristic.

Our trader made two mistakes. First, he allowed the news background to influence his trading decision. Second, he failed to give the system enough time to work. In effect, he took his eye off the ball at the wrong time, a mistake that left him with an unprofitable performance.

Anyone who has traded in the markets will recognize this failure to stay the course as a fairly common form of weakness that periodically attacks all traders. How many times have we seen investment books or software programs that promise their readers and users instant gratification? It is doubtful that any purchasers of such merchandise ever profit to the extent of their expectations. To start, most such schemes or systems do not deliver what they promise, but those that do are rarely practiced in the recommended way. Hopeful investors and traders may start off with the best intentions but will rarely stick with their plans. They see the evidence that the system works, but they do not have the patience and discipline to follow the rules.

This phenomenon is not limited to the financial markets. Many health-conscious people, for example, purchase expensive exercise equipment with the objective of getting fit or losing weight. After an initial bout of enthusiasm, however, they lose interest, relegating the equipment to the basement, garage, or attic. It's one thing to know what to do, but it is quite another thing to put our knowledge into action.

In Figure 6–1 we saw that it is normal for a bull market to be interrupted by countercyclical movements known as secondary reactions. This idea of a primary uptrend consisting of a series of rising peaks and troughs also indicates that even if a purchase is made at the top of a rally, such mistakes are only temporary, because the rising trend will eventually bail us out. This leads us to another aspect of "keeping your eye on the ball."

Most of the time it is not possible to have a firm opinion about the direction of the main trend, but when you do, it is usually very unwise to position yourself against it. Let's take a look at a system that I first introduced in *Technical Analysis Explained*. It involves a very simple idea of buying and selling the pound sterling based on a mechanical technique. The rules are described in Table 6–2. The arrows in Figure 6–5 represent the buy and sell signals between 1974 and 1976. This system has been tested back to the early 1970s and would have been very profitable. I calculated that by 1980 anyone who had followed it religiously using a margin of 10% and reinvesting the profits would have turned an initial $10,000 investment into more than $1,000,000. Since then, the system has done even better.

The principle point I am trying to make is that a close examination of the performance shows that the profits have come

Table 6–2 Rules for Buying and Selling the Pound Sterling

Rule 1

Go long when the pound is above its 10-week moving average *and* 13-week rate of change is above 0 and 6-week rate of change is above 0.

Rule 2

Go short when *all* conditions in Rule 1 are reversed, i.e., price below 10-week moving average and both rates of change are negative.

almost entirely from buy signals that have occurred in the direction of the main trend. In Figure 6–6 the top series is the equity line. It shows how an initial $1,000 investment would have fared by following the system on a nonleveraged basis between 1980 and 1992. Some counter-cyclical signals are flagged by the arrows. Note that these reflect the largest losing trades.

This principle of trading in the direction of the underlying trend applies to any intermediate trading system and to most short-term ones as well. Obviously, it is not always possible to have a firm opinion as to the direction of the main trend. When you do, however, it is clearly of paramount importance to trade in its direction, however tempting it may be to do otherwise.

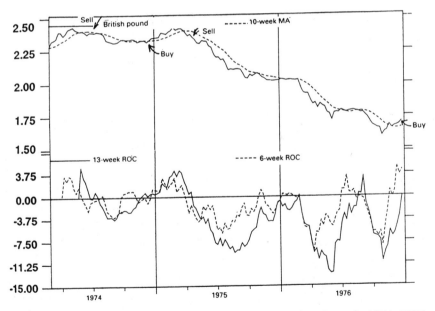

Figure 6–5 Mechanical Trading System for the Pound 1974–1976. Source: Pring, Martin J. (1991). *Technical Analysis Explained*. New York: McGraw-Hill.

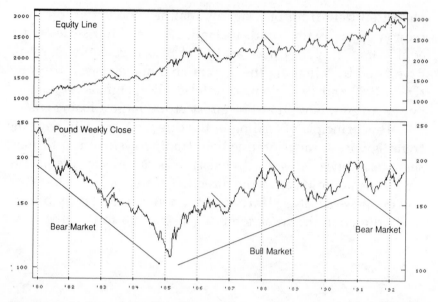

Figure 6–6 Pound Trading System. Source: *Pring Market Review*. This chart has been plotted from the Metastock Professional charting package. The system testing abilities are covered in the "System Testing" segment of the *Exploring Metastock Professional II* video by the author (International Institute for Economic Research, P.O. Box 329, Washington Depot, CT 06794, reproduced with permission.)

◆ Keep Your Eye on the Ball, but Remain Flexible

The idea of staying on a predetermined and well-tested course is sensible, but it is also important to keep an open mind because underlying financial conditions can and do change. This advice may sound somewhat contradictory, enabling us even to do some Monday morning quarterbacking as conditions suit. But that is not really the case.

Most of the time, anticipations of business-cycle conditions propel the financial markets. The economy is not responsive like a car or a speedboat. It's more like an oil tanker; it takes time to change direction. Consequently, any indicators that you are monitoring also will have the tendency to move slowly and deliberately. Some are bound to fail from time to time and that is why no investment decision should be based on one indicator alone but on a consensus.

Occasionally, though, institutional changes will affect the reliability of a specific indicator. Under such circumstances, it makes sense to disregard the indicator's signals, since they are unlikely to be as reliable as they were in the past. A classic example of this occurred in the 1980s when stock-index futures and other derivative products were introduced. These products resulted in some brand new trading and arbitrage activities, the most notable of which was program trading. Not surprisingly, this new activity distorted some of the indicators that market technicians had been using with great success since the 1930s. The most notable casualty was the short-interest ratio. (The ratio of the short interest to average daily trading volume for the month.)

Similar institutional distortions occurred in the 1970s when inflation was rampant. Reported earnings, for example, failed to take into account inflationary conditions. Profits were thus greatly exaggerated when large but unsustainable inventory gains unduly overstated the true earnings picture. Investors basing an approach on price–earnings ratios without regard for this important change could easily have run into trouble. They may have had their eye on the ball when selecting a stock in the sense that the selection criteria remained the same. Environmental changes, however, may have greatly distorted the quality of the stock's earnings.

Another example of an institutional change occurred with the growing popularity of money-market funds in the 1970s and early 1980s. Originally these deposits were not included in the money supply numbers. As the amount of cash squirreled away in these funds increased, the money supply numbers became more and more distorted. Eventually, money market funds were incorporated into some measures of money supply. However, anyone who continued blindly to use changes in the money supply as a basis for making investment decisions prior to these definitional changes could have been badly misinformed.

These are all examples of the importance not only of following your chosen investment approach but also of periodically reviewing it in case any significant and fundamental economic changes may have taken place.

◆ *This Time It's Different*

One of the worst traps to snare any investor is departing from a tested methodology or philosophical approach and then rationalizing the decision by saying, "This time it's different." All too often, some rationalization for even higher prices will seize the imagination of the crowd after a market has reached and often exceeded its normal technical or fundamental benchmarks. Such arguments are usually compelling, because they appear when optimism is rampant and everyone expects prices to move higher. The arguments are typically based on hope rather than on the facts, which are conveniently overlooked. The "new era" thinking is therefore welcomed with open arms, and little thought is given to the underlying investing concept, or the fact that betting on a "first-time" event usually has disastrous consequences.

A classic example occurred in the 1920s when many investors believed that stock prices had reached a new plateau because the outlook for business continued to be very positive. Few individuals concerned themselves with the fact that stock valuations were excessive and margin debt extremely high. Merger mania and similar phantom concepts captured the imagination of the public who were prepared to take their eyes off the ball by accepting the delusory concept of a "new era."

In the early 1970s, money managers fell in love with the "Nifty Fifty." These were companies whose consistent growth rates and sound financial standing made them so-called one-decision stocks. Examples included Avon, Xerox, and Polaroid. During this mania, the price–earnings ratios of these stocks were bid up to extremely unrealistic levels, but no matter how expensive they became, prices continued to advance. Their valuation was not only excessive in historical terms but in relation to the rest of the market as well. Not surprisingly, they suffered considerable damage in the 1973–1974 bear market, and most took a decade before they returned to their former highs.

In situations similar in nature to those of the 1920s and the 1970s, the warning signs come early—usually too early—because a lot of investors will correctly recognize the sign of an impending top and get out. The problem is that prices continue to advance making it appear that they will never come down. These same investors then return to the market at precisely the wrong time, forgetting all the principles that had encouraged them to get out earlier. In effect, they have chosen to take their eyes off the ball and then must deal with the consequences of their actions. In both examples, the underlying rationale for higher stock prices was false, since prices were way beyond normal benchmarks of valuation.

◆ *Random Economic Numbers Play Havoc with Your Financial Health*

One sure way to get into trouble is to make investment decisions based on single economic numbers with no regard for the underlying trend. So often these days, we see markets that have rallied or reacted in anticipation of good or bad economic news. When the number is released and the reported data counter expectations, the market reacts almost instantly as it unwinds the speculative positions previously set up. Such wild action is catnip to media that thrive on volatility and excitement, but not for the investor or trader caught up in this process. The investor who is able to keep his eye on the ball and maintain perspective should actually be in a position to capitalize on such discrepancies.

◆ *Summary*

It is easy to become sidestepped by events and news stories going on around us. Unexpected price fluctuations stimulate our emotions and are another source of distraction. In such situations, we must make sure that we are not incorrectly drawn into believing that the main trend has reversed. A warm day in January does not mean that spring has arrived, neither does an isolated piece of good news denote that a bear market is over. We have to learn to step back and sort out the woods from the trees.

If we are following a particular approach or methodology, whether it be a trading system or a longer term fundamental philosophy, it is also important to stick with it. Otherwise we lose our basis for making sound decisions.

Part II

THE WALL STREET HERD

7

A New Look at Contrary Opinion

The law of an organized, or psychological, crowd is mental unity. The individuals composing the crowd lose their conscious personality under the influence of emotion and are ready to act as one, directed by the low, crowd intelligence.

—*Thomas Templeton Hoyne*

The Theory of Contrary Opinion was first promulgated by Humphrey Neill, who combined his own experience and observations on the stock market with those of Charles Mackay, Gustav Le Bon, and Gabriel Tarde. Today it is popularly accepted that since the "crowd" is wrong at major market turning points, everyone wants to be a contrarian. In the world of investing, to be caught with the crowd in this day and age is the equivalent of admitting a terrible sin.

As so often happens when a concept or a theory is popularized, however, the basic idea becomes distorted. Those market participants who have not had the benefit of reading Neill and other writers on the subject do not realize that they may be on shaky ground. Neill pointed out that the crowd (i.e., the majority of investors or traders) is actually correct most of the time; it is at turning points that they get things wrong.

This last distinction is the essence of Neill's theory. Once an opinion is formed, it is imitated by the majority. This process can extend to such a degree that eventually virtually everyone agrees to its validity. As Neill put it, "When everyone thinks alike, everyone is likely to be wrong." He writes, "When masses of people succumb to an idea, they often run off at a tangent because of their emotions. When people stop to *think* (italics added) things through, they are very similar in their decisions" (Neill, 1980).

I have emphasized the word "think" because the practice of contrary opinion is an art and not a science. To be a true contrarian involves study, creativity, wide experience, and, above all, patience; no two market situations are ever alike. We know that history repeats, but never in exactly the same way. Hence you cannot mechanistically conclude, "I am bearish because everyone else is bullish."

Knowing when to go contrary is of primary importance. Many of us believe that the particular methodology that we are using in the market ought consistently to work for us. Unfortunately, as we discovered earlier, there is no perfect approach to investing, because the formation of a correct contrary opinion can be a difficult and at times elusive task. Even if we are able to correctly assess where the crowd stands, this knowledge can still result in frustration, because the crowd frequently moves to an extreme well ahead of an important market turning point. Many clever stock market operators correctly knew that the situation was getting out of control in 1928; they had concluded that stocks were overvalued and discounting the hereafter. They were right, but their timing was early. Unfortunately, many investors got sucked in just before the final, fateful top. Economic trends are often very slow in reversing and manias take prices not just past reasonable valuations but to ridiculous and irrational ones as well.

In a timely bearish article in published in *Barron's* in September 1987, John Schultz wrote, "The guiding light of investment contrarianism is not that the majority view—the conventional, or received, wisdom—is always wrong. Rather, it's that majority opinion tends to solidify into a dogma while its basic premises begin to lose their original validity and so become progressively more mispriced in the marketplace."

These trends occur because investors tend to move in crowds that by nature are driven by herd instincts and the desire for instant wealth. If left to their own devices, individuals isolated from the crowds would act in a far more rational way. For example, if you saw a house that sold one year ago for $50,000 now priced at $100,000, you would judge it to be expensive. But if you knew that an identical one down the road just fetched $120,000, the price of $100,000 would seem cheap. This feeling would be especially true if you were bombarded by both friends and stockbrokers telling you of the killing they have made in real estate, along with the rosy forecasts from the media and real estate agents. Even though you might know intuitively that house prices can't continue to double forever, you would become caught up in the excitement of the moment.

Under those circumstances, it is difficult for an individual to think independently from such an established line of reasoning. As Neill put it, the art of Contrary Opinion "consists in training your mind to ruminate in directions opposite to the general public opinions and to weigh your conclusions in the light of current manifestations of human behavior." A good contrarian should not "go opposite" for its own sake, but should learn to *think* in reverse. By taking the reverse side, you will come out with reasons why the crowd *may* be wrong. If the rationale holds water, the chances are that going contrary will work.

Why is the crowd usually wrong? The answer is that when virtually everyone has taken the position the market is headed in a certain direction, there is no one left to push the trend any further. The next step is that a countertrend initiates a new trend in the opposite direction. This idea applies not only to markets, but to political, social, religious, and military trends as well.

Let's take an example of an economy that has been in recession for a long period. At such times the media typically tell of layoffs, weak car sales, bankruptcies, and other signs of hard times. The economic forecasts are almost unanimously and universally grim, and it seems as if all events are working in a self-perpetuating, downward spiral. This is the classic environment in which the majority are extremely despondent. The feeling grows that the economy will never turn up again or, at best, the recovery will be extremely weak.

And the contrarian? He would look up, not down. The contrarian would ask, "What could go right? What normally happens in desperate economic times?" The answer is that once people realize that hard times are coming, they take steps to protect themselves from disaster; hence, they cut inventories, lay off workers, pay off debts, and take other steps to economize. It is these very actions that contribute to the weak economic climate. But once these measures are taken, those businesses and individuals who made them are then in a position to experience tremendous profitability when the economy reaches a balance between demand and supply and starts to improve. As Neill puts it, "In historic financial eras, it has been significant how, when conditions were slumping that, under the pall of discouragement, economics were righting themselves underneath to the ensuing revival and recovery."

The same problem occurs in the equity, or any other market. No investors want to hold stocks if they think that prices are in for a prolonged decline. Naturally, they sell. When everyone who wants to sell has done so, there is only one direction in which prices can go, and that's up. The reason for this is that changes in equity prices are caused by the attitude of market participants to the emerging fundamentals. The reversal in prices is always based on the realization by more and more people that the underlying assumptions of a weakening economy are false. Going into the bear market, many investors vow to buy stocks when interest rates begin to fall since this is a known precursor of an improving economy and stock market. By the time interest rates have peaked, equity prices have declined. So much of the economic news is so bad that the same investors either forget—or become carried away by the fear and panic enveloping them—to even think of buying stocks. The Theory of Contrary Opinion thus requires us to *go against our natural instincts*—a difficult task indeed.

I have only touched on a few of the elements of Contrary Opinion and will pursue the subject in greater detail later. First, however, I would like to consider two examples of manic crowd behavior to illustrate the fickleness and gullibility of crowd instincts in a more graphic way.

◆ *The Florida Land Boom*

The Florida land boom began in the early 1920s when America had started to enjoy a long period of prosperity. For many years, it was the custom of wealthy Northeasterners to visit such glamorous Florida sun resorts as Miami and Palm Beach in winter. Prior to World War I, they had been joined by well-to-do midwestern farmers and northern manufacturers. In the early 1920s, this flow of visitors grew to include just about everyone.

Initially, Florida was considered a paradise. The way of life was very relaxed and visitors could soak up the sun all day while their neighbors at home were laboring in the harsh conditions of a northern winter. Land prices in Florida were substantially below the national average so it was an easy decision for many people to buy some parcels, either to settle permanently or to use as a potential second home. Naturally, as demand increased, land prices rose.

The boom started on a sound basis as prices still represented good value compared with other regions, and there was plenty of undeveloped land that could be added later to the real estate stock. Between 1923 and 1926, Florida's population grew to 1,290,350, an increase of 25%. Real estate prices grew even faster. Gradually, word spread and land prices began to escalate. In *Psychology and the Stock Market*, David Dreman cites the example of a lot in Miami Beach purchased for $800 that was resold several years later (in 1924) for $150,000. Another lot located near Miami was purchased for $25 in 1896 and sold in 1925 for $125,000.

As is normal in such situations, stories spread of instant wealth and rapid capital gains. After all, the economic outlook for the country as a whole was favorable and land prices were low. Developers rushed into a 100-mile strip stretching from Palm Beach to Coral Gables. Projects sprang up overnight as swamps were drained and new roads were constructed.

A major selling factor was the limited amount of American land lying in the subtropical belt. This scarcity added to the land's perceived value and carried a tremendous emotional appeal that would eventually push prices to undreamt-of levels. Scarcity is a key ingredient in giving a mania both credibility and the capability to grab the imagination.

A sure sign of a mature land boom is an unrealistic number of real estate agents. In 1925, Miami provided employment for 25,000 brokers and more than 2,000 offices. Since the entire Miami population was estimated to be 75,000, this meant that there was one broker for every three residents. The broker–resident ratio was one of signs that prices could not continue climbing forever. Others included overburdened rail, shipping, and utility facilities. By 1926, the boom went bust and prices began their decline. Yet, the frenzy continued.

Dreman also reports that one man quadrupled his money on a beachfront lot within a week. This type of speculation in real estate is typical of a topping-out process when people often buy properties with no intention of developing, building, or living in them. Properties could be purchased with a down payment as low as 10%. Binders, a form of buyer's option, were issued that enabled the purchaser to sell the property immediately. This type of speculative activity could not continue forever. In these situations, prices eventually rise so high that more land than can reasonably be absorbed is forced on the market. A similar phenomenon occurred at the end of the Bunker-Hunt silver boom in 1980. When the price of silver reached $30 or so, individuals flooded the market with their silverware to have it melted down. The price had lost touch with reality.

However, it is extremely difficult for anyone bound up in such frenzied activity to think objectively, especially when some of the most respected financial minds in the country also fail to recognize the impending danger. Roger Babson, a leading money manager and commentator, declared the land boom to be sound. Successful speculators such as Jesse Livermore, who should have known better, also went along with the crowd. J. C. Penney and William Jennings Bryan were also willing participants. With prices rising and endorsements from respected "experts," it is little wonder that virtually everyone wanted a piece of the action. Few people at the time questioned that these so-called real estate experts had gained their reputations in fields other than real estate.

As prices rose, so did confidence. The effect of this rise in the confidence level typically showed up in the way in which loans were granted. Early on, bankers tend to be quite cautious, but as prices increase they become so confident that they approve loans less on the ability of the borrower to repay them than on their underlying equity. Of course, the procedure should work the other way because the higher prices go, the greater the likelihood that the borrower will default. Bankers also become carried away by the sheer pressure of competition. If they are unwilling to offer the money, a competitor almost certainly will. Bankers, being human, cannot help being affected by the frenzy going on around them, so they grant more and more "risk-free" loans as their outlet for participating in the boom. This psychology is not limited to the real estate area. We have seen it in the early 1980s in loans granted to what economists call *less developed countries* and in investments in the leveraged buyout (LBO) craze of the late 1980s.

Manias such as the Florida land boom are eventually brought to a close as rising prices bring out more and more marginal supply. Sooner or later, some of the more heavily leveraged players begin to come unstuck, thereby putting even greater supply on the market. We have to remember that people have prepared themselves only for prices to move in one direction. When they start to drop, what looked to the bankers like a comfortable 10% margin of safety evaporates overnight, as prices move below the value of outstanding mortgages. During the boom, everyone

115

is aware of all the bullish arguments, because they have been widely advertised. This means that once the tide turns, literally no new buyers are available.

One of the characteristics of manias, especially in their final days, is that they are usually riddled with fraud. In the Florida case, this took the form of false advertisements and other sharp practices. The uncovering of such dishonesty adds fuel to the downward spiral in prices. At the culmination of the new-issues boom in the late 1960s, this took the form of Ponzi schemes associated with the IOS mutual fund company. The late 1980s LBO mania was associated with unscrupulous insider trading activity and so forth. As the bubble is blown up, there is less and less margin for error. In the case of Florida, the property market was hit with two hurricanes late in the decade.

We will draw on some more lessons and characteristics of manias later, but first we will examine another instance of crowd psychology gone mad.

◆ The South Sea Bubble

One of the requirements of any financial mania is a revolutionary idea or concept that offers the possibilities of untold growth and quick and easy gains. We have already seen this in the example of the Florida land boom where the idea of a limited amount of American property in a subtropical region captured virtually everyone's imagination. A similar fantasy swept Britain in the early part of the eighteenth century.

At that time, it was commonly believed that one of the growth areas was trade with the South America and the South Pacific. In 1711, the South Sea Company was formed. In its charter, the company was granted exclusive rights to English trade with the Spanish colonies of South America and the South Pacific. Purchasers of the stock not only participated in a market with prospects of unlimited growth but also received a monopoly on that market. It is little wonder that the company's promoters found many willing participants.

In return for these trading rights, the South Sea Company had undertaken to pay part of the English national debt. In effect, it was buying the rights to trade. In reality, the actual rights were not as attractive as the directors made out. Spain did control a vast and wealthy territory, but the nation allowed almost no trade with foreigners. As it turned out, the company was allowed only to trade in slaves and to send just one ship per year. Even then, the profits were to be shared with Spain.

This policy impeded the company's activities, so in 1719 it again approached the English government and offered to pay off more debt as compensation for more trading rights. Holders of government debt were then offered stock in the South Sea Company. The government was happy because the debt was being paid off, and the debt holders were content because the price of the South Sea stock continued to appreciate.

Having twice successfully tried this creative financing method, the directors were then tempted to promote an exchange of the remainder of the national debt for more company stock. For this operation to become successful, it was necessary to push the price of the stock to higher and higher levels. Since the growth in profits was limited, the only way this could be achieved would be through the introduction of new concessions. The rumor mill now began to flood with stories such as Spain's willingness to give the company some major bases in Peru. Images of gold and silver flowing from South America into the company's coffers began to take hold of the imagination.

By September 1720, the issue price had reached £1,000, an eightfold increase in six months. Sharply rising prices always catch the attention of the financial community, but this was something different. Talk of the South Sea boom was on everyone's lips. The mania developed to such an extreme that it became unfashionable *not* to own shares. There was, therefore, a strong social, as well as financial, pressure to go along with the scheme. In the Florida land boom, anyone who stepped back from the crowd and viewed the situation objectively could see from such a simple statistic as the broker–resident ratio that the situation had reached an unreal stage. The same could be said of the South Sea Bubble. At the height of the mania, the value of the company's stock was the equivalent of five times the available cash not just in England but in the whole of Europe. It is obvious with the objectivity of hindsight that this was an unrealistic situation. However, it is difficult for investors caught up in such a flood of emotion to become detached because they are continually being proved wrong by higher and higher prices.

Responsible people who correctly identify such bubbles are often taken seriously at first but are later ridiculed as prices work their frenzied way to their peak. Commentators such as Le Bon and Neill have noted that there is a relationship of sorts between the degree to which a mania can develop and the ability of people to back up their beliefs in that mania with facts. For example, if I look out of my window and see a green lawn, it will be difficult for anyone to persuade me that it is a swimming pool. I know from experience what a lawn looks like, and it is nothing like a swimming pool. On the other hand, if the facts are debatable, such as the future growth of the South Sea Company, it is possible that I could be persuaded to make an investment. My broker, for instance, could point to some new arguments of which I was previously unaware. If I can see that the company has had a good record and that the price has consistently advanced, I may become more interested. When I hear that prominent investors are also on board and that everyone around me is positive, the idea becomes very difficult to resist. When the question becomes not *whether* the price will go up but *when* and *by how much*, it is time for some reflection and objective thinking.

As 1720 progressed, belief in a bright future began to grow, so it was only natural for others to issue new stock in the hope that investors would bite. Greed, it seems, has no bounds because fast and easy gains become addictive. Flotations began for all kinds of projects, and companies were organized for such endeavors as draining Irish bogs, importing jackasses from Spain, and trading in human hair. It didn't much matter what the company was going to do. There was a surplus of funds and few places to put them, so a public that had already seen shares in the South Sea Company skyrocket, was anxious not to miss out on the next investment boom. Once again, we see the law of supply and demand coming into play, rising prices in the South Sea Company raised the prices of equities in general. Other companies were then in a good position to bring their stock to market. These new issues quickly sopped up the surplus funds just as did the marginal land in Florida and the silverware in 1980. The craze seemed to reach its height when a London printer decided to float an issue offering investors the opportunity to participate in "an undertaking of great advantage." Even though no one actually knew what it was, he raised £2,000 in six hours, a huge sum in those days. He then left for Europe and was never heard of again.

This increase in fraud is typical of the later stages of a financial mania as an ever-gullible public becomes an easier and easier mark. The fraud was not just confined to small operators but by now had extended to the directors of the South Sea Company itself. They had bribed many public figures to get the concessions they needed but were now irritated by the way these new companies were absorbing money that would otherwise have gone to supporting the price of South Sea Company stock. In taking steps to expose some of the frauds being committed by the smaller "bubbles," the directors raised some questions in the minds of their own shareholders as to whether the South Sea Company was just a giant version of the newcomers.

Within a month, the mood had quickly reversed as people finally began to question the willingness of Spain to grant concessions. Positive rumors were replaced by negative ones, and the price of the stock began a precipitous slide. By the end of September it had reached £129/share. Thousands of investors were ruined, and a government investigation found that there had been widespread fraud. Many banks had loaned money on the basis of collateral provided by South Sea stock. When the stock tumbled there was no collateral, and so many banks failed. Even the Bank of England itself narrowly escaped financial ruin.

◆ Ingredients for a Mania

These are two examples of financial manias. There are many others such as the famous Dutch tulip mania in the seventeenth century, John Law's Mississippi scheme and the bull market in the 1920s. No two instances are identical, but they all share some common characteristics. We do need to stress that even though these experiences all represent extremes, they are nevertheless indicative of day-to-day market psychology. The principal difference between a mania and a more common emotional fluctuation is that the mania lasts much longer and goes to a far greater extreme.

The elements that make up a mania can be summarized as follows under two headings—"The Bubble Inflates" and "The Bubble Bursts."

The Bubble Inflates

1. A believable concept offers a revolutionary and unlimited path to growth and riches.

2. A surplus of funds exists alongside a shortage of opportunities. This channels the attention of a sufficient number of people with money to trigger the immediate and attention-getting rise in price. These are the germs that spread the contagion.

3. The idea cannot be irrefutably disproved by the facts but is sufficiently complex that it is necessary for the average person to ask the opinions of others to justify its validity.

4. Once the mania gets underway, the idea has sufficient power and compelling belief to spread from a minority to the majority as the crowd seeks to *imitate* its leaders.

5. The price fluctuates from traditional levels of overvaluation to entirely new ground.

6. The new price levels are sanctioned by individuals considered by society to be leaders or experts, thereby giving the bubble an official imprimatur.

7. There is a fear of missing out. The flagship or centerpiece of the bubble is copied or cloned as new schemes and projects attempt to ride on the coattails of the original. They are readily embraced, especially by those who have not yet participated.

8. Lending practices by banks and other financial institutions deteriorate as loans are made indiscriminately. Collateral is valued at inflated and unsustainably high values. A vulnerable debt pyramid is a necessary catalyst for the bust when it eventually begins.

9. A cult figure emerges, symbolic of the bubble. In the Mississippi scheme, it was John Law himself; in the 1920s, famous stock operators such as Jesse Livermore. In the late 1960s, Bernie Cornfield symbolized the so-called mutual fund "gunslingers," and more recently Michael Milken represented the late-1980s LBO craze.

10. The bubble lasts longer than the expectations of virtually everyone. Commentators who warned of trouble in 1928 were initially taken seriously but were way too early and were discredited in the early part of 1929.

11. An atmosphere of fast, easy gains almost invariably results in shady business practices and fraud being practiced by the perpetrators of the original scheme, for example, the insider scandals associated with the 1980s LBO mania. We have already seen that fraud played some part in the South Sea Bubble and the Florida land boom. The Mississippi scheme was also based on similar practices.

12. At the height of the bubble, the possibility exists that even the most objective person can come up with a simple but eyecatching statistic proving that the madness is unsustainable. The broker–resident ratio in Florida in the 1920s and the value of South Sea Stock relative to Europe's total available cash are two examples. In our own time, we note that in the late 1980s, the value of the land encompassing the Emperor's Palace in Tokyo was equivalent to the total value of all New York. Just before the Japanese stock market peak in 1990, price–earnings ratios

reached historic proportions, not just by Western standards but by Japanese ones as well.

The Bubble Bursts

1. There is a rise in prices sufficient to encourage an influx of new supply. In the case of the stock market, new issues are offered to investors at an increasing rate. If viable companies cannot be found, money is raised for concepts. We saw this kind of activity in 1720 but it was just as relevant at the end of the new issues boom in 1968–1969. The scale may have been smaller but the principles were identical. In effect, it is possible to lower investment standards because an increasingly gullible public is demanding new vehicles for instant wealth. A different example occurred in 1980 at the height of the silver boom. In this instance, increased supply took the form of ordinary people finding prices far too attractive as they rushed to sell the family silver to be melted down into bars that could then be sold at higher prices.

2. Another cause comes from a rise in the cost of interest, either as a result of the increasing demand for credit or from the curtailment of supply from an increasingly skeptical government or both.

3. Prices do not just fall, they collapse. The "concept" stocks are exposed for what they are—concepts. Collateral for loans evaporates overnight. Bankers not only are reluctant to expand credit for new ventures but also try to protect themselves by calling in existing loans. The result is a self-feeding downward price spiral as everyone heads for the exit at the same time.

4. Inevitably fraud and other shady dealings are exposed. These sometimes represent a cornerstone of the debt pyramid, the removal of which is a primary cause of the price collapse. At other times, they are ancillary or contributing factors that adversely affect the general level of confidence.

5. The government or other quasi-government agencies occasionally intervene to try to shore up confidence. Such activity

merely gives cooler heads the chance to unload before the real price decline sets in. We saw this in November 1929 when a group of major banks headed by J. P. Morgan attempted to support the market. Anticipating the bursting of his own bubble, John Law staged an elaborate parade in Paris but only kept the bubble afloat for a few days. In more recent times during lesser crises, we have grown accustomed to government jawboning. Such actions and words can only be aimed at the symptoms of the problem, since the problem itself has usually progressed beyond the point at which it can be corrected other than by a painful adjustment in prices.

◆ *Some Further Thoughts on Contrary Opinion*

The preceding examples represent extremes, but the basic tenets just listed are common to all market trends and fads. In the case of manias, we are dealing in years, but many market movements develop in a much shorter time and are far less intense. In his classic book *The Art of Contrary Thinking*, Humphrey Neill states that the theory is based on several of what he calls "social laws." These are:

1. A group of people, or "crowd," is subject to instincts that individuals acting on their own would never be.

2. People involuntarily follow the impulses of the crowd, that is, they succumb to the herd instinct.

3. Contagion and imitation of the minority make individuals susceptible to suggestion, commands, customs, and emotional appeals.

4. When gathered as a group or crowd, people rarely reason but follow blindly and emotionally what is suggested or asserted to them.

In practicing the Theory of Contrary Opinion, we must first be aware of these laws and then structure our thinking to put ourselves in a stronger position to combat them. This means, for example, that we need to be skeptical of the headlines and must try to identify the reasoning behind them. Obviously some common sense is in order. For example, if we read the headline "Plane Crash Kills Five Executives; Stock Price Plummets," the chances are good that the crash has been caused by some mechanical or human failure that has nothing to do with the operations of the company. On the other hand, "Chairman Fires CEO; Stock Price Plummets" may indeed require a closer examination. The market has taken the firing as an indication of civil war within the company and so the stock has declined. On the other hand, perhaps the chairman is sending a signal to the world that a constructive shakeup is underway from which the company will eventually benefit. The lesson is that we should not take a negative stance just because the news seems bearish and prices decline. Perhaps such a view would be justified, but we should at least take a look at the opposing case before taking action.

Of course, it is very difficult to take an opposite view from those around us because evidence of the new contrary trend has not yet emerged, either in the form of a change in the price trend or in the facts themselves. In the case of the CEO firing, it may take months before the results of the shakeup and the rationale behind it begin to emerge. It is good to remember that the crowd will already have sold the stock in anticipation of the worst, so the selling will be over long before the turnaround is apparent. The market, like a good contrarian, *anticipates* what will happen.

It is very difficult for most of us to anticipate a future event by taking action right now, even when the event is more or less certain to take place. For example, we all know that the grass will begin to grow again in the summer, but how many of us take the time and effort to buy a new lawn mower when there is a sale on mowers in January? A few farsighted souls take advantage of this type of deal but the vast majority of us wait until the last moment, even though we know that logically we should buy ahead of time at the more advantageous price. It does not require a great leap of imagination to see how difficult it is to buy into a stock when there is absolutely no certainty of the expected outcome.

Further compounding our reluctance to act is the attitude of those around us. By definition they will almost always disagree with our contrary opinion, sometimes violently. Occasionally the vehemence of the response is itself a sign that you might be on to something. I remember writing a bullish bond article for *Barron's* in 1985. The following week a reader felt so strongly about the article that he wrote a poem denouncing it. In the late 1980s, Bob Prechter, the well-known market letter writer wrote a bearish article on the gold price for the same publication. He suffered a greater tirade. Both articles turned out to be accurate. I can also point to articles with incorrect predictions where there was no response or outburst whatsoever.

One other difficulty in taking a contrary stance is that it often takes a long time before your view is vindicated. It is only natural for this to underpin your faith, because you begin to fear that these contrary views have no basis. Starting off on the path of contrary thinking is quite difficult, because man is a habitual animal. William James in an essay entitled "Habit" noted "the universally admitted fact that any sequence of mental action which has frequently repeated tends to perpetuate itself; so that we find ourselves automatically prompted to think, feel and do what we have been accustomed to think, feel or do under like circumstances, with out any consciously formed purpose, or anticipation of results." As Neill pointed out, "Habits push our minds into ruts—and it takes a considerable amount of force and time to get out of the ruts." Consequently, if we wish to think differently from the crowd, we need to develop a mechanism to stop us from slipping back into bad habits.

Neill cites some additional reasons for our failures to anticipate. First, individual opinions are of little value since they are so frequently incorrect. Second, human character weaknesses such as fear, greed, pride of opinion, and the like prevent the average person from maintaining an objective stance. He opined that "subjective reasoning leads to opinionated conclusions."

Third, if we stand stubbornly by our own opinion, we are likely to defend it regardless of its merit. Many of us are unwilling to admit a mistake.

Neill concluded that if individual opinions are so suscepti-ble to flaws, one should "go opposite" to the crowd, which is so often wrong. This is not as easy as it sounds because you cannot go opposite if you haven't successfully dealt with your own bi-ases. For example, if you hold the view that gold prices are in a bull market, it will do you little good to hunt around for bearish articles and then declare yours to be a contrary view. In this case, you would have made the facts fit your own opinion instead of forming your opinion from the facts.

By the same token, it does little good to say, "I'm bearish be-cause everyone else is bullish." This may be correct but we have to remember that the crowd is right during the trend and is only wrong at both ends, that is, when it really counts. We still need to justify our bearish view based on a logical and well-reasoned argument.

In 1946, the Securities and Exchange Commission examined the mailings of 166 brokers and investment advisors during the week of August 26–September 3. Of that number 4.1% were bear-ish. An investor could certainly have used this survey as a basis for believing that the crowd was positioned in a bullish direction. This belief also could be backed up by facts: The Federal Reserve Board had already indicated it was tightening monetary policy by raising the discount rate, equities were selling at an expensive price/earnings multiple, and some speculation had begun to ap-pear. The market declined by 26 points, the next week, and the bear market was underway.

It is not so much that nearly 96% of the brokers and advisors were bullish but more that their opinions were either influenced by or reflected the opinion of the vast majority of market partici-pants. Thus virtually everyone who had contemplated buying had already done so. Once the smoke had cleared, people began to anticipate a tighter Federal Reserve rate; they could now "see" that stocks were overvalued, and the market began to decline. In effect, the argument on which the bullish case rested could no longer hold water.

◆ Requirements for Contrary Thinking

Consider the Alternatives

It has been said that if you can't think through a subject, you are through thinking. The contrary approach requires a person to look and weigh up the alternatives instead of taking someone else's word for it. One method is to take the prominently held consensus, whether it be financial, economic, political, social, or philosophical, and ask what may happen to change that outlook. Don't stop at the first alternative but try to think of as many plausible alternative scenarios as possible. Going through this exercise will help you recognize which one is more likely to come to pass, when some vital clues that are invisible to the unthinking majority start to materialize.

One problem that we all face is that we were conditioned at an early age to believe everything we read in our schoolbooks and hear from our teachers. As Neill put it, "We bred the habit of unthinking acquiescence rather than exercising such intelligence as we might have." Very few of us take the trouble of looking at both aspects of an argument. We either derive our opinions second-hand from what we hear or read or conveniently take the side that is consistent with our personal philosophical or political beliefs.

Don't Extrapolate the Future from the Present

Part of the process of anticipating the market's twists and turns involves assessing when the prevailing price trend is about to reverse. Most of us gain greater confidence as prices move up not only because our accounts show more paper profits helping us to feel more at ease with our financial position but also because rising prices are an apparent vindication of our judgment. Since the markets discount the good news on the way up, the longer a bull trend continues, the more positive the news background is likely to be. This makes it difficult to anticipate a turn since we all have a tendency to extrapolate from present conditions. Many market analysts get locked into models or other analytical frameworks based on previous experience and have a similar problem.

In the late 1980s, the economy experienced a long recovery that was well above its normal two- to three-year span. This led many economists to conclude that the business cycle had been repealed. The argument rested on the so-called rolling economy in which alternating regional declines would result in a self-correcting economy. Under such an environment, the overall growth rate for the economy would simply slow and not actually contract. A similar theory based on global economies also pronounced the international business cycle to be dead. A long recession did emerge in the middle of 1990 and 1991. In retrospect, this whole exercise had represented one of projecting what was the prevailing trend of economic recovery well into the future.

You will be amazed if you read past periodicals and newspapers how often the prevailing conditions produced the opinions of the day. The press rarely makes any effort to report things that would cause a change in the future. One exception occurs after an unexpectedly sharp price reversal has taken place. Media spokespersons, who are always looking for an excuse to justify price changes, will then say, for example, "Bond prices fell sharply yesterday because speculators were worried about the resurgence of inflation." In this example, the analysis of the future is based on a knee-jerk reaction to a price change rather than a reasoned analysis of why inflation might be a problem in the future.

We are, to a large degree, unconsciously influenced by what is taking place at the moment. If prices are rising, the bullish arguments and commentators are plastered all over the financial pages. Conversely, it is the bears who are quoted as prices plummet. It therefore becomes the job of the contrarian not to confuse cause and effect.

Remember That Events, Not People, Control the Future

In this era of public relations and "spin doctors" when people in authority are able to manipulate the news with timed announcements, photo opportunities, and leaks, there is a natural tendency to believe that personalities are in control of events. In most cases, though, it is the events that drive the leaders. External circumstances control the attitude of individuals and crowds, so it is important for contrarians to analyze events just as much as viewpoints, personalities, and sentiment.

In his famous treatise on crowds, Le Bon wrote, "A great number of historical events are often miscomprehended . . . because we seek to interpret them in the light of a logic which in reality has very little influence on their genesis." We constantly look to the government as a source of problem solving but usually find it wanting. If logic played any part in governmental decision making, the Vietnam War would not have escalated to the extent that it did, nor would the Soviet invasion of Afghanistan have taken place. Often those in power find that they have to react to events. It is how they cope with those events that separates the great from the rest of us. Sound reasoning rarely plays a part in social trends, otherwise we would have solved such problems as racial prejudice and nationalism long ago. These dilemmas are essentially the result of emotions and attitudes rather than logic. Is it little wonder that many devastating wars have arisen from religious conflicts based on beliefs rather than knowledge?

Brooks Adams, in *The Law of Civilization and Decay* (1897), also encapsulated this feeling in his preface: "Another conviction forced on my mind, by the examination of long periods of history, was the exceedingly small part played by conscious thought in molding the fate of men. At the moment of action the human being almost invariably obeys an instinct, like an animal; only after action has ceased does he reflect."

Humphrey Neill summed up the role of events in *The Ruminator*. "Events control actions and attitudes of individuals and crowds. Contrarians therefore look for the contrary guidance in the *events* as well as in the analysis of viewpoints, sentiment and activities of those concerned."

People Like to Conform

One reason that people grouped together act as crowds is that they love to conform. In a way, this is a form of imitation. In the 1950s, virtually every male wore short hair; long hair was considered to be antisocial. In the 1960s, many influential rock groups made long hair fashionable so that many who had worn their hair short in the 1950s now found themselves imitating and conforming by growing it long. The same sort of thing happens at committee meetings. Most people feel much safer going along with the majority so as not to rock the boat, or, in the case of corporate meetings, jeopardize their careers.

In the financial markets, we look for opinions from prominent analysts and other experts. We forget that they are as fallible as the next person. We often overlook that such people often have a personal motive for holding their views. An example of this would be the portfolio manager or strategist who is already invested in the stocks that he is recommending.

Where Do Opinions Come From?

Themes in the market and other general opinions find their origins in sudden events, a sharp move in price either up or down, or from ideas radiating slowly from a small group of opinion makers. This latter phenomenon is somewhat akin to throwing a stone in a still pond and watching the ripples spread into a widening circle. The contrarian should take advantage of this ripple of knowledge by skimming through a number of financial periodicals for an opinion that is likely to catch the imagination of the public when it spreads further.

A good source of such concentrated uniformity of opinion comes from forums or conferences. I remember attending an international conference of market technicians in October 1990. Equity markets around the world had fallen sharply that September due to the Persian Gulf crisis. Many attendees had either lost their jobs or feared a potential loss, and sentiment was among the most negative and one sided that I have ever experienced at a conference of this nature. It was difficult to buck the prevailing opinion, but as it turned out, that was the correct thing to do. The U.S. stock market, for example, was in the final throes of a primary bear trend and therefore presented an outstanding buying opportunity. One of the principal reasons for the negativism was the fear that oil prices would rise and that this would in turn result in an inflationary increase in interest rates. What happened was that interest rates fell because of weak economic conditions, the Fed eased in a series of cuts in the discount rate, and the stock market took off.

In the world of fashion, different styles grow and wane in popularity, and the world of buying and selling stocks is no different. Various industries become popular with investors and just as quickly lose their luster. In the late 1970s, food and tobacco stocks offered tremendous value and for the most part had very consistent growth records. Even so, they were considered to be dull and unexciting because they went nowhere. By the beginning of the 1990s, these same stocks had become "musts" in any institutional portfolio. Technology stocks were the darlings in 1983, but that was to be their peak in popularity for many years to come. It is the job of the contrarian to find the positive aspects of these groups when they are out of favor, and vice versa.

I distinctly remember reading an article on oil stocks in the financial press at the close of 1980. At the time, oil had everything going for it such as shortages and an increase in world demand. You name it and it was fully documented in the article. It was *very difficult not to believe that oil stocks were headed much higher.* As it turned out, that happened to be the peak in oil stocks for many years. It was necessary to look for the contrary arguments because the bullish ones had already been factored into the price. If an argument appears in the popular press, you can be sure that everyone who wants to buy is already on board. And that, if you will, is the time to look at the other side of the argument.

History Repeats, but Contrarians Must Be Careful

The study of previous market experiences indicates that history does indeed repeat but rarely does it repeat itself exactly. If we take this truism too literally, we can find ourselves in trouble, because the aspect of repeating past mistakes has to be carefully thought through by comparing the facts in the two situations. For example, people rarely repeat the same mistake on consecutive occasions because they can remember back to their last unfortunate market experience. So they vow never to make the same mistake again. In Chapter 6, we cited several examples of this phenomenon.

If the Theory of Contrary Opinion Becomes Too Popular, Will It Fail to Work?

Contrary opinion in a mechanistic sense has already become popular, but forming a contrary opinion is an art not a science so it does not readily lend itself to a mechanistic or simplistic approach. It is one thing to point to a news story and take the opposite point of view or to take the position that "everyone is bearish so I am bullish." It is quite another to see that majority opinion has solidified into a dogma for which there is no longer a basis in fact. The true theory of contrary opinion is unlikely to become widely practiced because it involves creative thinking, and most people when given the choice, prefer to follow and imitate rather than reflect.

The majority will always find it easier to follow views that appear in the papers or on the television than to think through a number of alternative scenarios for themselves. To give Humphrey Neill the last word, "The Theory of Contrary Opinion will never become so popular that it destroys its own usefulness. Anything that you have to work hard at and to think hard about, to make it workable, is never going to become common practice."

8

When to Go Contrary

◆

*I*t is one thing to understand that going contrary can be profitable. It is quite another to know when to do it. In this chapter, you will find a few guideposts to point you in the right direction. These guideposts are not found easily; there is no fail-safe way to establish the exact moment when the crowd will be proved wrong. Market prices are determined by the evolving attitudes of individuals who may be either temporarily in or out of the market. The hopes, fears, and expectations of these people, and their attitudes toward those expectations are all factored into the price. Trends in psychological attitudes have a tendency to feed on themselves. In many instances, it is possible to point to a market trend that has reached what we might call a normal extreme. The widely held view appears to be well-established, and the market seems to have fully discounted this point of view; yet for some seemingly irrational reason, the movement in crowd psychology continues beyond normal bounds. More and more participants are drawn in, and this conventional view becomes increasingly solidified.

Fortunately, these extreme situations, in which normal levels of valuation and rationality are thrown to the wind, do not occur very often. The bull market of the 1920s in the United States, and the Japanese equity boom of the 1980s are two such market crazes that readily come to mind. Another example would be the spectacular run-up in precious metal prices that culminated in the 1980 blowoff. In each of these examples, rational expectations were abandoned early on, and the markets took on a life of their own before the inevitable crash. These situations demonstrate one of the key problems facing the contrarian—calling a market turn too early—in these examples, far too early.

In a way, forming a well-considered contrary opinion is similar to establishing an informal measure of market risk. When all participants agree on a specific outlook, it means that they are all positioned to take advantage of it. In the case of a negative outcome, they will already have sought protection either through a direct sale, by hedging their investments, or a combination of the two. In such instances, the odds are good that the prevailing trend will head in the opposite direction, because there are fewer people to sustain it. In those situations where the trend continues on its course, participants begin to feed on new and freshly developed arguments that help to sustain their belief in the consensus. In extreme cases, these newfound arguments combine with the allure of rapidly moving prices to entice more players onto the field.

When I was a broker in Canada back in the early 1970s, for example, no one was particularly interested in gold, which was selling for about $100 at the time. Few people understood its role in the monetary system; most were interested in stocks or bonds. By the end of 1979, attitudes had changed. Participation in the gold market had greatly expanded from the usual speculators in the futures markets. Swiss banks had heavily involved their clients, and the public was now queuing up in the banks to purchase the yellow metal. Opinion on gold as an inflationary hedge had not only solidified but had attracted and seduced a naive public into the market as well.

When the question changes from "whether" the price will rise or fall to "when and by how much," thoughtful people should consider closing out their positions. In the preceding example, that point would probably have been reached when gold was selling in the $300–$400 range. That, of course, would have been far too early, because the price eventually touched $850. However, the contrarian recognizes that it is far better to be early and right than late and wrong. Therefore, the major drawback of the contrary approach is that you often find yourself prematurely liquidating a position.

This problem is less critical at market bottoms where values are sound and prices reverse quickly. When a bearish opinion solidifies, people tend to throw stocks and other investments away at virtually any price. Moreover, sharp price setbacks tend to be self-feeding for a while, since lower prices force those with leveraged positions to liquidate. Fear is a stronger motivator than greed, so the "early" contrarian does not usually have long to wait before prices return to their break-even point. In such situations, he will have the confidence to hold on, since the purchases will undoubtedly be made at an unsustainably low level of valuation. This valuation could take the form of an unusually high dividend yield for stocks, a very high interest rate for bonds, or, in the instance of a commodity, a price that is well below the prevailing level of production costs.

Knowing when to "go contrary" then, is a difficult and elusive task. For this reason, it is best to integrate the contrary approach with other methodologies of market analysis. The degree to which a consensus becomes solidified is in a sense a measure of market risk, and what is risky can become more so before the prevailing trend has run its course. Combining the contrary approach with other approaches such as historically accepted measures of valuation can therefore represent a useful confirmation. For example, if stocks are yielding less than 3%, interest rates have begun to rise, and the view on the street is that stocks have nowhere else to go but up, there is an excellent chance that a major peak in equities is close at hand. When valuations are high, this is another way of saying that the consensus has reached an extreme.

◆ Determining Whether the Consensus Is at a Short- or a Long-Term Turning Point

One task that the contrarian must accomplish is to decide whether the consensus is of short- or long-term significance. For example, a recently released government report on the employment picture may indicate that the economy is stronger than most people expected. As a result, bond prices, which do not respond well to favorable economic news, start to sell off sharply. At this point, speculators in the bond market begin to get very discouraged. Not only are prices declining, but a rumor of a pickup in the inflation numbers has now begun making the rounds. The bond market declines even more. The consensus among traders has, in the space of a few days or a week, moved strongly to the bearish side. The chances are, though, that this is only a short-term top.

We do not know the details of the general economic picture from this example, but major peaks in bond prices require a lot more evidence that the economy is turning than one economic report and the rumor of a second. Such turning points are usually associated with a general belief that the economy will not recover for some time. Typically a turn has been previously but prematurely anticipated by the majority. When there is no follow-through to these initial signs, people lose heart. This "give-up" phase is often the contrarian's best tip that a recovery is, in fact, on the way.

In any market situation, there are always the structural optimists, or bulls, and the structural pessimists, or bears. These are the people who have a permanent bias in one direction or another. As the recession progresses, the structural bulls notice that the leading indicators have begun to turn up and take heart from this. When the numbers do improve and then temporarily reverse, this solidifies the opinion of the bears, but more importantly it also convinces a significant number of the structural bulls as well. The significance of this "give-up" stage is that it broadens the number of people holding the consensus to the point that expectations of a weak economy and higher bond prices become a forgone conclusion. The question is no longer "whether" but "when and by how much?"

The consensus that forms at a short-term market turning point appears to expect that "the correction will continue." There seems to be an underlying feeling that prices will eventually move higher, but conventional wisdom insists, "Don't buy yet.

Prices will become more attractive in the next few weeks." Invariably they do not, and the next leg of the bull market gets underway to the great surprise of the majority of investors. In these
instances, be on the lookout for headlines in the financial press
predicting a correction. When this becomes a fairly widespread
expectation, you can be sure that a major rally is not far off.

The consensus around major tops and bottoms is a much
more contagious affair. Instead of headlines and articles expect
to see cover stories in major magazines and features on the
evening news. In the case of bearish trends, confirmation is often
seen in the indignant reactions of politicians. They usually act
right at the end of the trend. Do you remember President Gerald
Ford's WIN (Whip Inflation Now) buttons that appeared right at
the peak of the 1971–1974 jump in the rate of consumer price inflation? Talk of a new era or justifications that "it's different this
time and valuations are not important because . . ." abound. We
shall examine some of these concepts later, but in essence they
all represent signs of major turning points in the markets. Even
so, some of them may appear well before the actual price peak,
others will coincide with the peak, and some may actually lag a
little. Regardless of the actual timing, such signs represent a
warning that the true contrarian ignores at his peril.

I have addressed the subject of when to go contrary in somewhat general terms. We now turn to some more specific, practical
methods of assessing when a consensus view has moved too far in
one direction. As described in Chapter 7, the major problem arises
because it is not possible to set hard and fast rules: Forming a contrary opinion is an art and not a science. No two instances are the
same in a character sense and no manias or crowd movements
end at the same place. Figure 8–1 represents a typical oscillator
used in technical analysis. It moves from one extreme to another.
A glance at the chart tells us that when the oscillator reaches the
overbought and oversold dashed lines, the probabilities favor that
the prevailing trend of prices is coming to an end. However, there
are some instances when it continues much further, such as the
overbought reading in early 1990. Trying to judge when a consensus has moved too far is a very similar matter. What could

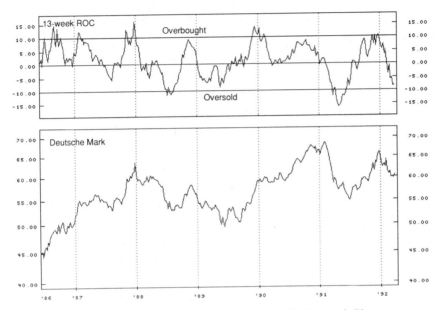

Figure 8–1 The Deutsche Mark and 13-Week Rate of Change as an Example of a Typical Oscillator. Source: *Pring Market Review*.

normally be interpreted as an extreme in crowd psychology can often move to an even greater extreme before the tide eventually turns. With this important caveat in mind, we can now proceed.

◆ *Headlines, Cover Stories, and the Media*

The role of the media is to report news and opinion, not to make predictions and forecasts. If the media perform their task well, then they should be reflecting the opinions and views of their readers, or constituents. The more widespread and intense the views and opinions, the more prominently they should be featured. We would surely expect to see stories about the stock market featured in the financial press such as *The Wall Street Journal*. This in itself tells us little. On the other hand, when a feature article on the equity market appears in general-circulation publications such as *Time, Newsweek,* or *U.S. News and World Report,* we should take note because the story has begun to circulate well beyond the usual financial circles. It reflects that the general public may be about to imitate the "experts." The interesting thing about such stories is that they invariably occur after a substantial price movement has taken place. The article may explain why prices have risen so much and in a roundabout way will reflect the conventional wisdom, thereby giving the general public some powerful reasons they too should buy. To the contrarian, the appearance of such stories is not a signal to buy; rather, it is a sign that is time to think about selling.

When market stories reach the front pages of general purpose newspapers or the covers of magazines, the implications are far greater than if the stories appear in the financial press. Several years ago, I did some research to try to come up with a contrarian media index. The idea was that if a specific story or theme appeared in the popular media a sufficient number of times, then it was likely that the market was about to reverse. Unfortunately, I was unable to correlate such stories with reversals in the markets. Sometimes my index worked very well. On other occasions, there was a huge lag between the cover stories and the market reversal, and sometimes there was no reversal at all. This underscores the point that the formulation of a true and accurate contrary opinion is very much an art form that can only be achieved with much experience and a great deal of creative thinking.

Paul Macrae Montgomery is a stock market analyst based in Newport News, Virginia, who specializes in what we might call "cover-story analysis." In the June 3, 1991 issue of *Barron's*, Montgomery claimed that there is a significant correlation between *Time* cover stories and major reversals in the stock market. His research, which begins with magazine issues from 1923, indicates that when a bullish cover is featured, the market usually rallies at an annual rate of about 17% for a month or two and then reverses. Note that the annualized gain of 17% for two months translates into an actual gain of about 3%. According to Montgomery, then, the appearance of the story breaks pretty close to the final peak. On the other hand, bearish covers are followed by annualized declines of 30% for a month or so (i.e., about double the rate of market rises that follow bullish stories). The interesting point is that over a one-year period the market moves an average 80% in the opposite direction to the theme of the cover story.

Needless to say, these examples occur at major market turning points. By the very nature of the situation, it would be unrealistic to expect a widely published story to signal a short-term turning point. To make the cover of a major magazine, the article has to represent news to which more or less everyone can relate. A major stock market selloff or a huge bull market clearly fits the bill. Other examples cited by Montgomery are the famous "Crash" cover story in November 1987 and a feature article on the "Match King," Ivar Krueger, the day before the 1929 market crash. Krueger was featured because he had just lent $75 million to France to help stabilize the currency, and $125 million to Germany to support his match manufacturing monopoly. This high rolling activity is typical of a long-term peak in speculative activity. Just after the *Time* cover story appeared, the price of Kreuger & Troll's stock plummeted from $35 to $5 within 24 months.

Cover stories sometimes focus on interest rates. In March 1982, for example, an article entitled "Interest Rate Anguish" featured Paul Volcker, then chairman of the Federal Reserve Board. Treasury Bills were yielding 12.5%, but a year later they had fallen to 8.5%.

I have also found the track record of *Business Week* magazine to be an equally accurate indicator of major market changes. Perhaps the most famous such piece was one entitled the "Death of Equities" in 1977 when the Dow was selling at less than a thousand. Montgomery cites a 1984 cover story warning of disaster in the government bond market (i.e., implying that investors should avoid government bonds). It was, but for those who did not buy, because yields fell from 14% to less than 7.5% within two years. In this instance, the bond market reversed its downward path within a few days of the story's publication, but trend reversals in other instances usually take much more time. If the story seems to fit the overall market environment, you should begin nibbling away at your holdings or liquidating, depending on the signal.

When emotions reach an extreme, we should expect to see an extreme movement in prices in the opposite direction to the prevailing trend. In the 1984 *Business Week* article just discussed, the report in some places turned into a forecast by saying, "Investors can do little but brace for further depression of the prices of their bonds. . . ." In this instance, the writer was so utterly convinced that prices would decline that he felt it necessary to overstep his function as a reporter and make a prediction. This is most unusual and provided strong anecdotal evidence that emotions had run too far.

In more recent times, the November 1990 cover of this same magazine was right on a contrarian target when it published "The Future of Wall Street" following a sharp market retreat. The article was not only instructive in the sense that it featured a Wall Street story during a bear market. That was bullish in itself. What was of equal significance for stock pickers was that the article was pointing out why brokerage stocks, the principal beneficiary of a bull market, would be under pressure. During the next bull market, brokerage stocks obliged by putting in one of the best performances of any industry group.

Cover stories that do not appear to have any direct bearing on the markets or the economy can also help in discerning the market's mood. Features about the United States or its embodiment—the President—can often reveal how we think about ourselves. For example, Americans reached an emotional high for several months during and after the 1984 Los Angeles Olympic games, a mood certainly reflected in the news coverage. In February 1985, the dollar ended a super bull market and began a terrible decline within a matter of months.

Covers featuring upbeat and confident presidents also reflect a similar mood in the country. In this vein, George Bush was featured on the cover of *Time* during the summer of 1989. The article lauded him for being smarter and less ideological than Ronald Reagan. The market responded with a sharp selloff. In January 1991, a cover story depicted President Bush as "two-faced," "wavering," and "confused." This also reflected the mood of the country, and that uncertainty also pervaded the stock market. This sentiment had already been discounted by the stock market, which then proceeded to experience a very powerful rally. In effect, if the nation, either directly or indirectly through its elected officials, is reflected in a cover story as ebullient and confident, expect the market to decline. On the other hand, if the story reflects a lack of national confidence and will to tackle its seemingly insoluble problems, expect a rally.

I should add that you should not rely on all cover stories with such precision. *Time*'s famous "Birth of the Bull" cover in the fall of 1982 was not followed by a general market collapse but by a long-term bull market. This emphasizes that one should not go contrary just for the sake of going contrary. It is mandatory to examine the facts and come up with some reasonable alternative scenarios. In the case of the "Birth of the Bull," the economic and valuation conditions were totally inconsistent with a major market top. The dividend yield on the S&P Composite Index at 5.1%, for example, was closer to the historical level of undervaluation than overvaluation. Moreover, interest rates had just begun to plunge and the economic news was very poor—all signs of a major market bottom. The only aspect that did not fit was the "Birth of the Bull" cover. In this case it was being featured because of a tremendous rally on Wall Street accompanied by record volume, not because the consensus had moved to the superbullish camp.

Even when conditions appear to be in tune with a cover story, a rally is not necessarily guaranteed. In the summer of 1991, *Fortune* featured the CEO of IBM on its cover. This seemed to confirm the general opinion that the company had been going through a difficult period from which it might not emerge quickly. The price of Big Blue's stock had sunk from $140 to about $100 at the time of the article. With a yield of close to 5%, the market had already gone a long way toward factoring in all the bad news. As this chapter is being written a year later, IBM is no higher in price. This is not to say that IBM's stock will not rise but more to underscore that cover stories cannot normally be relied on as exact timing devices. They require patience. The contrarian value investor can afford the time and in this case is being rewarded with a dividend yield that is almost twice as much as the market itself.

We also need to be careful in our cover story analysis when there is very little general news. Somebody has to appear on the cover of *Fortune,* so if there is very little competition for the front page, a market or economically related story may well creep in by default. The impact is likely to be far less significant under such circumstances.

◆ *Thin-Reed Indicators*

Cover stories are a high-profile tool put at the disposal of contrarians, but some less obvious ones, in their own way, can be equally as valuable.

A classic example was featured in the November 1990 edition of *Investment Vision* (now *Worth Magazine*). The article was written by Contrarius, a pseudonym for Leo Dwarsky, formerly portfolio manager of the Fidelity contra-fund. He made the point that stock groups move in and out of fashion just like styles of clothing. The article featured Campbell Soup, whose stock had quadrupled between 1958 and 1962 reaching a price/earnings multiple of 30 at its peak. In the ensuing 19 years, earnings grew consistently. There was only one down year. This certainly justified its rating as a growth stock even though the momentum of the earnings growth had begun to slow. Surprisingly, by 1981 the stock was selling for about 40% less than it did in 1962. Investors had lost complete interest in the stock.

Dwarsky then tells us of a "thin-reed" indicator that provided a vital clue that the consensus had solidified in the bearish camp. He received a report on Campbell Soup that read as follows: "Campbell Soup—Deleted from Coverage. Investment Opinion: In preparation for an expanded coverage of the consumer area, we are deleting Campbell from our coverage."

That was it. A perfectly good national company that had consistently improved its earnings over the period of several decades was suddenly being deleted from coverage. It indicated that the stock was out of favor with the institutional community. The real kicker was that the consumer area itself was being expanded and yet a key consumer stock, Campbell, was being dropped. Research houses thrive on commissions and if there were no commissions to be gleaned from Campbell, better not to cover it. Needless to say, the stock appreciated by 900% in the next 9 years.

Another form of thin-reed indicator occurs when you read a story in a general-purpose magazine that is highly technical or specialized in nature. For example, a story on stock index futures or options would not be out of place in a financial publication such as *The Wall Street Journal*. They appear there all the time. However, it would be somewhat out of the ordinary to see such a feature in a general-purpose publication such as *Newsweek* or *Time*. Such an item generally indicates that an investment idea that is normally confined to a select number of speculators and professionals now has a more widespread acceptance. For "widespread," the contrarian should read "potential reversal."

Another specialist concept that could fall into this category might be a cross-currency trade. Usually the dollar is traded against the German deutschemark. Consequently, a story featuring the benefits of trading the mark against the yen or the Canadian dollar against the pound would represent a strong thin-reed indicator that the prevailing market trend was about to reverse.

The so-called Ted Spread is another favorite. This transaction involves the simultaneous buying of Treasury Bill futures and selling of Eurodollars. The idea is that, if some financial crisis is brewing, investors will rush to embrace the quality of Treasury securities to avoid Eurodollars, which are an investment of poorer quality. If speculators are able to get in on this trend early enough, they can expect to make some reasonable profits. This is the kind of stuff that is featured quite often in financial publications but only makes its way to general purpose magazines and newspapers when there is a story attached to it. That inevitably means close to a major turning point. The reversal of such trends in the relative performance of Treasury Bills to Eurodollars obviously has a lot of relevance to the small number of individuals playing the spread but it can also have wider implications for interest rates, the stock market, and the economy. Presumably, if the major players are concerned that something like the Ted Spread is widening, the appearance of the story means that confidence is at a trough and so too should be the stock market.

Other thin-reed indicators may include a story on a relatively obscure market such as lumber or sugar. There is a natural consumer interest if the prices of these commodities have risen. The chances are that they will have reached the peak by the time the popular press has got around to extrapolating recent trends. I remember in the early 1980s seeing a story on the price of sugar being featured on the *CBS Evening News*. This occurred after a huge run up in the price had taken place. The story "broke" almost to the day of a major peak. It is doubtful whether sugar has been featured on the program since.

Not all such indicators are as timely and useful. In 1990, for example, a gold fund was liquidated because of a general lack of interest in the precious metal. Also several major brokerage houses in New York and London deleted their gold coverage in a manner similar to the Campbell Soup example cited earlier. The gold price did rise for a few weeks after these developments, but not nearly to the extent that might have been expected. By the same token, the price did not go down either, choosing to languish in the $345 to $370 area for the next year or so. In this sense, the thin reed along with the cover story on IBM mentioned earlier told us that these markets were sold out and were a low-risk play. They did not, as they usually do, signal that a major rally was underway.

◆ Best-Selling Books

When trying to form a contrary opinion, it is very important to attempt to gauge the mood of the general public. The media can provide us with some useful clues but some of the best signals of all come from the best-seller list.

Perhaps the first indicator in this direction occurred in the 1920s at the height of the bull market when *Common Stocks as Long-Term Investments,* by Edgar Lawrence Smith, saw widespread approval. The thesis of the book was that over the long haul stocks had outperformed bonds and that is where investors should put their money. His argument has been proved to be correct since that time because stocks have continued to outperform bonds since 1929. The problem was that the book's popularity indicated that the general public obviously understood the bullish argument for equities. In the next decade, bonds handsomely outperformed stocks.

Best-seller signals of this nature do not come around very often, largely because market trends do not move to a manic extreme that frequently. Adam Smith's *Money Game* was a classic in that respect, reaching the best-seller list at the time of the speculative stock market bubble in 1868. William Donahue's book on money market funds in the early 1980s hit the best-seller list right at the period of the postwar peak in interest rates. It represents a classic indicator of a fairly technical book that would not normally be expected to sell more than a few thousand copies. Yet it reached the best-seller list and in doing so indicated that the public was probably reaching a peak in its desire for money market funds. I do not mean to cast any aspersions on the book but merely draw your attention to its unusual and unexpected success.

Another book that caught the attention of the public was Ravi Batra's forecast of a major depression right at the time of the 1987 crash. As it turned out, the market, far from declining, managed to rally over the next few years, doubling in price from its crash lows.

◆ Sentiment Indicators

A final avenue that we need to cover in our quest for a more timely basis on which to form a contrary opinion is data obtained from polling various professionals about their views.

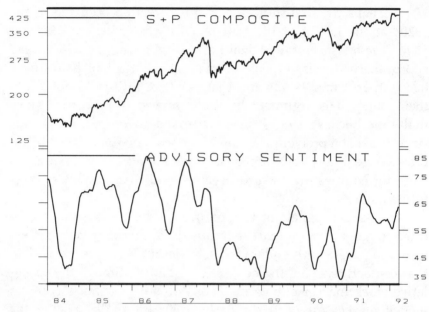

Figure 8–2 S&P Composite versus Advisory Sentiment 1984–1991 (10-Week Moving Average of Bulls Divided by Bulls + Bears). Source: *Pring Market Review.*

Investor's Intelligence, * founded by the late Abe Cohen, pioneered the approach of gauging how many of the numerous newsletters he read were bullish or bearish on the market. These data have been available on a continuous basis since the early 1960s. The results for more recent years have been plotted in Figure 8–2 and compared with the market's performance. The concept is quite simple. When the majority of market letter writers are bullish, it represents a danger signal so it is time to think about selling, and vice versa. The chart shows that this is easier said than done, because there are many periods such as mid-1985 and mid-1986 when people were bullish and yet the market did not decline, and those such as early 1990 when most investors were bearish yet the market did not rally. The indicator, then, is far from perfect. Sometimes it is right on the mark and sometimes very early. It

---

Investor's Intelligence, Chartcraft, Inc., New Rochelle, NY 10801.

therefore makes more sense to use it as a complement to other measures of market sentiment and contrary opinion.

Figure 8–3 shows another sentiment indicator. Published by *Market Vane*, this is a four-week moving average of the percentage of bond traders who are market bulls. The published data are expressed on a percentage basis. I have subtracted 50 from the total so the resulting series moves from positive to negative territory. The opinions expressed in this survey are of a far shorter time horizon than the *Investor Intelligence* data and therefore are significantly more volatile. They match the swings in bond prices quite well, but it is difficult to obtain a precise timing device from this activity. In short, such data need to be combined with other indicators and approaches if a meaningful use is to be made of it.

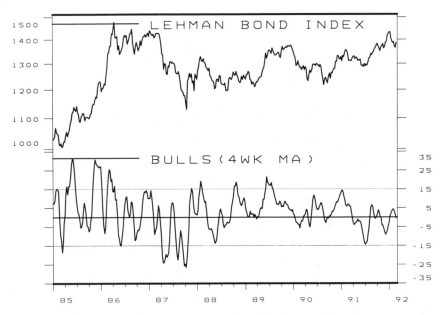

Figure 8–3 Lehman Bond Index and Bullish Bond Consensus 1985–1992. Chart Source: *Pring Market Review.* Source for Bullish Consensus: *Market Vane's* poll of futures-trading advisors, Haddaday Publications, Pasadena, CA 91101.

◆ Sentiment at the End of Recessions

I mentioned in an earlier chapter that it pays to be skeptical when reading comments volunteered by "experts" because such prognostications can often be misleading. In the January 1992 edition of the *Bank Credit Analyst*,* the editors researched several publications to find out what was being said at the end of the 1969–1970, 1973–1974, and 1981–1982 recessions.

1969–1970

The jobs picture continues to deteriorate—almost every major industry cut back on its work force in October. . . . The October numbers are worse than they look. *Business Week, November 14, 1970*

Business statistics of current activity look sour—so do those which point to prospective activity. Orders for durable goods are dismal. . . . There are few (businesspeople) who expect an economic turnaround before the end of 1971. *Business Week, November 28, 1970*

The (staff) projections still suggested that the average rate of growth in real GNP over the three quarters ending in mid-1971 would be relatively low. *Minutes of the December 15, 1970, meeting of the Federal Open Market Committee*

Mr. Paul McCracken (head of the Council of Economic Advisers) is telling everyone—including the President—that the job of re-stimulating the economy next year will be more difficult than most people had thought. . . . (There is) strength in housing construction and in spending by state and local governments, but sluggishness elsewhere. *The Economist, December 19, 1970*

The editor noted, "The recession trough was recorded in November 1970. Real GNP rose by 9$\frac{1}{2}$% between the fourth quarters of 1970 and 1971."

---

*Bank Credit Analyst, January, 1992.

1974–1975

The decline in industrial production is particularly worrying because it is still on an accelerating trend, and it can no longer be pinned on any single industrial sector. . . . Low interest rates have done nothing for the money supply which has dipped marginally in the past two months. The economy, frighteningly, seems to be going its own way, shrugging off the help being doled out to it by the Administration. *The Economist, February 22, 1975*

Whenever the upturn in the American economy comes it will not, according to even the most optimistic predictions, be before summer. That means at least four more months of dire economic statistics telling much the same story of deepening recession as the latest February figures. . . . While the Federal reserve is proudly trumpeting its apparent victory over inflation, its worry is how to pump enough money back into the economy. If the private sector is not going to take the lead, then the government must. Congress itself is playing with increasingly generous sums to inject into the economy. *The Economist, March 15, 1975*

The information reviewed at this meeting suggested that real output of goods and services was continuing to fall sharply in the first quarter of 1975. . . . Staff projections, like those of a month earlier, suggested that real economic activity would recede further in the second quarter. . . . *Minutes of the March 18, 1975, meeting of the Federal Open Market Committee*

A sharp contraction in employment in February indicates that the production decline and inventory readjustment is proceeding rapidly; there is scant evidence of an impending improvement in business. . . . There is little question that the labor market is deteriorating. . . . Moreover, the contraction in jobs is widespread, suggesting that further declines lie ahead. *Business Week, March 24, 1975*

It is yet far from clear when the recession will bottom out and how far down the low point will be. *Business Week, April 7, 1975*

The editor's note read, "The recession reached a bottom in March 1975. Real GNP rose by 13$1/2$% between the first quarters of 1975 and 1976."

1981–1982

The Fed's view is that without some stimulus, economic activity will not pick up in the near future. The 1% rise in retail sales in September was mostly clearance sales of cut-price cars. Consumer confidence is low and spending is slack. *The Economist, October 16, 1982*

The battered economy isn't picking up yet. There are still very few signs that business activity is improving. On balance, in fact, it looks as if the decline in manufacturing is still not over. *Business Week, November 8, 1982*

The staff projections . . . suggested that real GNP would grow moderately during 1983, but that any recovery in the months just ahead was likely to be quite limited. . . . Many members continued to stress that there were substantial risks of a shortfall from the projection. Considerable emphasis was given to the widespread signs of weakness in economic activity and to the continuing absence of evidence that an economic recovery might be under way. *Minutes of the November 16, 1982, meeting of the Federal Open Market Committee.*

The data have been suggesting it for weeks. There is as yet no general recovery in business. To confirm it, the fourth quarter started off on the downside. *Business Week, November 29, 1982*

Across the nation, the bottom is dropping out of the budgets of state and local governments. . . . The result is likely to be new rounds of spending cuts, layoffs and tax increases despite efforts to adjust to rising unemployment and falling federal aid during the past two years. *Business Week, November 29, 1982*

The editor noted, "The recession reached a bottom in November 1982. Real GNP rose by 10^1/$_2$% between the fourth quarters of 1982 and 1983. State and local finances improved dramatically in 1983.

The average person taking these comments at face value would be badly misled. On the other hand, the contrarian, taking a more skeptical line, would see them as an established viewpoint deserving of consideration from the opposite perspective. The quotations are self-explanatory and stand on their

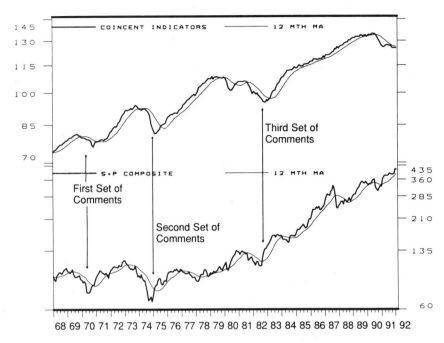

Figure 8–4 Economic Forecasts versus the Commerce Department's Coincident Indicators and the Stock Market. Source: *Pring Market Review.*

own. Figure 8–4 shows when the comments were made and what happened to the economy and stock market afterward.

◆ *Summary*

Forming a contrary viewpoint for exact timing purposes is a difficult task. In this respect, we need to combine a study of the media and the attitudes of friends and associates together with indicators such as valuation that give a good historical perspective of when an extreme has been reached. When all the pieces are more or less consistent and it is possible to come up with some alternative and credible scenarios, the chances are that the market or stock in question is about to reverse its prevailing trend.

9

How to Profit from Newsbreaks

*F*rom time to time, you may have heard or read a news account of a market development along these lines: "Despite a jump in the discount rate, stocks rallied sharply on Wall Street," or, "IBM announced today that earnings were up 10%, but IBM shares declined by $1.50. Analysts were at a loss to account for this reaction." These reports are typical of the way any market might react to news. This type of seemingly irrational price action is certainly not the sort of thing that a logical person would expect to happen, though. If the news is good, presumably the stock should go up, and if it's bad, certainly then it should go down.

These seemingly inexplicable reactions occur because the market, or, we should say, market participants, are always looking ahead and anticipating all facets of the news and the events behind the headlines. Consequently, when the IBM earnings were announced, the figure was something that most observers had expected, and so they had already bought the stock. Some, who were not aware of the "good news," decided to purchase on the announcement. Others, however, had been waiting for that exact moment to unload the stock and used the IBM earnings report as an excuse to sell.

Occasionally, these types of announcements will generate greater buying strength, in which case the stock may close the trading day up in value, but probably well down from the high achieved just after the announcement. No matter. Most people expected the news and had decided to use the event to unload stock on those individuals or institutions who were unexpectedly impressed with the earnings report. Why? Perhaps these same investors believed that this represented a peak in earnings for a while. The announcement was therefore a God-given chance to sell into strength at a very favorable price. In any event, from the point of view of the market observer, the key is that the news was good and therefore the stock *ought* to have risen in value. That it didn't was a sign of weakness. After all, if the price is unable to rally on good news what *would* induce it to go up? This is a very difficult concept for most people to grasp, even those with many years of experience in the markets. If the news is good at the time, it always seems foolish to sell, but in retrospect that is usually the smart thing to do.

On the day of the August 1991 coup against President Gorbachev in the former Soviet Union, the gold price ran up $4 to $6 during the morning but closed the day in New York only 50 cents higher than its value at the start of the day. This was two days before the coup collapsed, so there was still plenty to worry about. Few observers would have guessed at the time that the revolt would soon be over. The gold price, which was moderately oversold at the time, *ought to have had a field day* since it almost always responds positively to disquieting world events.

In the inflationary 1970s, such news could have been expected to result in a $20 to $30 increase. As that first day of the coup came to an end, there was a great deal of uncertainty and the price barely budged. The event was totally unexpected by the market, so it could not be argued that the coup had been factored into the price. No, there was clearly something bearish in the supply–demand relationship. Buyers were not being enticed back into the market by this "bullish" news for the metal, but sellers were there ready to offer all the gold that anyone wanted. The failure of the price to rally on the news was a bearish sign. Later that week the coup failed, and the price continued on its way down. Figure 9–1 shows that it did not decline that much and eventually returned to the precoup levels, but

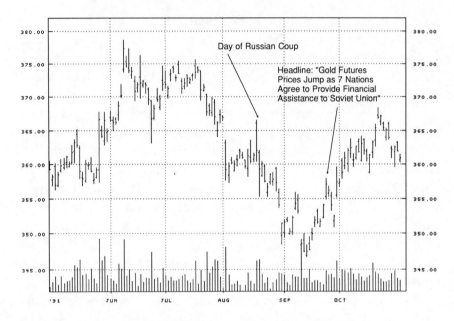

Figure 9–1 The Gold Price 1991. Source: *Pring Market Review.*

from a short-term point of view, selling on "good" news was the correct thing to do.

◆ News Known Is News Discounted

All financial markets look ahead in an attempt to anticipate future events. This practice is called "discounting." At first, this process involves a few farsighted individuals who have a good sense of the chronological sequence of events that usually transpires in a typical market cycle. Such individuals also have experience in gauging how the perceptions of other market participants might change as events unfold. As time passes, the probable outcome becomes more widely expected and therefore discounted by more and more people. Finally, the event takes place or is announced, and participants start to anticipate the next one. This is a simplification of what actually takes place, since prices are determined by the interaction of a number of different events, economic trends, and psychological background factors. If it were possible to isolate the discounting mechanism to one or two events, forecasting any market would be a relatively simple matter because everyone would play the same game, meaning that the discounting process would be instantaneous.

Academicians have long claimed that financial markets are efficient. The efficient-market theory states that a specific market or security digests all the information likely to affect it, so that this knowledge is immediately and efficiently factored into the current price. Proponents of the theory claim that it is not possible to make money in the markets by anticipating events because they are in effect already accounted for in the prices. The markets, they conclude, are therefore a "random walk."

I cannot disagree with the hypothesis that markets are to some extent efficient. Anyone who believes that the earnings of his favorite stock are going to plunge would be illogical if he did not sell at least part of his position and buy it back later at a more favorable price. There are two flaws in the efficient-market hypothesis. First the same information is not given to everyone at the same time. News takes time before it can be widely disseminated. Second, not everyone will interpret the information the same way when it is received. Remember, for example, how most people take the news at face value, while the contrarian will look behind the headlines to see whether there are any reasonable, alternative scenarios to those being followed by the crowd.

Let's take the example of XYZ stock. For the past six months, XYZ has been trading in the $10 to $12 range. One particularly bright analyst discovers that the company will soon be in a position to cut costs dramatically because of a new product that it is about to introduce to the market. As a result, he starts to recommend the stock to a few of his select clients. This incremental demand is enough to push its price above that $10 to $12 trading range. Other analysts gradually pick up the scent, and the price advances a little further. Then the company announces some unexpectedly bad earnings, and the price slides. Miraculously, the decline is very brief, and the price again resumes its advance. This occurs because the knowledgeable people who are aware of the forthcoming development see the decline as an unexpected opportunity to pick up some stock at what they consider to be bargain prices. One of the key points to grasp here is that a market or a stock that can quickly absorb bad news is usually in a strong technical position. Such action in effect represents a very positive sign.

Later, more investors begin to hear about the company as retail brokers spread the news to their customers. During this whole period, the price continues to advance. Consequently, by the time the company is ready to make the announcement, almost everyone is expecting it, so the news comes as no surprise. When the product introduction finally appears in the newspapers, the event is common knowledge. Only newspaper readers who have not previously been privy to the information are likely to be buyers. After that point, there is no one left who is likely to make a purchase based on the news.

You can see that it is not the announcement of the news event that causes the price to rise, but the expectation of the announcement. Money was not made on the day of the announcement. It was made days or weeks or months before, depending on where you stood in the information line. You can now appreciate that a lot of those people who bought in anticipation of the news are now tempted to take profits. If they want to do this in sufficient numbers, the price will decline. In this instance, the selloff triggered by a bullish announcement is a sign of technical weakness.

The other principal reason the efficient-market theory is flawed is that prices are determined by the *attitude* of market participants to expected future events. We have noted how many people react to news in a knee-jerk fashion and how others take the time to reflect. In the example of the CEO firing cited in Chapter 7, we found that there was a silver lining behind a news event that on the surface seemed quite bearish. Other examples abound.

The fact is that investors in the stock market tend to be very fashion conscious. They were prepared to bid up the prices of technology companies between 1982 and 1983, but a change of attitude meant that high-tech stocks were out of favor for the remainder of that decade. Food stocks saw consistent growth rates in the 1970s, yet they did not find favor with investors until the next decade. The only explanation for most of these apparent inconsistencies is investor attitudes, not efficient-market theory.

Sometimes the market's response to news is delayed. In October 1973, the Organization of Petroleum Exporting Countries (OPEC) announced an embargo on oil exports to the United States because of America's support for Israel in the Arab–Israeli war. Logically, the market should have declined immediately, but it actually took several days between the announcement of the embargo and the start of the dramatic stock selloff that followed. The facts were known, yet people did not begin to react immediately. Eventually attitudes changed, and prices sank. Another example occurred in December 1991 when the Fed lowered the discount rate by a huge and unexpected 1%. The market immediately responded with a small rally that day but the explosion in prices did not occur until later. On the other hand, the market's response to Saddam Hussein's invasion of Kuwait was more or less instantaneous.

The efficient-market theory makes no allowances for these idiosyncrasies of human nature. There is no question that markets have a tendency to be efficient, but the examples cited here indicate that efficiency alone cannot account for all the causes behind price movements. Markets are usually efficient in the sense that it is very difficult to prosper from specific announcements that have a reasonable chance of being foreseen. A substantial amount of research has been done on this subject. One study at the University of Notre Dame by Dean Frank, Frank Rielly, and Eugene Drzyminski indicated that stock prices rapidly factored in new information on world events. The speed at which this happens keeps investors from raking in above-average returns based on such information. Other studies have also concluded that attempting to capitalize on public announcements, earnings reports, and the like have little chance of beating the market.

The problem with any of these research efforts is how to quantify the importance of a news item. It may be a bullish but more or less insignificant item and thereby have little or no effect on the price. On the other hand, much of the news may already have been leaked. Quite often, companies will "prepare" analysts for a forthcoming development of which they were previously unaware.

In this respect, Dr. Patrick Gaughan, at Fairleigh Dickinson University, showed that the closing value of stocks was not related to news published on a specific day in *The Wall Street Journal*. Instead, using multivariate analysis, he was able to show that prices one or two days prior to the publication of the news were statistically related. Drawing on these data, he concluded, "It is not that news in daily financial publications does not have an impact on security prices. News is most important to these markets. However, the markets often have access to more timely sources of news than the printed word." In this short-term study Dr. Gaughan therefore proved the point that markets usually factor in the likely effect of a news announcement before it happens.

◆ How Can We Profit from Analyzing the Market's Response to the News?

We have already learned that it is very difficult to profit from a news announcement because in most instances such information will almost invariably be factored into the price. Of course, some news events, such as natural disasters, assassinations, and other random occurrences cannot be foreseen and therefore are not discounted. Even in these instances, the market's response can be very instructive. Good news that fails to induce a rally should be interpreted as a bearish sign. On the other hand, bearish news that does not result in a decline or causes a decline that is a short-lived one with a quick recovery is a sign of strength. After President Eisenhower's heart attack in the early 1950s, the market sold off but rallied quickly. Anyone who had bought at "pre-announcement" prices after the President's heart attack would have done very well. The same was true for investors after John F. Kennedy's assassination, on November 22, 1963. The market's initial reaction was to sell off sharply, but the selling wave lasted for only a short while and then prices began to climb.

In both examples the market was able to digest such horrible news and take it in its stride was a positive factor. In effect, both instances represented a strong signal to buy. This price action after the assassination resulted in two things. First, the initial selling panic got rid of the weak holders—those who reacted in a knee-jerk fashion. When the market moved back above the preassassination level, it indicated that this type of selling had been completed. Second, that the market was able to take such potentially destabilizing news in stride demonstrated that it was technically strong and was likely to move higher. At that time, the rationale was that Lyndon Johnson had taken over and appeared to be in control of the situation. Since the market abhors uncertainty, this perception was greeted as a very positive factor. The real reason is more likely that the economy was in the early stages of a long-term recovery, a factor that the market was very much aware of. Had the economy had been on the verge of a recession, it is doubtful whether the market would have taken the news so heroically.

Just contrast the preceding response to the reaction of the market to the resignation of President Nixon during the 1973–1974 recession. When Vice President Gerald Ford assumed the presidency, he performed every bit as well as Johnson. However, the background of rising interest rates and a declining economy meant that stocks faced a bear market. The timing of Nixon's resignation may have been surprising, but the act was by no means unexpected, unlike Kennedy's assassination or Eisenhower's heart attack. Consequently, the market was able to discount this possibility ahead of time. Even though Ford performed well, the tide of the bear market proved to be overwhelming, and prices continued to decline. The way that a market responds to a news event therefore can be very enlightening in telling us whether the primary price trend is up or down.

Another example of the market's response to news came on January 16, 1991, at the outbreak of actual hostilities in the Persian Gulf War. Wars are not always predictable but in this case the Iraqis had been given a January 15 deadline to withdraw from Kuwait. Since they did not, it was predictable that at some point the United States and its allies would begin shooting. When war did break out, the market exploded in a manner contrary to almost everyone's expectation.

Why was this? The answer lies in an analysis of the events and investor perceptions leading up to the war. Remember, the possibilities of war were known well ahead of time. The market had actually bottomed in October 1990. As the deadline grew closer in the opening weeks of 1991 many investors decided to sell, thereby pushing the market down. Not only was there a general sense of uncertainty, but professional wisdom at the time anticipated a further 100–150 point decline on the breakout of hostilities. This eventuality, it was argued, would provide a wonderful buying opportunity. The problem was that everyone else had the same idea. In a rather perverse way the market responded to the war by exploding. One reason the market did not act as anticipated was that the attack took place at night when the New York market was closed. The initial response in Japan was precisely what people had expected, that is, an initial selloff followed by a rally. By the time the New York Stock Exchange opened, selling in the global equity markets had given way to a buying frenzy as the European markets began to explode. This left no chance for American investors to buy at fire-sale prices.

We also have to note that January 15 had been preceded by extreme pessimism. Consequently, a significant number of traders were holding short positions and were forced to cover their borrowings at the opening on January 16. The morning of January 15 was a classic example of market participants all pointed in one direction. Bulls had liquidated and bears were heavily short. As people began to discern that the market was not going to collapse, these positions quickly unwound. The shorts covered and the sold-out bulls, realizing that they were not going to get the chance to get back in at bargain prices, started to reaccumulate their positions.

The rationale that was used to justify the price rise was that the United States was likely to win the war hands down with its superior technology. In addition, consumer confidence, which had been buffeted by the thought of war and the prevailing recession, would bounce back, thereby resulting in a recovery. The fact was that the Federal Reserve had already eased monetary policy, sowing the seeds for a recovery. The explosion of prices on January 16 was therefore nothing less than a powerful confirmation that a bull market was underway.

Another point arising out of this example derives from the old Wall Street adage that the market rarely discounts the same event twice. In this instance, the market had sufficient time between August and October 1990 to discount the negative aspects of the war. When hostilities finally broke out, it was time for market participants to focus their attention on something else. This is not surprising when you think about how most people react and worry about predictable events. Most students taking an exam at the end of term begin to worry about it rather early. As a result, they study hard in preparation for the exam. This is not to say that they do not worry about the ordeal about to confront them. Their apprehension may even get a little more intense just before the exam. However, the point of greatest concern comes early on and is the triggering point for taking action, that is, studying. If it were possible to measure the degree of anxiety, you would see that it would be most intense just before the process of studying begins. Once the period of study has begun, the students realize that the exam is not as difficult a hurdle as they had first thought. This does not rule out the possibility of renewed nervousness just before the exam. However, the solid preparation that takes place gradually gives them the confidence that they can pass. In a similar way, markets prepare for any ordeal that lies ahead by declining in price. People take defensive action by selling, so that when the event takes place, all those who were concerned have had a chance to get out, leaving the market free to discount the next event.

The market's reaction to news can be very revealing in relation to stories in the financial press. One interesting exercise is to follow feature stories in the Money & Investing section of *The Wall Street Journal*. The commodity pages, for example, usually focus on a specific commodity with an accompanying chart. The commodity making the headline has usually experienced a sharp price move during the previous day or over the course of the previous two or three weeks. To justify the coverage, the commodity must experience a sharp price movement based on some news event. In Figure 9–1 the gold price clearly experienced a pretty good run prior to September 21st, the day it was featured. The headline on the commodity page read, "Gold Futures Prices Jump as 7 Nations Agree to Provide Financial Assistance to Soviet Union." Obviously, the price had been running up in anticipation of this event. Now that it was public knowledge, the chances of additional near-term gains were greatly reduced. Figure 9–1 shows that this did in fact prove to be the case, for the price retreated for a few days after the story ran.

A similar example is shown in Figure 9–2, but this time for wheat following a large drop. The headline reads, "Wheat Futures Prices Skid to a 13-Year Low." Again, the day the story broke proved to be a good reversal signal. These classic examples are used to prove a point, but as with most approaches to market analysis *The Wall Street Journal* cannot be used as a fail-safe contrary mechanism. My point is this: If a market is featured in such a way after a prolonged price trend—be it up or down—this should serve as a warning flag that the trend *may* be about to make an about-face. If the market in question closes in the *opposite* direction to that indicated by the story, chances are that the trend will reverse. A news story is but one indicator, but it unquestionably represents a warning about entering the market at that particular time. Generally, the odds will favor those taking the opposite side of the prevailing trend, especially when the headline refers to a 5-year high, 10-year low, and so on.

Quite often, we find that a poor earnings announcement results in an initial selloff but that the price finishes the day on the plus side. Usually such action is accompanied by particularly

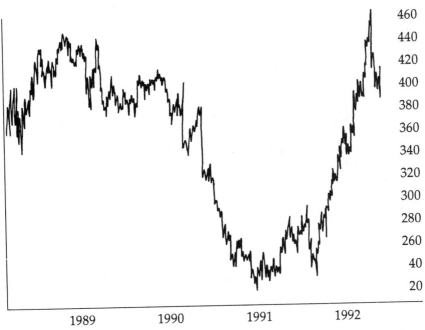

460
440
420
400
380
360
340
320
300
280
260
40
20

1989   1990   1991   1992

Figure 9–2 Wheat Prices 1990. Source: Commodity Trend Service, P.O. Box 32309, Palm Beach Gardens, FL 33420.

heavy trading volume. The reason often is that investors were expecting the bad news and had been holding off until it was out of the way. Of course, this has the effect of putting pressure on the price because buyers were waiting until the announcement was made. Once the bad news is out, those investors in the know begin to accumulate the stock and the trend reverses.

The price action of stocks—or, in fact, any financial market following an important announcement—can be very revealing. We have already learned that if a market moves in the direction contrary to the course that an uninformed observer might expect that market has already factored in the good or bad news and a new price trend has probably begun. Whether that trend will last for a short or a long time is another matter. On the other hand, the market may be expecting bad news and get even worse news than is generally expected. In this instance, one of two things may happen. Either prices continue to sell off, in which case little can be learned from the technical position since the price is reacting in a perfectly logical way. Or, if the news is quickly absorbed and prices go on to make new "postannouncement highs," then this indicates a very strong technical position, and we should expect to see significantly higher prices. Examples of this phenomenon were discussed earlier with XYZ stock and the market's response to the Kennedy assassination. In both cases, market participants were able to look over the short-term hurdle and focus instead on a bullish long-term picture.

The same is true in reverse, where the market reacts perversely to the most bullish news imaginable. I remember as a broker in Canada in 1973 receiving unbelievable earnings on two stocks, Chrysler and a small Canadian electronic manufacturer, Electrohome. In both instances, the earnings were way above expectations, but the stocks still declined. At the time, I could not understand why this was so, but having seen so many glaring examples since, I have found that it is generally not a wise policy to ignore such blatant signs of technical weakness. The reason that Chrysler and Electrohome sold off on the good news was that investors were looking ahead to the next recession and were not willing to hold the stocks no matter how good the current news.

10

Dealing with Brokers and Money Managers the Smart Way

*E*ven though most investors and traders place their buy and sell orders through a broker, they think very little about that relationship and how it might influence their success or failure. Rarely do they consider that the broker is the last person they speak to before a buy or sell order is placed or executed. Many investors also make the false assumption that the broker not only is knowledgeable but also is in a far better position to gather information than they are.

The association between client and money manager is also a crucial one that does not get the attention it deserves. In this chapter, we will examine these relationships in closer detail, pointing out the dangers and describing some guidelines that will help you to develop both a better understanding of these roles and a more profitable partnership.

◆ The Role of the Broker

The role of broker can fit either within two extremes or at one or the other end of these extremes. At one end his function is that of order taker, at the other he might have total discretion over the account. There is less potential for misunderstandings at the extremes because the bulk of the ground rules would already have been set. If the broker merely executes orders, this implies that the client is making all the decisions. Consequently, he can do little "damage" by giving poor advice. At the other extreme, the client hands everything over to the broker. Once that decision has been taken, the broker's role is that of money manager. In this instance, there is little he can do to affect the client's decision-making process until he is either fired or resigns the account.

Most client–broker relationships lie within these two extremes, so a combination of these roles is played by the broker. It is in this middle ground that the psychological dynamics of the relationship can shape investment success or failure.

It is amazing how most people pay scant attention to the selection of a broker, yet one small, suggestive sentence can result in the gain or loss of thousands of dollars. A suitable broker is usually selected by word of mouth, typically by referral. This process may also take place through a phone solicitation or the follow-up of an ad in response to a clever sales pitch. Neither of these introductions is likely to lead to investment success unless the client happens to be particularly fortunate. I class myself as one of the lucky ones in that respect for I found my broker through an ad in *The Wall Street Journal*. Our relationship has been alive and well for more than 12 years. We have our ups and downs but generally speaking each of us knows what is expected of the other. This is definitely the exception rather than the rule, however. I used to be a broker myself, and I can think of many former colleagues with whom I would like to pursue a social relationship but precious few with whom I would like to work on a professional basis.

An inexperienced trader or investor will undoubtedly rely on a broker's advice for his initial trade. If that broker is incompetent or motivated by the thought of some quick commissions, the odds of success will be considerably diminished. Even accounts that have been exposed to the markets for years can suffer. For example, the failure of an account executive to call at the right time, or to correctly enter an order can be crucial. This is especially true in the futures markets where leverage leaves virtually no margin for error.

Keep in mind that brokers are usually paid on a commission basis. Consequently, if they are not completing orders, they are generating little or no income. When business is slow, even the most ethical of brokers cannot counsel you without the tiniest thought of the commissions influencing their advice. The pressure to sell can sometimes be even more intense since many firms bring underwritings to the market and require brokers to sell an allotment whether the broker believes it to be a good investment or not. He cannot be legally forced to sell such issues, of course. Nevertheless, the pressure from management and the competition from peers are sufficient to trigger a significant number of "borderline" sales. Moreover, most of these new issues carry a generous commission that cannot but contribute to an even greater conflict of interest.

Another problem that we all run into occurs when, after very careful consideration, we call our broker with an order to buy or sell a specific security. The next thing we know is that he has managed to talk us into something else. This is by no means an unethical practice, but one by which a broker can inadvertently and, probably with the best of intentions, sway us into making a wrong decision.

You may wonder why I assume that the account executive will give you the wrong, rather than the right, advice. This happens because the broker is literally sitting in the "crowd." He watches the newswires, probably listens to the financial channels, is inundated with the firm's research, and is heavily influenced by his fellow account executives. The odds that he will give you the right advice are therefore pretty poor.

Several factors influence the broker. For instance, investors commonly do not recognize that most of them are really conduits for their research departments. Recommendations to clients are not necessarily made on the basis of what the broker himself thinks but more on what "our research department likes." If this isn't running with the herd, I don't know what is!

Peer pressure is another unhealthy influence so far as the client is concerned. Usually, one particular broker in the office takes the lead, because he is either a successful salesperson or has had a few lucky recommendations. This is enough to set the ball rolling as the urge to imitate this "leader" becomes irresistible. There are two problems here. First, the broker who is following the leader usually recommends the stock more on the basis that the leading broker is selling it than on its own merits as he sees it. Second, the very spirit of this competitive activity means that sales are being made purely to generate volume in a competitive spirit, not because a stock is the appropriate security for a specific portfolio. Managements, of course, love this competitive atmosphere since it generates more commissions. It is questionable whether this is also true for the poor clients.

I do not mean to imply that there are no brokers that can think for themselves, merely that they are a rare breed. After all, the brokerage community is, in psychological terms, a cross-section of the rest of the population. Why should it be blessed with an abundance of independent thinkers? Brokers are hired principally to generate sales, not to think creatively. Better for the management to do the thinking by placing some juicy commission-generating ideas on the broker's plate. Since members of this select breed of independent thinkers are few and far between, it is of paramount importance that you either learn to think for yourself or give full discretion to a professional who can. By all means consider a broker's recommendations and include them as part of your decision-making process, but don't give the advice greater significance than it deserves.

◆ How to Choose a Broker

The first place to start is to examine the type of firm with which your prospective broker is associated. You should give top priority to ensuring that the firm is stable. This is not an easy matter since the size of the company is not necessarily a good indication of the firm's financial standing. In recent years, we have witnessed many mergers of major brokerages as well as the failures of futures brokers. One method for testing the stability of a firm is to evaluate how aggressive they might be in their advertising and recommendations. Get hold of some of their promotional material or research. Compare this with other brokers' material, and a pattern will probably emerge. Generally speaking, the greater the hype and the more aggressive the recommendations, the more vulnerable a firm is likely to be. A firm that is willing to risk its customers' money in questionable ventures is unlikely to have its own financial house in order. Also, if a firm is going through some difficult times, your broker cannot but help to be caught up in the office gossip and politics. This is bound to adversely affect his ability to service his clients.

A second area to consider is the firm's capability to provide you with information—not the information that *they* want you to have, but the type of information that is helpful to *you*. After all, you will be paying for this material indirectly through commissions, so it should be tailored to your needs as much as possible.

The level of the commission structure can also be a serious consideration since it often reflects the kind of service that the firm provides. If you are just placing orders and are acting as your own information source, then it makes no sense to deal with a broker who offers lots of research but charges you high commissions for it. Commissions are not the only cost of doing business; poor executions can, and often do, represent an even greater expense. This is especially important for short-term traders where high turnover means that transaction costs have a greater effect on the ultimate outcome. It is usually better to pay a little more for commissions if you are satisfied that the orders are prompt and properly executed.

Establishing the competence of executions is a difficult matter. Even in the best circumstances, the execution of orders can, and often does, go wrong. Do not expect your broker to be perfect. However, if a pattern of poor executions starts to appear, you are advised to question seriously whether you should continue to retain his services. Still, if you have a long-time horizon and do not place orders very often, these commission and execution factors will be far less important.

Finally, choosing a firm that can provide you with up-to-date reports of your account and with *readable* monthly statements can help you tremendously in doing a more efficient job of managing your money.

Once you have settled on a firm, the next step is to choose an account executive (AE). I realize that you may select the AE first, but even in this case it is also prudent to check out the firm itself. If a broker is going to do a good job in helping you to manage your portfolio, he first needs to know quite a bit about you, your financial position, and your investment objectives. If he does not have the important facts on your financial background, he will not be able to tailor his recommendations to your requirements. If he asks for the order first and then ask questions about you, a red flag should immediately go up in your mind.

You, in turn, need to know some things about the broker. Is your business important to him? If so, you need to know how many active accounts he has, their average size, and so forth. If you are a small account and his average size is much greater, perhaps he will not be able to find the time to service you properly. It is also helpful to have an understanding of his investment philosophy, so ask him to explain it. If he likes charts and you like balance sheets, you may not have much in common. Also, by asking him what he thinks drives the market, you may find out that he has no idea and therefore no philosophy. This is an indication of someone who blindly follows the crowd.

We usually think of a broker solely as a source of recommendations, but even if you make your own decisions, he can still be helpful in other areas. In my own case, for example, I like to make my own decisions but am terrible at record keeping. This is a role that my broker, a former accountant, is happy to fulfill. He also provides me with information that I cannot get for myself. He watches the markets closely while I get on with the job of publishing a newsletter. Even with this necessary detachment, he is my eyes and ears, reporting faithfully when some prespecified market condition materializes. In this way, I have someone watching the markets for me, and my time is not taken up looking at computer screens. Alternatively, you may be new to the markets and require your broker to fulfill an educational function.

A broker–client relationship should be a customized one, tailored to your needs and desires. You are the only one who can establish such criteria, but once you have, you are in a better position to locate a broker who can fulfill these needs.

The potential for clashes is always present, even in the best of relationships. If your personality and that of the account executive are different, it's much more likely that you will have disagreements. This aspect is crucial because such clashes introduce emotions that are bound to affect your investment performance adversely. Let's suppose, for example, that you decide to buy XYZ stock contrary to your broker's recommendation. If you do not have a good rapport with him, you will find it difficult to sell the stock because you will have to admit, not only to yourself, but to the broker that you've made a mistake. Selling a stock at a loss is difficult enough, but when you also have a personal hurdle to overcome with the broker, it may be the last straw that precludes you from making the sale. Alternatively, you might want to buy ABC for perfectly logical reasons, but are afraid to do so because you know that your broker doesn't like the stock or the industry. These types of conflicts are bound to arise from time to time even with the best relationships. However, if your philosophies and personalities are markedly unlike, the potential for losses to materialize will be that much greater.

Your first step in establishing a relationship is to agree on the ground rules. Don't *assume* that your broker will fulfill all the functions you want him to. You should state clearly and precisely what you expect of him and ask him what he expects of you. Always be completely frank about your views and expectations. A good broker–client relationship should mirror a partnership, because that is what it really is. Competent brokers realize that maximum long-term commissions are a direct function of the success of their clients. It's a fact that when they are making money, most people trade more; and when their equity is declining, they are far less active. A broker may talk his client into executing numerous transactions, but if the client loses money, he will either trade less or move the account to another broker.

We have discussed the relationship with the broker from your point of view, but his reaction to you can be equally important. For example, he may recommend a stock to you and later the price will drop. His rationale for the recommendation may have been perfectly logical and justifiable, but a conscientious broker is bound to feel some sense of regret concerning the purchase. In such circumstances, you must communicate to him that you do not blame him for the result and continue to believe that he was acting in your best interest. If you don't, he will hesitate before calling you next time even though he might have some valuable information about one of the companies you hold, or a recommendation that will turn out to be profitable. Consequently, if you do not have an open, friendly, approachable, and frank relationship with him, it means that an unnecessary and unprofitable barrier has been set up between you.

You have to begin by deciding what role you want the broker to perform. If you want him to provide research, you should tell him so. If you want him to inform you promptly concerning order executions, he should be informed of this as well. Just think about all the services that you need or don't need and let him know. It's just as important to let him know the things that you do not need, so you will not be unduly bothered and he will have more time to perform the tasks that you feel to be of greater value.

◆ Money Managers versus Clients

The psychological dynamics between a money manager and client can be as crucial as those between a broker and client. You might assume that once you have handed over your account to be professionally managed that everything will work smoothly. This may be true if the manager has sold you on his philosophy and then performs satisfactorily. Unfortunately, this is rarely the case. In previous chapters, I stressed that success in the financial markets requires a totally objective and flexible outlook. When a money manager takes on a new account, he faces more than the twin battles of beating the markets and mastering his own emotions that the rest of us have to deal with. He also has a third challenge revolving around his relationship with the client. This does not imply that the manager is in an adversarial role with his client, for such a relationship could never be maintained for very long. The problem is more subtle. The manager often finds himself asking, "What does my client want? What will he think if I buy company XYZ and then sell it at a small loss because my view has changed?"

If the manager is buying and selling for his own account, he does not have to worry about such matters, since he has to answer only to himself. However, when managing an account, he has to look over his shoulder continually and worry about what the client may be thinking. Consequently, the objectivity he may have obtained for himself stands a good chance of being replaced by concerns about his relationship with his client. Even though the client may have researched the track record and philosophy of the money manager and they have a good personal relationship, problems can still arise because many clients continually second-guess what the manager is doing.

The client places his assets under management because he does not have the time, expertise, or aptitude to invest for himself. If the manager is a real pro, he will be constantly going against the crowd. He will be buying when the news is bad and selling when it is good. If the client doesn't have an aptitude for investing, he will more than likely be of the opposite frame of mind. When prices decline, the news background is invariably negative; so it is little wonder that we find the customer calling up the manager when he has just made some purchases at fairly depressed levels. The manager, for his part, is also questioning his new acquisitions, because it is rarely easy to buy at the bottom. The client's call expressing uneasiness therefore clouds the manager's judgment and adversely affects his confidence. Whereas he might have plucked up the courage to buy some more stocks at bargain basement prices, this kind of concern is likely to make him hold back and make purchases when prices and the client's comfort level are much higher.

Client–manager relationships can interfere with a successful investment program in numerous ways. There are two approaches for avoiding some of these dilemmas. The first is for you, as the potential client, to make sure that your investment objectives are not only realistic but are also consistent with the investment philosophy of the firm that you have selected to manage your money. Second, once you have made the decision to give the manager discretion, let him get on with his job. Avoid the temptation to interfere. Obviously, this does not mean that you cannot or should not periodically critique his performance, but you do need to give him the benefit of the doubt in questionable circumstances. The media and fast-talking brokers have led many of us to expect instant success, but that is rarely the case. Quick profits usually arise from being in the right place at the right time—luck rarely strikes in the same place twice.

If you compare the long-term performances of cash, stocks, and bonds, you will find that stocks offer the best rate of return. If you then analyze the performance of the stock market over the past 100 years, you will learn two things: First, the market can be extremely volatile over short periods; second, the longer the time horizon, the less the volatility and the greater the reward. Consequently, if you allow your manager to concentrate on the big picture and do not worry him with day-to-day concerns, he will be in a far better position to give you the superior results you demand. In effect, the longer the time horizon, the greater the opportunity for the long run (upward) trend to offset short-term volatility.

If the manager does not perform after a period of two years or so, you need to reassess your relationship with him. It may be that his particular investment philosophy is still relevant, but that it has produced below-average returns over the past two years. This can happen to the best of investment approaches and is a simple fact of life. Table 10–1, for example, shows the total return performance of both stocks and bonds using Stock and Bond

Table 10–1   Record of Return Performance on Stocks and Bonds

Record of Buy and Sell Signals				
Date	Buy	Date	Sell	S&P Gain (Loss)
Jan. 54	25.46	Jun. 55	39.78	14.32
Nov. 57	40.35	Feb. 59	54.77	14.42
Jun. 60	57.26	Apr. 62	68.05	10.79
Nov. 62	60.04	Feb. 65	86.75	26.71
Mar. 67	89.42	Jul. 68	100.30	10.88
Jul. 70	75.72	Nov. 72	115.05	39.33
Dec. 74	67.07	Sep. 77	96.23	29.16
May 80	107.69	Mar. 81	133.19	25.50
Dec. 81	123.79	Jan. 84	166.76	42.97
Nov. 84	165.87	Jul. 87	309.47	143.60
Nov. 89	340.33	Aug. 90	323.47	(16.86)
Dec. 90	328.33	?	?	?
Total Gain				340.82
Buy/Hold Gain				298.01
Net Gain				42.81

Bond Barometer Performance				
Date	Buy At*	Date	Sell At	% Gain (Loss)
Oct. 53	245.08	Dec. 54	232.67	7.2
Aug. 57	205.70	Sep. 58	200.42	(2.6)
Apr. 60	183.60	Jul. 61	194.13	5.7
Mar. 62	189.72	Jul. 63	189.72	0
Jan. 67	175.37	Nov. 67	139.74	(20.3)
Jul. 70	115.31	Oct. 72	132.05	14.5
Oct. 74	95.62	Aug. 77	104.65	9.4
May 80	76.7	Nov. 80	64.34	(16.11)
Nov. 81	59.02	Jul. 83	69.07	17.0
Nov. 84	69.13	Apr. 87	95.94	38.8
Jul. 89	97.67	Jul. 90	93.27	(4.5)
Nov. 90	93.54	?	?	?
Total Gain				36.83
Buy/Hold Gain (loss)				(61.94)
Net Barometer Gain				98.77

*Index based on 20-year perpetual bond with an 8% coupon.
Source: Pring-Turner Capital Group, Walnut Creek, California.

Barometer models that I developed. We use them in the Pring Turner Capital Group, the money management firm with which I am associated, to allocate assets in our clients' portfolios. The overall performance is fairly good, but if we consider the results for some specific time periods, such as 1967–1968 and 1980 for bonds, we can see that there have been a number of instances where the performance has been disappointing. This underscores that even the well-designed models for investment approaches can and do fail from time to time. Remember, there is no Holy Grail.

Success comes at the margin through hard work and patience; it builds incrementally through the compounding process. Your expectations as a client going into a money-management relationship are probably more crucial to the success of the project than those of your manager. Most people err on the optimistic side, believing that high returns can be earned with very little risk; they also prefer stable returns over unpredictable ones. This immediately sets up a conflict because high returns are predominately a function of risk, and the higher the risk, the greater the volatility and hence the unpredictability. Stability comes with a cost and that cost is a lower rate of return. One way of getting around this problem is to give your manager time, because the passage of time is the mortal enemy of volatility and the friend of superior risk-adjusted rates of return.

◆ Matching Your Needs with the Management Philosophy

The first requirement when selecting a manager is to tell him your investment objectives and, as best you can, your ability to tolerate risk and volatility. He can then judge whether his philosophy is consistent with your objectives and character. For example, you may tell him that you want to retire in 10 years on an annual income of $50,000. At an 8% rate of interest, this would require a capital amount of $400,000 at retirement. Your current capital is $100,000. Achieving that objective will require a gain of $300,000. Since the average annual total return from stocks since

1926 has been around 9%, it will mean that the manager has to take above average risks to achieve that objective. If you also let him know that you are afraid to take big risks, your objectives are clearly unrealistic and will need to be modified. Consequently, the starting point for the discussion should be your ability to tolerate risk rather than your investment objectives. The level of risk tolerance puts a cap on a realistic expected total return. Once you establish your tolerance level, the appropriate return commensurate with that risk can be calculated from historical data. It is then possible to set a more realistic investment objective.

If your objectives are consistent with the investment philosophy of the money manager, it is important to fully accept the broad concepts. If you say you agree with his philosophy and sign a contract with him even though you do not fully accept his investment outlook, conflicts are sure to arise. For example, if the manager has a conservative approach and regards the maintenance of principal as the guiding light of his philosophy, you will become frustrated at this safety-first strategy if riskier small-growth stocks begin to take off. You will read about the great gains being achieved by this market sector and will be disappointed in not being able to participate. The manager cannot be faulted for this, because it is alien to his investment universe. This type of conflict is a recipe for trouble. Only by fully buying the philosophy and making a commitment to stay the course will you allow the relationship a chance of success.

Even though a manager hates to turn away prospective clients, it is in his long-run interest to indicate that you should look to someone else if your philosophies and risk-tolerance levels are different from his. An unhappy client will leave sooner or later anyway and difficult clients drain managers of the energy and emotion that they need to devote to the market and their other clients. By succumbing to the temptation of taking on a large client that does not fit the client profile, the manager will jeopardize the performance of all his other accounts.

Part III

STAYING ONE STEP AHEAD

11

What Makes a Great Trader or Investor?

He who knows much about others may be learned, but he who understands himself is more intelligent. He who controls others may be more powerful, but he who has mastered himself is mightier still.

—Lao-tsu

Just as there is no Holy Grail—that is, no easy path to quick wealth—there is no secret or formula that history's great traders and investors have called on to propel them to their great achievements. Each success story is unique. Some of their stories are just that: tales, myths, or legends.

The famous quip by former New York Yankee catcher Yogi Berra—"It's not over till it's over"—is just as relevant to careers in the financial world as it is to those in the world of sports. Jesse Livermore, for example, was a legend in his time, but he died bankrupt. He certainly could be classed as a successful trader in his heyday; indeed, he made and lost several fortunes, yet both died a broken man. Is this how we ought to judge success? Is this what we want for ourselves? I hope not.

The problem is that many of us use money as a vehicle to work out our basic internal needs, but in fact money cannot offer us such solace.

It can offer a short-term antidote, but it can never alleviate insecurity, loneliness, or other forms of mental dependency. If you are unsure what is stopping you from becoming wealthy, you will remain a victim of money. If you do not know what you want from money, it is unlikely that you will be able to achieve your financial goals. To follow in the footsteps of the truly great traders and investors, you will have to change your habits and attitudes. Otherwise, you will remain at the starting gate.

The quotation by the Chinese philosopher Lao-tse that begins this chapter summarizes the secrets of the market wizards. They understand themselves and in doing so have mastered their emotions. Not being perfect, they make mistakes like the rest of us. The difference is that their mistakes are less costly because they have learned to recognize low-risk ideas and quickly bail out of them if they do not turn out as expected.

Successful traders and investors possess confidence and a strong sense of self-esteem. They have feelings of personal worth. A truly successful trader or investor does not crave recognition in a wide sense; many, in fact, shun publicity.

As Kathleen Gurney put it in the March 1988 issue of *Personal Investor*, "The money masters are in control; they know themselves and their money styles. They are aware of who they are, where they have been and where they are going. Their money sense of themselves is both positive and secure." Gurney adds that it is this self-assurance that makes them secure that their decisions are the correct ones.

In *Money Masters*, John Train reiterates the view that there is no one secret to success in the market. He believes that basically two investment attitudes mark successful investors: Either they can study with focused care and imagination what is under their microscope at the moment, or they see their work as "an exercise in cautious futurology—peering into the fog a little farther than the crowd." In addition, Train rebuts the argument that these individuals are lucky. It is true that being in the right place at the right time can result in some spectacular success stories. However, to maintain a position at the top for a long time can only be achieved with hard work, lots of study, and a consistent performance.

Working hard and working smart are different things. In his book, *Peak Performers,* Dr. Charles Garfield sets out his conclusions from interviews with more than 300 successful individuals in business, sports, arts, and education. He found great differences between a workaholic, who is addicted to activity, and a peak performer, who is committed to results. In the book, he lists six basic attributes common to individuals who achieve peak performance. Since these characteristics are common to all forms of successful activity, including trading, they are worth repeating:

1. *A Commitment to a Mission.* This ultimate source of success was common to all respondents. In deciding their missions, peak performers have first to decide what they really care about and what they want to accomplish. The motivation for their mission is not expertise but a personal choice based on preference.

2. *Results in Real Time.* Peak performers establish realistic, measurable goals and act in a deliberate manner in order to achieve them.

3. *Self-Management through Self-Mastery.* Each peak performer was able to demonstrate an ability for self-observation. This involved both the ability to grasp the big picture and small details. Survey participants were also able to utilize the technique of mental rehearsal in which the most desired outcome of an event and the most effective way of achieving it are first orchestrated mentally.

4. *Team Building and Team Playing.* This characteristic is but prevalent in traders and investors who often act alone. But it is an important trait as well in larger organizations where it is necessary to delegate investment functions. Team builders are able to delegate to empower, stretching the abilities of others and encouraging educated risk taking.

5. *Course Correction.* This refers to the ability to initiate change and to learn from past mistakes.

6. *Change Management.* Peak performers have the ability to anticipate and deal with rapid, external changes caused by new technology or other factors and to construct alternative outcomes.

Summarizing his conclusions, Garfield states that what motivates an individual to fulfill his talents is a strong commitment to values. "These values—the old fashioned and very real qualities that make up a person's and organization's character—are the leverage point for the whole internal impulse to excel, to put a mission on its course."

Dr. K. Van Tharp, a research psychologist, has spent considerable time studying the psychology of high achievers and has had extensive exposure to successful traders. He has tested many of them to determine whether there is a correlation between their success and specific personality traits.

Tharp's work covered three basic areas: psychology, management discipline, and decision making. The researcher discovered that successful traders in their psychological makeup showed a well-rounded personal life, a positive attitude, a motivation to make money, a lack of internal conflict, and a willingness to take responsibility for results. Risk control and patience were key factors in the area of management discipline, Tharp found. Finally, sound decision making requires a good understanding of technical factors and the market, an ability to make unbiased choices, and independent thinking derived from competence.

Tharp's research also uncovered the characteristics common to losing traders. They appear to be highly stressed, a trait that impairs their ability to make sound decisions. They also tend to be pessimists, to have personality conflicts, and to blame others when things go wrong. Furthermore, losers tend to be crowd followers, are easily discouraged, and rarely establish a set of rules to follow. The psychologist emphasizes that a losing trader need not exhibit all these characteristics. One or two of them will suffice.

Generally speaking, Tharp's work confirms many of the ideas put forth by the other experts described in this chapter. Like Tharp, they conclude that successful traders and investors hold most if not all the following beliefs:

◆ Money itself is not important.

◆ Trading or investing is a game, hobby, or "love" above all else.

◆ Profits are a fringe benefit.

◆ Losing money is an accepted aspect of playing the market.

◆ Mental rehearsal helps in anticipating all possible outcomes.

◆ A high level of self-confidence enables them to convince themselves that they have "won" the game before it has begun.

There is, of course, a big difference between justifiable and unjustifiable confidence. Justifiable confidence comes from a coherent set of beliefs, usually encapsulated in a methodology or trading approach that has been soundly tested. Well-founded confidence springs from a commitment to do well. This means that you are certain that you are doing the right thing and are prepared to make some sacrifices to accomplish your goals.

◆ The Opposite Side: Why Do "Stars" Self-Destruct?

We can better appreciate what motivates successful traders and investors by looking at the other side of the coin and examining why "stars" tend to self-destruct. Perhaps two classic examples of this tendency are the entertainers, Elvis Presley and Marilyn Monroe. Both enjoyed unprecedented international fame, substantial wealth, and the adoration of millions of fans. Tragically, both ended their lives with an overdose of drugs.

In an article in *New Dimensions* in 1990, Roy Masters comes to grips with this seeming dilemma. He points out that stars with tendencies to self-destruct have attributes that are the exact opposite of those common to successful market operators. The financial wizards have put their acts together and are comfortable with themselves. They know that if they carry psychological baggage their goals will be unattainable, so they make continuous efforts—partly conscious, partly subconscious—to improve themselves by observing themselves.

On the other hand, as Masters points out, the stars are the victims of their own successes. We know that everyone loves to be loved, but, writes the author, "There is something strangely negative and destructive about being unconditionally loved by everyone, being constantly reminded that you are wonderful and can do no wrong." This state, he goes on to warn us, reinforces a person's worst attributes. The very reason these self-destructive stars began to seek this unconditional love and adoration may well have been to avoid confronting their problems. Eventually, they discover that this type of "success" is the ultimate betrayer, for they are still miserable, guilty, or angry. Yet, as Masters puts it, "There is no more promised land to look for." Either the high they experienced no longer satisfies them, or, more tragically, they begin to decline.

In a paragraph near the end of the article, Masters confirms what really makes a successful operator. "Contrary to popular misconception, there is nothing inherently wrong with attaining fame, great wealth, or power. But a great deal of maturity is necessary to deal with and hold on to power and wealth without going crazy. And such maturity is acquired gradually through a certain crucial process." In effect, Masters is stating that these self-destructive stars haven't got their act together, while traders and investors with a long history of success do. Whereas the stars obtain their wealth very quickly with relatively little effort, market wizards earn theirs through hard work over a longer time. Market operators often go broke or are on the verge of giving up before they become established. They pay their dues by learning from their mistakes, while the stars succeed only in temporarily covering up their problems. Under the surface, these problems then intensify in a potentially destructive manner.

◆ *The Attributes of Great Traders and Investors*

Being a market wizard involves no real secret. The rules and explanations are set out in this book. If you study the operations and methodology of any of the successful names, either historical or current, the same old characteristics come to the fore. We will examine a few case studies later, but first here are a few thoughts on attributes that are common to them all. In a sense, I am repeating some of the principles outlined earlier in this chapter, but they are so important that they deserve highlighting to reinforce the message.

First, every successful market operator is interested in the markets and how they work, not because they promise instant or even distant wealth but because of the fascinating inner workings and the challenges they offer. To quote a *Wall Street Journal* article by commodities specialist Stanley Angrist: "[Successful traders] share a surprisingly large number of attitudes in regards to why they do it. For example, almost all claim that they do not trade for the money, but view the market as a difficult game that is changing constantly. They are by now rich and diversified enough to afford this attitude."

In a published interview with Jesse Livermore, Richard Wyckoff points out that the eminent investor operated in a fashion similar to that of a merchant who, "accurately foreseeing the future demand for certain goods, purchases his line and patiently awaits the time when he may realize a profit." He quotes Livermore: "There is no magic about success. No man can succeed unless he acquires a fundamental knowledge of economics and conditions of every sort."

To us mere mortals, this highlights the point that if we trade purely for the monetary gain, we are placing low odds on our potential for success. In effect, anyone who puts undue emphasis on making money is likely to be consumed by that desire. This strong emotion will override any attempt at maintaining objectivity. It is better in such circumstances to try to overcome this natural desire and trade or invest in smaller positions where the money stakes are less. Only when we have begun to appreciate the market as a challenge in its own right will we be in a position to take a more aggressive stance.

A second characteristic is that almost all successful traders and investors are loners. They more or less have to be, because they are constantly called on to take positions opposite to those held by the majority or by the consensus view of the market. To buy low and sell high, they must be able to go against the crowd. Being a loner, of course, is not enough. They also need to be creative and imaginative independent thinkers. There is no point in bucking the crowd just for the sake of being contrary. The investor also needs to rationalize why the crowd might be wrong and what the alternative outcomes are likely to be. These money masters therefore have the ability or the knack to justify their contrariness. This then gives them the confidence to hold on to the position and swim upstream against the current of popular opinion.

Third, all great investors and traders utilize a philosophy or methodology. It was once said that all roads lead to Rome but that none of them start at the same place. When we examine the different trading and investment approaches followed by the money masters, we find that their goals—to accumulate wealth— are identical but their paths to that destination are vastly different. It does not matter which approach an investor takes as long as it works and the individual practitioner feels at home with it. Because he is comfortable with his methodology, he is able to work at it and refine it to its highest degree of efficiency. In effect, he has to be utterly dedicated to his chosen craft, for only then can he truly excel.

Fourth, to achieve success in the markets, investors must be disciplined and patient. This advice sounds so simple, yet paradoxically it is difficult to practice. Discipline means constantly gathering new facts and sticking to your rules. This is easy to achieve over the short run but much more difficult to maintain.

The only way is to work at it time and again until it becomes a habit.

You know instinctively that jumping out of a speeding car will be hazardous to your health. Entering poorly reasoned trades when rules are cast aside can be just as devastating to your financial health. The difference is that you can easily perceive the danger from the speeding car, but the consequences of trading recklessly are less obvious. You can read this section through and through and agree with its every word, but it is unlikely that you will fear a trade executed contrary to your rules until you have experienced the pain of losing.

All great traders and investors also possess patience. A predator waits patiently for its prey, and when the time is right and the odds are in its favor, the predator pounces, ready for the kill. Skilled market operators move in a similar fashion. They do not trade or invest purely for the sake of trading or because they need the money. No, they wait for the right time and circumstance and then take action.

There is nothing mysterious in this. Let's consider an everyday example of planting vegetables. Gardeners know from experience that the optimum time to do this is in the spring. To plant in the summer would be too late and in the fall or winter no good at all. This is evident to us all. We know that to get the best results we have to be patient and wait until spring, when growing conditions are at their best. However badly we might want those vegetables, we know that it is pure madness to sow the seeds in the winter, because all chances of their survival will be lost.

Ironically, the dangers in the marketplace are equally great but in this instance we rarely have the patience to wait, largely because we are unaware of the dangers of getting in at the wrong time. If we were, then as rational beings, we would wait until the right moment just as we would wait for spring. That we are unaware of the dangers of impatience distinguishes us from the market wizards. They know and understand the dangers, the rest of us do not.

Fifth, all great market operators are realists. Once you have entered a position whether as a trade or investment there is always the temptation when things go wrong to delude yourself that everything is still okay. This self-delusion is far less pronounced and even nonexistent in successful market participants. They are quick to recognize when conditions change and the original reason for holding the position no longer exists. They are married to nothing and are not afraid to admit a mistake, however painful it may be at the time. In doing so, they recognize that to hold on will result in even greater pain down the road. This means that they religiously follow the rule to "cut your losses short." Most of us are afraid to admit to ourselves when an investment turns sour. We cling to the false hope that things will get better, rarely asking ourselves, "If I had the money right now, would I still want to be invested in XYZ Company?" Even when we ask that question, we can always find a mountain of excuses for holding on to the position—the coming ex-dividend date, the brokerage costs involved in getting out. The list goes on.

In *Money Masters,* John Train quotes Paul Cabot, "the dean of Boston's institutional investors," as saying, "First you have to get all the facts and then you've got to face the facts . . . not pipe dreams." He continues, "There is no way to be a realist unless you've experienced the many facets of reality, which means having attained a certain age. . . . The older you get the more you've had a chance to see how often there's a slip between the cup and the lip."

Sixth, all successful market operators seem to have the ability to think ahead and figure out what may lie ahead. This does not imply that they have a sixth sense that is unavailable to the rest of us; it is more a talent for mentally rehearsing some of the alternative scenarios. Most of us assume that the current conditions and therefore the prevailing trend in market prices will continue ad infinitum. The truly great market virtuosi on the other hand are constantly looking ahead to anticipate what could cause the prevailing trend to reverse. It is not so much that they are smarter than the rest of us or that they are clairvoyant. Rather, they have trained themselves to question the status quo constantly and to anticipate a possible change of course.

This training is a form of mental rehearsal for the next event. All possible scenarios are examined and the unlikely ones discarded. Then, when a change in conditions begins to take place, they are able to roll with the punches and take advantage of them. In effect, by trying to maintain a flexible outlook, the successful market operator is far less susceptible to the element of surprise.

◆ A Sampling of Market Wizards, Their Philosophies, and Their Rules for Success

Successful traders and investors share basically similar characteristics. I have treated these case studies individually because their time frames and methodologies are so different. I have chosen but five studies from many possible examples. I selected these people because they have all publicly given us the benefit of their approaches and philosophies in a lucid manner. For that we should be grateful.

◆ Investors

Warren Buffet

In *The Money Masters*, John Train refers to Warren Buffet as "the investor's investor." It is a title well earned. A $10,000 investment in Buffet's original partnership in 1956 would have grown to $300,000 by the time it was dissolved in 1969. In that year, he dissolved the partnership to concentrate on other investments, most notably his controlling interest in Berkshire Hathaway, which was originally a textile company but later became a holding company. The price of shares in that corporation have appreciated from $38 in 1971 to $9,000 in the early 1990s.

Apart from his talent for accumulating wealth, one of Buffet's outstanding attributes is his interest in educating his shareholders. His annual remarks to shareholders of Berkshire

Hathaway are legendary. He also used to write to the shareholders of the original partnership. Every year he communicated the following:

> I cannot promise results to partners, but I can and do promise this:
>
> a) Our investments will be chosen on the basis of value, not popularity.
>
> b) Our patterns of operation will attempt to reduce permanent capital loss (not short-term quotational loss) to a minimum.

In this missive, Buffet was telling his shareholders that he was a value player and contrarian as well as a long-term investor. Preservation of capital was uppermost in his mind as the principal investment objective.

One important attribute of a successful investor is to stay away from the markets when conditions are not conducive to his chosen approach. In 1969, when cheap stocks were difficult to find and speculation was running rampant, Buffet wrote to his partners:

> I am out of step with present conditions. . . . On one point, however, I am clear. I will not abandon a previous approach whose logic I understand even though it may mean forgoing large, and apparently easy profits, to embrace an approach which I don't fully understand, have not practiced successfully, and which possibly could lead to substantial permanent loss of capital.

These remarks are most revealing since they indicate Buffet's intention to stick to the rules that had made him successful and that he understood. He could have made money by playing the speculative game but decided against that, because he knew that he might not have been able to get out when things went wrong. Again, he was unwilling to risk his partners' capital. The remarks also demonstrate a willingness to weather the storm and patiently wait for the bargains that appear once the speculative flurry is over, dragging both sound and unsound companies down with it.

Buffet lists six qualities that he believes are necessary for investment success:

1. You must be animated by controlled greed and fascinated by the investment process. He believes that too much greed will control you but that too little will fail to motivate you.

2. You must have patience. His time frame is much longer than the average investor. He believes that you should buy into a company because you want to own it permanently, not because you think its stock will go up in price. His belief is that if you are right about the company and buy it at a sensible price, you will eventually see your stock appreciate.

3. Think independently. He believes that if you don't know enough to make your own decisions, you should not make any decisions at all. He also quotes Benjamin Graham (the father of fundamental analysis) "The fact that other people disagree with you makes you neither right nor wrong. You will be right if your facts and reasoning are correct."

4. You must have the security and self-confidence that comes from knowledge, without being rash or headstrong. In effect, he is telling us that if we do not have confidence in our decisions because they have been poorly thought out, we are likely to be spooked as soon as the price goes against us.

5. Accept it when you don't know something.

6. Be flexible as to the types of businesses you buy, but never pay more than they are worth.

Buffet also told Train that there are 11 characteristics of a healthy business. This list is somewhat out of the scope of this book, but it is worth mentioning because of its significance. Buffet says a good business:

1. Offers a good return on capital.

2. Sees its profits in cash.

3. Is understandable.

4. Has a strong franchise and thus freedom to price.

5. Doesn't require a genius to run it.

6. Delivers predictable earnings.

7. Should not be a natural target for regulation.

8. Should have low inventories and a high turnover of assets.

9. Should have owner-oriented management.

10. Offers a high rate of return on the total of inventories plus physical plant.

11. Is a royalty on the growth of others and requires little capital itself.

John Templeton

John Templeton's claim to investment fame comes largely from the success of his Templeton Growth Fund, which grew twentyfold between 1958 and 1978. Counting reinvestment of all distributions, it ranked as the top performing fund during this period. This marks the pinnacle of his achievements, but there are other highlights before and since then.

One of his unique and admirable characteristics among money masters is his establishment of an endowment that annually awards a prize for progress in religion. He likens spiritual growth to gardening—if you find a weed you get rid of it, and you do the same for a bad thought or emotion.

His philosophy is based on the premise that you buy only what is being thrown away and hold on for an average of four years. He recommends that investors search among many markets for the companies selling for the smallest fraction of their true worth. These stocks, he argues, can be found only in companies that are completely neglected, that analysts and other investors do not even consider following.

As I have pointed out, one of the keys to successful investing is retaining your objectivity. One way to accomplish this is to cut yourself off from street gossip and unwanted solicitations from your broker. John Templeton lives in the Bahamas and instructs brokers not to telephone him but to send him in writing what they think he would like to see. In *The Money Masters*, John Train tells us, "The distance from [Templeton's] large, cool, porticoed white house . . . to the roar and shouting of the floor of the stock exchange is measured in psychological light-years. The house itself and everything in it are a silent reproach to excitement and hyperactivity."

Flexibility is another talent that Templeton shares with other great investors. He was a pioneer in the global marketplace, choosing to invest in an undervalued Japanese equity market long before global investing became a household game.

An additional quality possessed by most successful investors is consistency. For example, Fundscope placed the Templeton Growth Fund in the top 20 out of a total of 400 organizations in making money in bull markets but in the top 5 for not losing it in bear markets. This performance is even more impressive because many of the competing funds also held bonds, which are less susceptible than equities to down markets.

Examining the lifestyles, beliefs, and investment philosophies of successful investors other than Buffet and Templeton reveals that patience, flexibility, and hard work are irreplaceable allies in the quest for success. Detachment is a much easier goal to achieve for these long-term investors than for the traders whom we shall soon turn to. Summarizing the careers of eight prominent investors in *The Money Masters*, Train concluded that they practiced 11 winning strategies, as follows:

1. Buy a stock only as a share in a good business that you know a lot about. In other words, buy the business, and

if you have done your homework properly, the price will take care of itself.

2. Buy when stocks have few friends—particularly the stock in question.

3. Be patient. Don't be rattled by fluctuations.

4. Invest, don't guess. A badly chosen investment will surely go against you. If you lack confidence in a stock because you have not done the proper research, you are likely to take a hit when it declines in price.

5. High yields are often a trap. Growing companies need all the cash flow they can get to plough back into the business. Paying out a high proportion of dividends robs them of those growth opportunities.

6. Buy only what is cheap right now or is almost sure to grow so fast that it very soon will be cheap at today's price.

7. If stocks in general are expensive, stand aside.

8. Keep an eye on what the smart money masters are doing.

9. Buy investment management if you find company analysis too difficult.

10. Pick an appropriate investment strategy and stick with it.

11. Be flexible.

◆ Traders

The time horizon for traders is much shorter and the pressure commensurately greater due to the leverage factor. Trading consumes much more energy than investing because of the constant need to refer to price quotes. Consequently, we find that trading is much more a young man's game than investing. We will now consider two traders who were interviewed by Jack D. Schwager in his classic book *Market Wizards*.

Ed Seykota

Ed Seykota lives near Lake Tahoe in Nevada. He is reputed to have achieved a total return of 250,000% on one $5,000 account between 1972 and 1988—a truly remarkable feat. After interviewing Seykota, Schwager came away with the conclusion that he was someone who had found meaning in his life and was living exactly the life he wanted to live. This emphasizes the point made earlier that successful traders and investors have a strong sense of self-esteem and feel good about themselves, in contrast to the fallen stars. Seykota does not have an investment philosophy such as Buffet or Templeton but relies on computer-generated, trend-following systems. He uses the systems to filter out buy and sell signals, then uses his own judgment to decide how he should act on those signals. This in a nutshell is his philosophy.

When asked for his rules of trading, he replied, "One, cutting losses; two, cutting losses; three, cutting losses." This is another way of saying "protect your capital," for if you can do this, at least you live to fight another battle. Another money-management technique that Seykota employs is always to place a protective stop once he has opened a position. In this way, he lets the market judge whether he is right or wrong. Also, in the interest of maintaining principal, he never risks more than 5% of his equity on any particular trade.

Asked how he handles a losing streak, Seykota answered that he cuts down his activity and waits it out. He opined that to try to play "catch up" is lethal. Later, he volunteered that a costly tendency of many traders is to get emotional over a loss and then try to get even with an overly large position. This kind of activity is doomed to failure, since it reduces objectivity to a minimum. Such traders are not highly geared, because they think it's a good low-risk idea. Instead they are highly leveraged because they want to recoup their lost money as quickly as possible.

Seykota's trading rules are:

1. Cut losses.

2. Ride winners.

3. Keep bets small.

4. Follow the rules without question.

5. Know when to break the rules.

The last two points appear to contradict each other, but Seykota, like other great traders, has a passion for self-improvement. He believes that a trader should be totally at home with his approach and with the rules that govern that approach. However, part of the self-appraisal process involves evolution, and this in turn means breaking the rules and substituting new ones. This subject is covered at the end of Chapter 12.

Seykota summed up his success this way: "I feel my success comes from my love of the markets. I am not a casual trader. It is my life. I have a passion for trading. It is not merely a hobby or even a career choice for me. There is no question that this is what I am supposed to do with my life."

Paul Tudor Jones

Paul Tudor Jones represents another incredible success story. After a successful career in the New York cotton pits, he retired to form a money-management firm in 1984. At the end of 1988, each original $1,000 investment had risen to $17,000. Funds under his management grew so large that he has made a habit of returning profits to clients. This reduces his management fees but enables him to do a better job of managing money. It is to his credit when so many in the business try to grab money for management at virtually any cost. This impartiality and detachment from money is part of the characteristics of several market wizards that we have considered.

In his interview with Jack Schwager, Jones sums up his trading rules as follows:

> Don't ever average losses. Decrease your trading volume when you are doing poorly; increase your volume when you are trading well. Never trade in situations where you don't have control, e.g., in front of a major economic report.

> If you have a losing position that is making you uncomfortable, get out, because you can always get back in. There is nothing better than a fresh start.

> Don't be too concerned about where you got into a position. The only relevant question is whether you are bullish or bearish on the position that day . . . . Who cares where I was long from? That has no relevance to whether the market environment is bullish or bearish right now, or to the risk/reward balance of a long position at the moment.

> The most important rule of trading is to play great defense, not great offense. Every day I assume the position I have is wrong. [If my positions] are going against me, then I have a game plan for getting out.

> Don't be a hero. Don't have an ego. Always question yourself and your ability. Don't ever feel you are very good. The second you do, you are dead.

Thus we have in five paragraphs not only the essence of Jones's thinking but a concise account of the characteristics of other great traders. The idea of only playing defense, for example, is another way of saying the number one objective is to protect your capital. So too is the statement, "I always assume every position I have is wrong." When later asked to provide advice to a novice trader, Jones replied in the same vein. "Don't focus on making money," he said, "focus on protecting what you have." He considers himself to be a market opportunist developing an idea on the market and pursuing it from a low-risk standpoint until he has been repeatedly proven wrong or until he changes his viewpoint.

Pride of opinion, as described in Chapter 4, can cause devastating financial losses. When questioned by Schwager about what made him different, Jones said, "I don't really care about the mistake I made three seconds ago. What I care about is what I am going to do from the very next moment on. I try to avoid any emotional attachment to any market. I avoid letting my trading opinions be influenced by comments I may have made on the record about a market."

This last statement is somewhat remarkable for there are few people who do not worry about what they are on record as saying. It shows the investor's ability to change his mind and not be married to a particular situation merely because he once held that belief. After all, flexibility is a virtue that keeps appearing in the psyche of great traders. Whereas loyalty to people is a great virtue, disloyalty to a market that does not act well is also to be recommended. To quote Jones once again: "[Cutting emotional attachment to a market] is important because it gives you a wide-open intellectual horizon to figure out what is really happening. It allows you to come in with a completely clean slate in choosing the correct forecast for that particular market."

Bob Prechter

Bob Prechter does not conveniently fit into the great trader category, because his primary career has been in the business of writing a market letter. Nonetheless, he won the U.S. Trading Championship in 1984, setting an all-time profit record with a four-month gain of 440% in a monitored, real-money options account. This does not compare with the consistent long-term gains of a Buffet, Seykota, or Jones, but many successful traders subscribe to his market letter and follow his Elliott Wave Methodology. More to the point, he is lucid and has provided his subscribers a list of trading requirements (as opposed to a list of trading rules).

I have already outlined several of the roles recommended by Prechter but this merely underlines that certain characteristics or requirements contribute to making a great trader. The more times we can see them surface in different successful individuals the more we will appreciate their relevance. The following are Bob Prechter's trading requirements:

1. *A Method.* By a "method," he is referring to an objectively defined mechanism that helps you to make a trading decision. Buffet's and Templeton's methods focus on the simple concept of buying undervalued companies that possess good potential for growth. Seykota has a short-term mechanical/technical system. All the money masters and marked wizards have some kind of method or philosophy on which to base their decisions. None is perfect, but when properly applied they earn their practitioners substantial profits.

2. *The Discipline to Follow the Method.* We have talked about discipline earlier in great depth so there is no need to elucidate further, except to say, as Prechter puts it, "Without discipline you really have no method in the first place."

3. *The Mental Fortitude to Accept That Losses Are Part of the Game.* Most people blame outside forces for their losses: Insiders, unexpected news events, stock manipulators, and the like are often singled out for abuse. Rarely are losses accepted as part of the game. We do not expect a baseball player to hit every ball so why should we expect to win on every trade? Prechter's point is that we should not only accept losses but also should anticipate them through sound money management.

4. *The Mental Fortitude to Accept Huge Gains.* This is his way of saying, "Let your profits run." The concept theorizes that you make a series of small trades with mixed results. Then a big one comes along where you make twice the usual profit. Your best friend and your broker tell you not to be greedy, but your system or method says to stay in. You get out but find that when the system goes negative you have lost the potential of the trade of a lifetime.

No doubt there has been some repetition in this chapter, but that's all to the good. The more emphasis placed on the characteristics that contribute to the makeup of a great trader or investor, the more believable they will become. And the more believable these attributes become, the more likely you will be to put these rules into practice and to adopt the characteristics. The most difficult hurdle is understanding that these money masters are in the game less for the money than they are for the challenge of the game and their passion for that challenge. This factor probably distinguishes most of us from these exceptional players, because we usually play the market for the money first and the challenge and love of the game second.

12

Nineteen Trading Rules for Greater Profits

Previous chapters have described how markets have a habit of finding out our weaknesses and exploiting them to the fullest. Successful traders are those who not only know the workings of the markets but who also have the *will* to put a plan into action and follow it religiously. Since trading in the market is basically a process of dealing with probabilities and beating the odds, anyone who participates in the market must make a conscious effort to set up some kind of structure that will help him master his emotions. If you recognize that you have a problem before taking on a trading position or making a long-term investment you will be in a better position to spot potential pitfalls. In this chapter, we will outline some rules that will help you do this. But remember that *reading and understanding the rules is not enough. You must also put them into practice.*

The rules described here are not the only ones, but they are generally considered to be the most important. It is assumed that at this stage you already have some rudimentary knowledge of how markets work and also a method for making trading decisions. It could be a technical, fundamental, or behaviorist approach. The vehicle is not important as long as it has been tested and as long as you feel comfortable with it. All the world's great religions try to lead us to essentially the same place (i.e., discovery of the truth), but their paths are different. So it is with methods and markets. All approaches have greater profitability as their objective, but each individual has to choose his own path. It is no good using a method practiced by a prominent trader or market newsletter writer if you do not feel completely comfortable with it, because when things become difficult, as they will surely do, you are far less likely to stay with it. Also, if you are lucky enough to choose a trading style or approach with which you feel totally at home, the chances are good that you will find the incentive to work a lot harder at it.

Selecting a methodology is usually not hard; executing it is. Mastering emotion is precisely what the rules are designed to do. Once you have a position in the market, it's easy to play mental games to avoid the pain of losing. Let's say you buy one gold contract at $350, expecting it to rally to $370. Instead, the price of gold falls to $345. This decline is justified by the media (which always has to have an excuse for price movements) as being due to Russian selling. An immediate emotional response by most people is to rationalize that the selling is probably over. After all, why would the Russians announce they were major sellers if they had not already sold? Consequently, *hope* for a rally would now replace the original analysis as a basis for being long in anticipation of a rise in the price. The rationalization and the hope are really protecting the trader from the dual pain of having to admit he was wrong and has to take a loss. This process also involves some denial of the reality of the situation. After all, the market did not move in the expected direction, and this implies that the original decision to go long was incorrect.

Another example of denying reality may occur where a trader, to get in with less risk, stalks a possible trade for several days, waiting for a small correction. Let's say that the item in question is the deutsche mark. Each day, the price works its way slowly and tantalizingly higher. Finally, a very bullish news story appears in the wire services saying that the German balance of payments has moved into surplus. This is the last straw for our now impatient trader. He can no longer control his enthusiasm and plunges into the market at substantially higher prices than he was prepared to pay only two or three days previously. It's a good bet that this represents an exhaustion move, since the market had been rallying in the previous week in anticipation of this good news. Naturally, the mark peaks out and leaves our trader with a nasty loss and the need to make an objective decision of where to limit the damage. It is very difficult to obtain an objective viewpoint in an emotionally charged climate. Better to establish and follow some rules that are aimed at preventing such a situation from arising.

Rules won't eliminate losses, but they will help reduce the level of emotion as they increase objectivity and consistency. If you can be more objective, there will be far less room for hope, greed, and fear to crowd out your better judgment. In Chapter 14, we list trading rules proposed by many different but knowledgeable sources. No one can truly learn the benefit of any set of rules or principles except through actual experience in the marketplace, so the listing and explanation of some of the guidelines in this chapter are really starting points to which you will hopefully return. Studies show that advertising is far more powerful when it is repeated on a sustained basis than when it appears in one or two isolated ads. The message being portrayed then stands a better chance of being embedded in the mind of the consumer. The inclusion of the trading rules in Chapter 14 is a way to mount a sustained advertising campaign on you. These same principles have been expounded by history's great traders and investors, all of whom have struggled with the difficult task of mastering their emotions. Because each person has his own style and approach, the lists are slightly different. But they all have the same objective, namely, maintaining objectivity, and clear independent thinking and achieving sound money management practices. That these same principles come from so many different sources, separated by time and professional pursuits, cannot be discounted as a mere coincidence. They are on the list because they work. They worked for legends such as Jesse Livermore and Bernard Baruch as well as successful traders practicing today. They can and will work for you, but only if you give them a chance. You are encouraged to refer to Chapter 14, but the remainder of this chapter will summarize the rules I think are most important. Before we begin, please remember that *no rule will work unless it is put into practice.* If the road to hell is paved with good intentions, almost certainly the road to financial ruin is, as well.

The following 19 rules can be roughly categorized into those that help you to master your emotions and those that aid in risk control. In other words, personal psychological management and money management.

◆ Psychological Management

Rule 1. When in Doubt, Stay Out

When trading the markets, it is important to have a certain level of confidence in what you are doing. Too much confidence will lead to carelessness and overtrading and is unwelcome. On the other hand, if you enter a position with little or no enthusiasm, you are setting yourself up for some knee-jerk reactions when bad news breaks. If there is the slightest doubt in your mind about entering a trade, then you should not initiate it, because you will not have the emotional fortitude to stay with it when things begin to go wrong. For instance, if you are in doubt, you will tend to concentrate on any negative breaking developments. As prices decline, you will get more and more discouraged. Consequently, when the price falls to a support, or buying, zone, you will be in more of a frame of mind to sell than to buy.

Alternatively, you may get into a position based on some solid research and in a confident, but not overly enthusiastic mode. Later, some new evidence comes to the fore that causes you to be less optimistic than before. In short, some doubt about the validity of the original rationale for getting in begins to creep in to your mind. It does not matter whether the position is above or below where you got in. The important thing is that you now begin to doubt your original rationale. Under such circumstances there is only one logical course of action—get out. You no longer have the fortitude that comes from a strong conviction.

This means that you will most likely head for the exits at the first sign of trouble.

It is important to remember that the *principal* reason that you are in the market is to make a profit. If the odds of that happening have decreased, then you have little justification for maintaining the position. After all, this is not your last chance to trade; there will *always be another opportunity down the road.*

Rule 2. Never Trade or Invest Based on Hope

This topic was covered in Chapter 2. It bears repeating as a trading rule since so many of us hold on to losing positions well after the original rationale for their initiation has vanished. The only reason for not selling is hope, and markets usually reward the hopeful with losses. When you find yourself in this situation, sell promptly.

Rule 3. Act on Your Own Judgment or Else Absolutely and Entirely on the Judgment of Another

It was established earlier that if you do not enter a trade or investment with total confidence, you are likely to be spooked out at the first sign of trouble. If you find yourself relying on your broker or friends for tips and advice, the chances are that you will not have carefully considered all of the ramifications. This means that you will not have the emotional fortification to be totally committed to the trade if things appear to go wrong. It is much better to consider all the arguments, both bullish and bearish, prior to making a commitment. In this way, you will be in a good position to judge whether the latest price setback is a result of a fundamental change in the overall situation or if it is merely part of the normal ebb and flow that any market goes through.

Brokers, friends, and others that you respect can be helpful in providing you with ideas but you are the one who should make the final decision. This means balancing out the pros and cons, listening to this opinion and that before coming to a carefully considered independent conclusion of your own. After all, if things go wrong, it's you who lose the money, not your friends.

This rule also cautions you from following tips or insider information. I have found that people invariably lose when they trade on such information. In the case of stocks, such tips usually revolve around takeover activity, the announcement of better-than-expected corporate earnings, or a lucrative contract. In a publicly held company, the chances that you as an individual will be privy to such information will be remote. Others will usually have been there before you, the news being already factored into the price. Moreover, the "good" news often gets exaggerated as it gets passed around. Quite often, the story is false or the event in question fails to materialize. Even if you do manage to obtain some insider news from which profits can be obtained, it is basically unethical and unfair to buy stock from someone who would not be selling it at that price had he been privy to the same information as yourself. This is far different from two people deciding to make an exchange based on an honest difference of opinion concerning the outlook for the company in question.

If you cannot make a decision based solely on your own judgment of the facts, and opinions of colleagues, friends, and brokers, you are better off turning your portfolio over to someone whom you have checked out thoroughly for integrity and competence.

Rule 4. Buy Low (into Weakness), Sell High (into Strength)

Everyone knows that if you buy low and sell high you are bound to make money. This is clearly not as easy as it sounds otherwise you wouldn't be reading this book. The idea that I am trying to get over here is something a little different; it might be better expressed as "Buy on weakness, sell on strength." When prices rise, so does confidence. Prices that progressively fall, on the other hand, attract a greater and greater amount of concern. The reason is that rising prices are usually accompanied by positive news making us feel more comfortable. We tend to downplay our fears at such times and therefore take on more risk. In his classic · book, *Psychology of the Stock Market*, G. C. Selden explains it so: "The greatest fault of ninety-nine out of one hundred active traders is being bullish at high prices and bearish at low prices. Therefore refuse to follow the market beyond what you consider a reasonable climax, no matter how large the possible profits that you may appear to be losing by inaction." These words are as true today as in 1912, when they were originally written. This is the way both the crowd and individuals tend to react. However, as discussed in Chapter 7, it pays to go the opposite way to the crowd whenever you can. Generally, this means buying on weakness and selling on strength. This rule is applicable for both initial positions and when adding.

Rule 5. Don't Overtrade

This topic was covered in Chapter 2, so there is no need to repeat the detailed explanation except to say that overtrading leads to a loss of perspective and considerable transaction costs.

Rule 6. After a Successful and Profitable Campaign, Take a Trading Vacation

Many traders find that accumulating profits is relatively easy; the difficult part is keeping them. I am confident if most traders were to show you a graph of their performance, it would look like the oscillator in Figure 8–1, that is, a series of giant sine waves running up and then falling down, because they failed to recognize when their luck and trading skills had peaked. In short, they did not know when to walk away from the table.

No person, however talented, can maintain a super trading performance forever. People operate in cycles in virtually every endeavor. Take baseball players—even the best have their off days, off weeks, and even off seasons. The same is true for traders. Therefore, make sure that you take a break after a successful campaign, returning to the markets six or eight weeks later. Your outlook is likely to be less overconfident, and you will also be able to take a more objective view of the markets.

Rule 7. Take a Periodic Mental Inventory to See How You Are Doing

Quite often we get so engrossed in our trading and investing that we lose sight of where we are going. It therefore makes sense to reflect occasionally on where we are headed and to make sure that we are doing the right thing. As part of this process, you might want to ask yourself some questions on the lines of the following. Am I able to afford the risks I am taking? Am I speculating or investing intelligently or am I gambling? Am I following the right system? Am I trying to buck the prevailing trend? Am I too close to the market? Am I overtrading?

There are many more questions you could ask, including the other rules cited in this chapter. This simple little exercise will help to draw your attention to any mistakes you might be making or rules that are being broken. In addition, it will serve to reinforce those rules in your mind so that they have a better chance of eventually becoming good habits.

Rule 8. Constantly Analyze Your Mistakes

When we are successful, we tend to think that this process arises from hard work or good judgment. Rarely do we attribute it to chance or the luck of being in the right place at the right time. On the other hand, when things go against us, we often blame our setbacks on bad luck or some convenient scapegoat. Of course, we should be questioning our own judgment first because that is the most likely source of any mistakes that may have been made. It is only when we have made a mistake that we can begin to take responsibility for our own actions and learn from those mistakes. You can read books on the psychology of markets ad infinitum, but only when you have gone through the pain of losing money and attributing it to a mistake are you likely take remedial action so it doesn't happen again.

This process of self-critique has to be a continuous one. After a brief time, chances are that you will be lulled back into a false sense of security as profits begin to roll in once again. In this type of situation, most people will again fall back into their old ways. It will therefore take more losses to reignite the self-examination process. Either the lesson will eventually sink in or your account will be so depleted that you will no longer be trading.

The greatest benefit of analyzing your transgressions therefore arises because failure is often the best teacher; it brings you back to the reality that if you had faithfully followed the rules, you would not be in your current predicament. What more natural course than to follow them next time around? Most mistakes arise because of emotional deficiencies—the fear of being wrong or of feeling a fool at having to having to face your broker or some other person with the loss. This is also true of professional money managers who not only have to deal with the vagaries of the market and with their own emotions but those of the client as well. This latter battle—the fear of losing the client—can often be the most devastating of all.

The first step is to face up to such fears, recognize that they are a destructive force, and take some steps to rectify them.

Rule 9. Don't Jump the Gun

In any investing or trading situation, there is always the temptation to put on a position before the particular discipline or methodology that we are using has given the all clear. Enthusiasm replaces prudence. This is a poor practice because it means that we are not, in actual fact, following the discipline but have decided that we know better. Rarely does this type of policy pay off. After all, why go to the trouble of researching a methodology or approach and setting up the rules if we are not prepared to follow them? When tempted to do so, you may debate with yourself that this is an exceptional situation and that it justifies taking immediate action. The problem is that these "exceptional" situations will keep occurring until they become an everyday experience. In effect, the discipline will have been totally abandoned.

Rule 10. Don't Try to Call Every Market Turn

In our natural desire to be market perfectionists, it is quite understandable that we should feel the need to call every market turn. Unfortunately, that task is quite unobtainable. If we find ourselves trying to guess every twist and turn in the price action, not only will it lead to frustration, but we will totally lose any sense of perspective.

◆ Money Management

Rule 11. Never Enter into a Position without First Establishing a Risk Reward

It is not possible to set out a specific mathematical ratio of expected profits to maximum acceptable losses in all cases. The decision should be taken with regard to the proportion of capital being risked in a particular trade or investment. Another factor would relate to the character makeup of the person concerned. Risk-averse individuals should not go into a high-reward high-risk venture and vice versa. Risk is always relative. What is a financially life-threatening risk for one person may be beer money for another. Generally speaking, you should use a good dose of common sense, making sure that the ratio is normally at least 3–1.

Rule 12. Cut Losses, Let Profits Run

This is probably the most widely known rule of all. It is also one of the most important. We enter any trade with the objective of making a profit, so when the position goes against us, it is natural to feel some kind of emotional pain. Many of us choose to ignore the loss, rationalizing that the market will come back. Sometimes we can justify the decline because the market came down "on low volume," or "it might have declined, but the action was good so I will hold on." Another favorite comes from rationalizing the reason for the decline. "That was a bad piece of news, but it was amazing how the market only came down 50%; it's obviously very strong technically." Occasionally, we wait for an event to take place as justification for making a decision. I remember getting very badly burned in the in the spring of 1980. The commodity markets were under pressure because Jimmy Carter had told people to stop using their credit cards. A morale-building announcement was expected any day, but in the meantime commodity prices kept on slipping and the announcement kept on being delayed. In the end, I sold out, but waiting for the announcement cost my account dearly. I should have considered the market's action in relation to my game plan when deciding whether to liquidate. Instead I allowed my losses to compound.

It's amazing how we can play games with our emotions by justifying almost anything. This is because we want prices to go higher (or lower if we are short), but we either forget or chose to ignore that the market is going to move in the direction that *it* wants to, not the way we desire. The market is totally objective, it is the participants who are emotional. We may *wish* for a rally but that has no bearing on the situation except that our wishes are bound to cloud our judgment.

We need to remember that if the market has gone down when we expected it to go up, it is a warning that the original analysis is flawed. If this is so, then there is no *rational* reason for still being in the position. We should cut our losses and liquidate.

This does not mean that every time we enter a position and see it go against us, we should sell. A good trader will establish a potential reward and acceptable risk before putting on a position. Part of this acceptance of risk involves the possibility and even probability that the market will decline before it advances. It would certainly be extremely optimistic for us to expect every trade to become profitable immediately we put it on. No, the rule about cutting losses really refers to the point at which these acceptable risks are exceeded, for it is only then that the market is telling us that our original analysis is probably at fault. Even after these predetermined benchmarks have been exceeded and you have been stopped out, there is still room for the element of doubt to creep back. Even though the market has now given its decision, some of us do not like to accept that our hopes and expectations will no longer be realized. In such circumstances, the temptation is to break away from this self-imposed discipline and get back into the market. This is often done at a higher level than the level at which the liquidation took place. Rising prices, remember, build confidence. However, my experience has been that if a carefully chosen stop point has been executed, it rarely pays to get back in. More times than not, it would have been more profitable to have taken the opposite side, but very few people possess the mental agility to do so.

Cutting losses is a fundamentally important money management technique, because it helps to protect capital and therefore enables us to fight another day.

Letting profits run really involves the same principle as cutting losses. When the market exceeds your downside cutoff point, it is a warning that you have made a mistake. On the other hand, as long as the general trend moves in your favor, the market is giving you a vote of confidence, so you should stay with the position and let your profits run. There is a famous saying that "the trend is your friend." In effect, this is another way of telling us to let our profits run. Trends, once in force have a habit of perpetuating but no one on earth can forecast their magnitude or duration, despite what you may read in newsletters and the media. As long as your analysis or methodology indicates that the trend continues to move in your favor, you have few grounds for selling unless it is to lock in some partial profits. Markets spend enough time waffling back and forth in confusing, frustrating, and unprofitable trading ranges to allow the trader the luxury of prematurely getting out of a good trending market.

The problem is that when many people have a profit, they want to take it there and then. The rationale is based on the theory that it is better to cash in now, otherwise the profit will get away. It is certainly true that you can never go broke taking a profit. Unfortunately, every trader and investor cannot avoid losing positions. A net profit situation can only be achieved if the profitable trades outweigh the negative ones, and usually a few highly profitable ones carry most traders. Taking profits too early therefore limits this potential.

It is interesting how most people are risk averse when it comes to taking profits and risk seeking when it comes to losses. They prefer a smaller but sure gain and are unwilling to take a wise gamble for a large gain. On the other hand, they are more willing to risk their capital for a large uncertain loss than for a certain small one.

Rule 13. Place Numerous Small Bets on Low-Risk Ideas

Since a high proportion of trades unavoidably will be unprofitable, it is a wise policy to make bets small so that a significant amount of capital is not risked on any one transaction. As a general rule, it is not advisable to risk more than 5% of your available capital on any one trade. This goes against the natural tendencies of many of us. In our quest for a large and quick profits, it seems much easier and more logical to put all our money on one horse.

It is also important to make sure that any trade or investment that you do make is a carefully thought out low-risk idea. The estimated potential reward should always be much greater (at least 3–1) than the maximum acceptable risk.

Rule 14. Look Down, Not Up

Most people enter a trade by calculating its probable upside and building that assumption into their expectations. As a result, they are setting themselves up for a disappointment. The question to ask when putting on a position is "What is the worst that can happen?" By looking down, not up, you are addressing what should be your number one objective: preserving your capital. If you erode your capital base, then you will have nothing left with which to grow. Almost all traders lose as many times as they win. The successful ones make more on the winning trades but more importantly lose less on the bad ones. By looking down, they are, in effect, assessing where they should cut their losses ahead of time. If this potential margin of error proves to be too great, they walk away from the trade.

I can remember many instances when I was extremely optimistic about the prospects for a trade. I knew in my mind that the market would tell me I was wrong, but the chart point would be considerably below my entry point. My expectations would be so positive that I would fool myself into believing that the market would "never go down that far because the trend was bullish." Invariably it would, and so I would pay a heavy price for not taking the worst possible scenario seriously. A series of painful experiences have taught me that it is better to look down first and look up later.

If you know that about half the trades that you put on are going to go against you, then it makes sense to try to make those mistakes as inexpensive as possible.

Rule 15. Never Trade or Invest More Than You Can Reasonably Afford to Lose

Any time that you risk capital that you cannot reasonably afford to lose, you are placing yourself at the mercy of the market. Your stress level will be very high, and you will lose all objectivity. Decisions will be emotional because you will be focused on monetary gains and the painful psychological consequences of a loss and will not be based on the facts as they really are.

Rule 16. Don't Fight the Trend

There is a well-known saying that a rising tide lifts all boats. In a market sense, it is as well to be trading in the direction of the market since a rising market, in effect, lifts all long positions. Going short in a bull market therefore entails considerable risk; for by definition unless you are agile enough to take profits at the appropriate time, a loss is certain.

The opposite is true in a bear market where rallies are often unpredictable and treacherous. If you study the results of most trading systems, you will see that the negative results inevitably come from positions that are put on in the opposite direction to the main trend. Obviously, you do not always have a firm opinion about the direction of the primary trend, but when you do, it is much more sensible not to trade against it.

Rule 17. Wherever Possible, Trade Liquid Markets

In general, you should always trade liquid markets, that is, where the difference between the bid and ask prices are usually narrow. Trading in illiquid or "thin" markets means that in addition to broker commissions, you are also paying some form of cost because of these wide spreads. You may think that this can be overcome through patiently waiting to buy at a specific price, as opposed to placing a market order. Nevertheless, when you decide to sell, you are more likely to be doing so under pressure, so the wide spread will make the cost of an immediate execution work against you. Illiquid markets can be ascertained by the amount of average daily volume transacted. Normally, anything less than 2,000 contracts per day is considered illiquid. It is also important to remember that in the futures markets, deferred contracts (i.e., those due for settlement some time into the future), can also be extremely illiquid even with such widely traded items such as Stock Index Futures or gold. It is therefore usually a better idea to trade in the nearby futures since the commission costs of "rolling over" into the next available contract on expiration is normally less than the cost of dealing with the wider spread.

Liquid markets imply a wide variety of participants with differing opinions, so there is usually someone with an opposite opinion to your own who is willing to take the other side of the trade. Illiquid markets can be very profitable if you happen to be on the right side, but if you are caught on the wrong side when some unexpected bad news materializes, the results can be devastating. This is especially true in the futures markets that are subject to daily price limit moves. Most of the time, markets trade within the limits, but it is amazing how they seem to exceed those limits when you personally have a position. When we talk of "liquid" markets, we mean that it is relatively easy to get in and out of a position most of the time. This does not imply that so-called liquid markets are always liquid. There are times when even the most liquid of all, such as the S&P Composite, bonds or gold move at such a frantic pace that it can be impossible to obtain an execution at anywhere close to the expected price. This situation often develops after the release of a government report. If the market has factored in, say a bullish number, but the report is bearish, then for a few moments there may be no liquidity whatsoever as the market adjusts to this new reality.

These situations seem to arise when most participants are positioned on the same side and the market has factored in seem very favorable expectations. When the bad news comes out, there is virtually no one to take the other side and yet seemingly everyone wants to get out at the same time. Only when the price has made a rapid and, for the majority, painful adjustment, does liquidity return to the marketplace. It therefore makes sense for those who have a short-term horizon to avoid potential situations of this nature, for you really have no control over the outcome. You are literally gambling on the content of a government report that will probably be revised anyway.

Rule 18. Never Meet a Margin Call

This important rule applies only to leveraged traders. Margin calls arise for two reasons. First, the market may have gone against you, which means that the equity in your account has fallen below the required level. Second, the margin requirement for the commodity or financial futures in your portfolio may have been raised. When your broker calls you with a margin call, you have two alternatives. The first is to send in sufficient funds to bring your account up to the required equity level. The second is to reduce the margin requirement by selling all or part of your position.

To make the correct choice, we have to examine why your account is in this unfortunate condition. If the call is being made because the market has gone against you, it means that either you have too much leverage and will therefore be on emotional tenterhooks with each twist and turn or your original premise for getting into the position no longer holds. Either way, meeting a margin call will have the effect of *increasing* your emotional commitment and is therefore undesirable. If your original decision was based on a false assessment, then the margin call should be viewed as a gentle reminder that you should deal with this problem by liquidating all or part of the position. The margin call may also arise not so much because your current position has gone against you but because the account has been allowed to dwindle slowly. The call then follows in the wake of a string of losses. In this type of situation, the prognostications are worse because the call does not reflect an isolated incident but the culmination of a deteriorating trend. A stronger dose of medicine is then called for. The best thing to do is to exit the markets completely for an extended period so that your emotional wounds can heal and objectivity can return. The length of the period will differ for the individual and the seriousness of the losses, but in general, a "vacation" of at least three weeks is appropriate.

Alternatively, the margin call may arise because you have just added some new positions. This implies that you have been overtrading or at best that you have not taken the new risk–reward potential into consideration. Whatever the reason, the finger points to poor money management.

Sometimes the equity in the account rises a little from the initial balance, but a margin call is still generated because the exchange minimums have been raised. You may think that such calls should be met because the market has moved in your direction and you were, in fact, correct. The raising of margin requirements is merely a technicality. This type of reasoning is incorrect, because margin requirements are raised for a reason. Ideally, the exchanges prefer to set low margin requirements, because this encourages more trading and therefore more commissions for the members. However, when conditions become more volatile, they must also take into consideration that traders are more likely to run into financial difficulties. The raising of the requirement is therefore a hedge against such losses. If conditions become more volatile, then it makes sense for you as a trader to take some more precautions. Quite often, a raising of the requirement is a signal itself that the prevailing trend is in the process of reversing.

Consequently, whatever the reason for the margin call, the rule remains the same: Never meet it by sending in more money.

Rule 19. If You Are Going to Place a Stop, Put It at a Logical, Not Convenient, Place

Traders often follow the discipline of predetermining where their downside risk might lie and place a stop-loss order slightly below that point. If the stop point has been determined with resort to some sound technical or fundamental analysis, this represents an intelligent method of operation. However, if you initiate the trade on the basis that you cannot afford to lose more than $300 and so place the stop at a point that limits the loss to $300, your odds of a winning trade will be greatly reduced. In this instance, you are not making decisions based on price action, where the market has the opportunity to tell you if you are wrong. Instead, you are picking an arbitrary point based on your own assessment of how much you can afford to lose. If the stop is triggered, it is not a vote by the market that you misjudged the trend, for quite clearly the market was not given enough leeway to come to such a verdict. Such stop points represent nothing less than a gamble that the price would not slip to such a level. The chances are that, having been stopped out, you would then see the market reverse direction to a degree that the trade would have ended up in the profitable camp.

Even traders who recognize this fallacy can be drawn into complex mental games where the sheer degree of their optimism causes them to rationalize incorrectly that their stops are in fact logically placed. It is not a bad habit therefore to ask yourself, "Is this really the best place to put the stop, or am I placing it here as a convenient place to limit my losses?"

◆ SUMMARY

We could add a 20th rule, which would be to follow the other 19 rules without question. It makes little sense to learn about and develop a set of rules if you fail to put them into practice. You would forfeit any sense of objectivity, independent thinking, perspective, and risk control that the rules are designed to deal with. To make sure, let's add a 21st rule: Follow the other 20 without question at all times!

13

Making a Plan and Sticking to It

◆

*I*f you have studied the ideas in this book, you now have a good understanding of the underlying psychological forces that drive markets and the kind of pitfalls you can easily stumble into if you are unable to master your natural emotional tendencies. All the reading in the world, though, will be of little use unless you can put it into practice. That's the difficult part: Execution involves tremendous effort. Starting out is often relatively easy because you gain strength from the initial enthusiasm gained from fresh ideas. The really hard part is the continual application of these ideas as the novelty wears off and some losses develop. The struggle to maintain newly learned disciplines is then at its most difficult.

This chapter has two objectives. The first is to help you organize your thought processes in a way that will better equip you to do battle with the markets (and therefore yourself). The second is to emphasize the necessity of constantly reminding yourself to follow up and review your activities. In this respect, it is vital to remember that it is the function of the market to search out and exploit your every weakness. To overcome this challenge, you have to be constantly on guard to limit those opportunities as much as possible. Only with constant surveillance and continuous review can you accomplish this task successfully. Eventually, such perseverance will be rewarded with a change of habit and thinking, but this will take several years to accomplish.

The remainder of this chapter is organized under the following headings, which we will consider in turn: "Setting Up Your Personal Investment Objectives," "Adopting an Investment or Trading Philosophy," "Establishing a Plan to Maximize Objectivity and Minimize Emotion," and "Establishing a Review Process."

This overall, four-point plan is relevant to both traders and long-term investors. The principal difference will be the amount of time between progress reviews. Obviously an active trader, in the market on a daily or even intraday basis will need to review his progress on a much more frequent basis than someone who makes transactions as infrequently as three or four times a year. Even on the latter schedule, it is important not only to review the progress you have made but also to monitor any major economic, financial, or technical changes that may have occurred. It is easy to slip into complacency by getting into the habit of closing your mind to what goes on in the markets.

◆ *Setting Up Your Personal Investment Objectives*

When we are uncertain about our goals, our minds become a battlefield of conflicting desires. In this mental environment, the result will be total paralysis that will make it impossible to achieve investment success. Therefore, it is necessary to develop specific objectives for our trading and investment activities. If correctly done, setting up investment objectives helps to transfer our energies from the external forces where we often allocate blame to the real source of our problems, namely ourselves. For example, if an individual has a large position in the stock market and some random event such as the 1991 summer coup in the Soviet Union comes along to push prices down significantly, it is natural to blame "the market." In such circumstances, we can rationalize the situation because we have no apparent control over it. The real issue, though, is ourselves, and until we can learn to come to grips with that problem, it will keep resurfacing.

Arnold Toynbee, the great British historian, recognized that fact in his principle of challenge and response. He spent a great deal of time studying the characteristics of rising and falling civilizations. He noted that all civilizations faced challenges from time to time. The difference between a civilization that was on the rise and one that was in decline was that the rising civilization was able to meet challenges successfully and move on. The declining civilization, on the other hand, either failed outright or inadequately met the challenge, which then would continually resurface and become a even greater burden.

An example of a classic challenge occurred in the fifteenth century. The Western world faced the dilemma of how to trade with the Orient when the land routes were barred by the Islamic Ottoman Empire. The challenge was met by Columbus. Although he failed to find the elusive route, he instead discovered a new continent, thus paving the way for others to develop it later. When it comes to meeting challenges, the position of an investor or trader is no different. If you continually make the same mistakes and do not learn (i.e., fail to overcome the challenges put forward by the markets), you are doomed to fail. Setting some realistic objectives can help to put some of these problems in perspective and lay the groundwork for success.

Investors

The starting point of any plan is to establish a set of objectives. After all, if you do not know where you are going and how long it is likely to take, how can you possibly make the correct investment decisions? These objectives should be established, keeping in mind your status in life, financial situation, and ability to tolerate risk.

The three principal investment objectives that almost everyone has are liquidity, income, and growth. The term "liquidity" refers to that portion of the portfolio that can easily be turned into cash to meet an unexpected expense. Both equities and bonds are liquid in the sense that they can be easily turned into cash. However, it is not always convenient to sell them. Perhaps there is a taxable gain that you do not wish to realize at present.

Alternatively, the market may be down, and you do not want to take a loss because you feel that prices will soon recover. Liquidity, therefore, has a broader meaning than just realizing a sale to make a payment. It implies that the principal amount will not materially change. In short, it can be counted on. Hence, you need to balance your portfolio to provide sufficient funds to meet such obligations without jeopardizing the overall investment plan.

Occasionally, you will need funds, for example, two or three years down the road, to pay college fees. In this sense, a liquid investment would be one that matures at a much later date. In this way, it would still provide the ability to make a payment, but the principal value could also be counted on, thereby meeting the dual test for a liquid asset.

The second investment objective, income, will depend a great deal on your own financial requirements. For example, if you are retired and are relying solely on social security payments, your income requirement will be a great deal higher than if you have your whole career ahead of you. You may also be quite young and in the process of taking a higher degree. With no other income source, the need for earnings from your portfolio will be of paramount importance. Once you have earned the degree and have a good income stream, you would then be wise to change your investment objective toward one of growth. A heavy income requirement is not therefore confined to widows and orphans.

The final objective is growth. Here we are faced with a trade-off. As a rule of thumb, the greater the potential reward, the more substantial the risk and the uncertainty. If you are young and earning a good living, you are clearly in a better position to assume more risk than someone who is retired. The young person not only has more time to recoup a lost investment but will also be blessed with a potential cash flow that can make up for past mistakes. The retired person does not have that luxury.

For most people, the objective of liquidity will be relatively unimportant, so the decision will rest on an appropriate balance between bonds and stocks. It is important to assess your particular stage in life and your financial requirements in setting goals. Equally as significant is the need to make sure that your goals are not only realistic but also consistent with your temperament.

For example, if the stock market has appreciated by 15% in the past five years, you may decide that you want your portfolio to grow at a more conservative rate of 12%. This may appear to be realistic on paper, but the problem is that the market has experienced a compounded annual growth rate closer to 9% historically. Since the return over the past few years has been way above normal, it is likely that the next few years will see average or, more likely, below average growth. Over time, market performance has a habit of regressing or returning to the mean, so after a few good years, it is reasonable to anticipate a couple of poor ones. Unrealistic expectations therefore can lead to disappointment when they are not met.

Temperament is another factor that should be considered when establishing investment objectives. For example, we know that the average return on equities historically has been about 9%. However, we also know that this increase did not take a straight line and that the rate of return was not consistent; there were peaks and valleys along the way. In some years, the gain can be as high as 25%, and in others, there can be an equal amount on the loss side. If you are unable to live with the loss years and find the stress too great, you will not be able to stay the course and so you will not achieve even a modest investment objective. This is why you must recognize your own ability for risk tolerance and build it into the plan at the outset. It may be unrealistic to expect an unduly high rate of return, but it is even more unrealistic to expect such a performance if you cannot live with the pressures and swings in the market.

The degree of risk that can undertaken comfortably will depend on your own character. It is a personal decision, for you are the only person who knows when worries about investments cause a knot in your stomach or result in sleepless nights and so forth. If anything, you should lean on the side of caution, because the loss of principal due to an overly aggressive stance will be far more painful than the fear of losing out. Losing out on a major rally does not take anything away from you, whereas losses in the market do.

Traders

Since positions held by traders are of much shorter time horizon than those of investors, their objectives will also differ. Liquidity and income are not important; the prospect of growth is the uppermost objective in the minds of traders. In this respect, the danger of unrealistic expectations and the concept of risk tolerance should be of primary importance. For instance, you could rationalize that because of the leverage potential for futures trading, the expected return should be equally as great and the results ought to be that much better. If the S&P Index gains an average of 9% per year, it should be possible working on 10% margin to average 90% (i.e., 10 times as much). In reality, it doesn't work that way because to earn the 9% return, it is necessary to sit through some pretty big bear markets that would more than wipe out the equity in the account. The smallest gyrations in markets can have a tremendous effect on the equity in leveraged accounts, so the ability of the trader to know his limits of risk tolerance is that much more crucial.

Since traders are in and out of the markets every day, often on an intraday basis, their need to establish a campaign plan is even greater than someone who has a longer time frame because such a highly volatile environment has little margin for error.

◆ Adopting an Investment or Trading Philosophy

Establishing investment objectives helps to tell you where you want to go and how long it will take you to get there. Adopting a philosophy or approach to trading or investing is the vehicle that will enable you to reach that destination.

As I have said, there are many religions in the world, each taking a different path in search of the truth. In the financial markets, there are also many different investment and trading approaches, each seeking the realization of profits. Your job is not to find the best, because they all have weaknesses. Instead, you need to choose an approach with which you are comfortable, provided, of course, that it works. Because of the leverage involved and the life-saving requirement of not permitting losses to continue, traders usually favor using technical analysis; this enables them to set objective "stop-loss" points. A long-term investor, on the other hand, can afford the luxury of buying a stock with a low price–earnings multiple and patiently waiting for the price to increase. Others prefer to buy companies with high growth rates and high price–earnings ratios, believing that the fast growth of the company will result in higher stock prices. Still another might involve the adoption of the Theory of Contrary Opinion, discussed in Chapters 7 and 8.

Your chances of success will be higher if you combine some concepts of contrary-opinion principles with your chosen approach. For example, if in using technical analysis, you use oversold conditions as a basis for making purchasing decisions, contrary analysis will represent a useful confirmation. If your indicators are pointing out that the market is oversold, but you cannot find much in the way of bearish sentiment, the chances of a meaningful bottom will be much less than if a negative or pessimistic story was splashed on the cover of a major magazine.

The most important thing is to satisfy yourself that your method works. This does not mean researching it back over a few months but making sure that it operated profitably over many different types of market conditions. This is far different from expecting it to work perfectly. We have already established that there is no holy grail. Every market participant, however, needs some kind of foundation for making informed and objective decisions. In practice, individual decisions should not be made in isolation or solely on gut feel, but as part of an overall approach. The outcome will then be a consistent series of rational judgments.

The second principle involved in the adoption of a philosophy is comfort in its use. If you feel perfectly at home and enjoy your adopted philosophy or approach, two benefits will accrue. First, enjoyment implies interest. Interest in turn will encourage you to explore and expand your knowledge of the subject. Second, you will not be receptive when the approach signals the need for action. For example, you may be sold on the idea of buying stocks with low price–earnings multiples. However, if you don't believe in the approach wholeheartedly, it's a good bet that you will find a reason *not to buy* when all your conditions for purchase have been met. The very nature of a market bottom is that it presents a host of reasons for not getting involved. You will need total confidence in your adopted approach, otherwise you will be unable you to overcome the psychological obstacles placed in your way.

An additional consideration is to make sure that your chosen approach is consistent with your temperament. Suppose, for example, that you like the idea of trading the markets on a leveraged basis using a simple 20-day, moving-average crossover system. You buy when the price crosses above the average and sell when it falls below. However, if you do not have the stomach to endure the losses that are bound to arise from losing signals, there is little point in your following the system because you will be certain to lose money. In a similar but opposite vein, you may find some appeal in the idea of buying low multiple stocks that are out of favor and waiting for them to appreciate over a long period of time. However, if you have a trading mentality and lack the patience to wait out the long time interval that is usually necessary between buying and selling, then this perfectly legitimate approach will not work for you, either. You should therefore make sure that your approach or philosophy is not likely to conflict with your personality. Bear in mind, it is much easier to change the methodology than your character makeup.

Another factor worth consideration is your innate abilities and how they might be applied to a specific methodology. Everyone has a different character makeup, where strengths and weaknesses are emphasized in a unique combination. You need to examine your own balance because doing so will help you to choose an appropriate investment or trading approach. For example, if you have an affinity for tape reading or charts, it makes a great deal of sense to adopt a system that incorporates these tools. Alternatively, you may pay a great deal of attention to details and require a substantial number of facts before coming to a decision. In that case, use a methodology that takes advantage of those skills.

The essence of any approach, whether from a trading or investing aspect, is to develop a low-risk idea. Only when you have figured out the odds of winning or losing can you approach the markets with any hope for success.

◆ Establishing a Plan to Maximize Objectivity and Minimize Emotion

The first step in establishing a plan is to adopt a method for distilling a multitude of ideas into one low-risk one. In a sense, the methodology is the framework under which you will be operating. The next step is to set up a written plan that anticipates and overcomes the psychological conflicts that inevitably lie ahead. (See Figure 13–1.)

The advantage of a written plan is that it enables you to be precise. Once it is written, you can easily review its various aspects to make sure that it is consistent, comprehensive, and logical. Having it laid out on a sheet of paper will also reveal whether it has any biases and make it easy to check whether you have taken all the steps.

Most people object to a written plan on the basis that they do not like following rules or that they are far too "intuitive" for such a thing. Others, with the best of intentions, choose to postpone writing the plan, which, of course, never gets written. Intuitive market participants often make good moves but then give back their gains in a series of poor decisions. Results are therefore inconsistent and haphazard.

The benefits of a clearly written and logical plan in such cases are self-evident. Those who do not like to follow rules and

The following quick test can help you decide your investment temperament and ability to take risks for the purposes of asset allocation. It was designed by William G. Droms, a professor of finance at Georgetown University. Value the seven statements on a scale of 1 to 5, from "strongly disagree" with a rating of 1 to 5 for "strongly agree." Then add up your points.

1. Earning a high long-term total return that will allow my capital to grow faster than the inflation rate is one of my most important investment objectives.

2. I would like an investment that provides me with an opportunity to defer taxation of capital gains and/or interest to future years.

3. I do not require a high level of current income from my investments.

4. My major investment goals are relatively long term.

5. I am willing to tolerate sharp up-and-down swings in the return on my investments in order to seek a higher return than would be expected from more stable investments.

6. I am willing to risk a short-term loss in return for a potentially higher rate of return in the long run.

7. I am financially able to accept a low level of liquidity in my investment portfolio.

The following are Mr. Drom's asset allocation recommendations:

Total Score	Money Market	Fixed Income	Equities
30 to 35	10	10	80
22 to 29	20	20	60
14 to 21	30	30	40
7 to 13	40	40	20

Equities include real estate, venture capital, international stocks, gold, domestic stocks. Fixed income investments include American and international bonds.

Figure 13–1 Test for Investment Temperament and Ability to Take Risks for Purposes of Asset Allocation. Source: William G. Droms, Georgetown University.

are unwilling to develop a written plan clearly lack the discipline for profitable market campaigns. Moreover, financial success in the markets requires consistency and you can achieve this only by religiously following a set of predetermined rules.

The establishment of a plan is not a one-step procedure unless by pure chance you hit on the exact formula. The chances are good that your plan will require modification as you learn more about yourself and how you deal with various market situations.

One of the most competent market psychologists, Van K. Tharp, has worked with some of the world's most accomplished traders and has published a course called "Successful Investing" based on his experiences. The course is intended to help traders overcome their weaknesses. Tharp states: "Most people tend to avoid working on themselves. It's too painful. Instead, the issue they have with themselves (e.g., security, self-worth) becomes an issue they have with the market (e.g., profits, losses) . . . . [the trader] simply transfers his problem, transmutes it and then has the same problem [but with a different manifestation]." As an aid in overcoming these very human problems, Tharp recommends that his students establish a plan that involves what he calls "the ten trading tasks." His ideas are essentially meant for traders, but the principles are equally valid for investors and others with a long time horizon. Tharp points out that your mental state and the kind of preparation you undergo before you put on a position will determine whether you are likely to win or lose on a consistent basis. Remember the task of developing a plan is to help you to become as disciplined and objective as possible.

Tharp's steps are a good basis on which to formulate a written plan. Seven of these steps are listed next.

Step 1. Self-Analysis

If you are planning to take a run on a familiar track and want to beat your previous record, logic would tell you not to attempt such a feat if you are sick with a fever. You would be much better advised to make the attempt when you were at your physical peak. The same principle holds true when dealing with markets. If you are psychologically run down due to illness or personal problems, the chances are that you are not going to be able to withstand the psychological turmoil that the markets will cause you. You will still be able to make decisions, but your confused state will reduce your ability to make sound ones at the margin; and it is at the margin that the dividing line is drawn between winners and losers. Consequently, whenever you feel overly stressed because of factors outside the market, you are advised to stay away or to make as few decisions as possible until your condition improves.

We learned in the section on crowd psychology that going against the crowd at the right time can be very profitable. These types of decision by their very nature demand great courage. Anyone who has experienced a profitable trade or investment from such circumstances knows that they are usually the most rewarding. This approach does not come without its contradictions, though. How do you know whether your discomfort in making these difficult decisions stems from simply going against the crowd or whether it's a result of an emotional family dispute?

One obvious solution is to reexamine the contrary case to see whether it makes sense. Tharp also suggests that people should develop a rating scale from 1 to 8 depending on how you feel about yourself on the day in question. Under this system, 1 is terrible and 8 is great. The idea is to spend a quiet 30 seconds in deep thought as to where you stand on the scale that particular day. Over a period of 30 days, you should then compare your daily ratings with your trading performance. Working on the assumption that there is a rough correlation, you are then in a position to establish an objective standard below which you should not trade. The principle of this method can be applied to market participants with a longer time horizon, but clearly the control period would have to be much lengthier as well.

Step 2. Mental Rehearsal

Whatever task you intend to accomplish, the odds of success will be greatly enhanced if you can rehearse it first. In this way, you will be in a better position to anticipate potential problems and will find its execution to be more or less automatic. If you can anticipate problems before they arise, your odds of successfully dealing with any that materialize will be much higher.

Before I give a seminar, for instance, I will typically go through the lecture mentally in my hotel room prior to the actual delivery. Then, if I find that things don't flow in the manner in which I intended, I can make changes. At this stage, I also try to anticipate questions that participants might throw at me. I cannot prepare for all eventualities in this way, but at least I can have confidence that I have mastered my material and am therefore in a better position to deliver it more confidently.

In the marketplace, a trader may anticipate that the market will go against his position. If so, under what conditions should he take losses, or at what price should he set a stop-loss? By mentally rehearsing all the possible alternative outcomes, this trader is then in a more objective position to deal with them and not be knocked psychologically off balance by an unexpected setback.

Step 3. Developing a Low-Risk Idea

We established earlier that the vehicle for establishing low-risk ideas was your chosen investment or trading approach. To carry out these ideas, you will need some information on which to base your decisions. If you follow charts, then you need the latest data either from a data vendor, so that you can plot it on a computer screen, or from a subscription chart service. If your forte is stock picking through fundamental analysis, then you need the data to help you to arrive at a sound decision, and so forth.

In developing these ideas, it helps to isolate yourself from the views of brokers, colleagues, and friends and to come to an independent conclusion. Too much contact with the media can also be a potential problem, since it can easily sway your perceptions away from your chosen objectives. Also, make sure that you have all the facts necessary to make that decision before proceeding. It is amazing how our natural biases perceive that the glass is half full, when in fact it is half empty. A few more facts can often help to offset any structural bullish or bearish biases that you may have.

Step 4. Stalking

Once a low-risk idea has been established through the chosen methodology, the next procedure is to set out the kind of conditions in which it can best be executed (i.e., when the odds of success are greatest). A guerrilla band may come to the conclusion that a low-risk place to attack the army is in town A, but they must then choose a time for the attack. In this case, a public holiday, when the army is celebrating, would greatly increase the odds of success. The element of surprise has been known to militarists from time immemorial, and stalking has been a trademark of predators as well. This idea of choosing when to fight the battle is also relevant to market participants.

Once you have chosen the low-risk idea, the task then becomes one of establishing the most opportune time to act. It may be right now or it may be later. Each situation has its own answer. A technician may decide that a stock is under long-term accumulation but is short-term overbought. In that case, the stalker's task is to wait for a correction to result in an oversold condition. A fundamentalist may come to the conclusion that XYZ Company is cheap, but that they are going to come out with some poor earnings. Better to stalk the investment until the bad news comes out and the price of the stock is temporarily driven down. It may well be that the markets' response to that news is very poor (see Chapter 9). In this case, the stalking should continue until the stock acts better. Alternatively, the exercise may be abandoned at this point in favor of a more attractive candidate.

Step 5. Action

Once the guiding criteria have been established and the required conditions have materialized, it is important to take action. The market will often move quickly at this point so it is important that you act decisively. If you have done your homework, you will have a fairly good idea of what your potential loss will be should the market go against you. In particularly volatile or "fast" markets, it is usually a good idea to place limits on your orders. Limit orders put a cap on how much you are willing to pay for an item. For example, you may have been stalking Company ABC and decide to buy on the day the earnings come out. It may well be that the results are better than the market expected and an order imbalance causes a delayed opening. If you have been doing your homework properly, you would have already established a ceiling price for your low-risk idea, so you need to incorporate this price in your purchase order to make sure that you do not overpay. Remember, even if the stock "gets away" from you, there will always be another opportunity at a later date. Do not under any circumstances allow the emotion of the moment to interfere with a well-thought-out, logical plan.

Step 6. Monitoring

Complacency is the enemy of traders and investors alike. Once the initial position has been taken, there is a temptation to relax in the belief that the task has already been accomplished. Of course, it is not over until the position has been closed out with a profit or loss. The nature of the monitoring task will depend to a large degree on the time frame under consideration. If you are a day trader, then 10 trading tasks will be executed perhaps two or three times a day. For the *long-term investor*, the process will be slower. Even for a person taking the long view, it is still mandatory to follow your position. Many people think that the long-term is a comfortable place to be and that they can hide from the market and not worry about their position. Nothing could be further from the truth. Tharp divides the monitoring process into detailed monitoring for traders and overview monitoring for others with a longer time horizon.

Detailed Monitoring. If the low-risk and stalking exercises have been correctly completed, the trade should move into the profit side more or less right away. Tharp suggests traders should rate the trade to see how it "feels" in a manner similar to the rating exercise in Step 1. This time instead of "1–8," the benchmarks are "easy to difficult." He suggests that the trader undertake this rating three times a day for the first three days at the opening, close, and midpoint of the trading day. If the trade does not feel "easy" after the third day, it will probably turn out to be a bad one.

Overview Monitoring. This level is more suitable for long-term traders and investors. This type of monitoring involves a periodic review of the broad trends in the market or stock in question. Is it responding favorably to good news? Is there any change in your outlook for the economy? Is the technical picture still strong? During this process, it is important to make sure that you can remain as objective as possible. The natural tendency is to emphasize the favorable aspects and turn a blind eye to the negative ones. Expectations have a tendency to be based on hope rather than rational arguments supported by solid facts. Therefore, do not under any circumstances interpret signals according to your expectations. Try as best as you can to look at them objectively. Pretend that you do not have the position you hold and see how it looks from that aspect.

As the monitoring process gets underway, survey the overall environment. As market events unfold, compare them with your original plan and study the implications of these events. You may find, for example, that the market moves against you, bringing the price back to a breakeven point. This need not be an unfavorable sign. Perhaps the news is unexpectedly bad, and the market sells off but holds at support and rebounds. A market that can do this is in good technical shape and should give you encouragement. On the other hand, a stock that sells off on a surprisingly good earnings report is to be questioned, and so forth. The monitoring process is no more than one of risk control. It is telling you to stay with a position, or it throws up reasons why you may need to sell. If you substitute monitoring for complacency, this healthy second process of self-enquiry will result in a far sounder campaign.

Step 7. Getting Out

In this phase, the rule of cutting your losses and letting profits run really begins to apply. Cutting losses applies when you have reached your point of maximum loss. One thing you cannot afford to do is take a big loss. Not only will it affect your mental balance for the next transaction but it also is the fastest way to lose principal. As I mentioned earlier, the first objective of any trading or investment program is to preserve your capital. Only risk capital when a low-risk/high-reward opportunity comes along.

A second reason that justifies liquidating a position occurs when the original rationale for entering the trade or investment market no longer exists. After all, if you bought XYZ Company because you were expecting profits to improve and they actually deteriorate, there is no reason for holding it any longer. In our minds, though, we often have difficulty in accepting this. Perhaps the price is down and we are unwilling to take a loss. Perhaps we feel uncomfortable in calling our broker and letting him know that what was a long-term investment is actually a short-term trade. Where pride of opinion is concerned, our minds can play many tricks on us.

Uncertainty is another factor that should influence you to get out. There is an old trading adage: "When in doubt get out." In any situation, there is always going to be some element of doubt. What we are talking about in this instance is a degree of doubt and uncertainty that is far greater than when the position was initiated. If you are unsure, then you have lost a great deal of the confidence and objectivity needed to continue. Under such circumstances, it is appropriate to reconsider whether it is in your best interest to continue with the position.

Letting profits run is a commendable objective, but you must remember that prices do not move up forever. It is therefore a good idea to establish some objectives at the outset as to what level to take profits. Originally, the position would have been initiated because the risk was considered to be low. If, because of a price rise, the risk is now judged to be correspondingly high, the position should be at least partially liquidated. Moreover, if you have run into some personal emotional problems, it means that your judgment will hampered. After all, if a poor psychological condition can be used as a justification for not entering the market, surely it is equally valid for protecting profits.

The task of taking profits should also be a natural consequence of following the plan. If you plan to buy a stock when it has a price–earnings multiple of 8 and sell it when it gets to 15, then the plan calls for liquidation when it reaches that point. Of course, the situation can be reassessed when the objective has been reached. Perhaps there are very good reasons for maintaining the position for greater gains, but you should at least go through the exercise.

The main thing is to focus on setting realistic goals and being consistent in trying to achieve them. This means staying with the plan and modifying it when necessary. Low-risk ideas are so few and far between that this fact in itself will protect you from the pitfalls of overtrading. Even when you have put the plan into action and have achieved some degree of success, you still must implement one more procedure.

◆ Establishing a Review Process

The principal objective of the review process is to establish whether you have faithfully followed the plan and to see whether it may have to be modified. This process has nothing to do with whether you made or lost money. It is there to examine whether you followed the rules. If you didn't follow the rules, then you have made mistakes. You need to ask yourself why you were unable to follow the rules. Perhaps you anticipated what the market was going to do rather than waiting for the market to give its signal as called for by the rules. Perhaps the plan did call for a specific purchase, but when you called your broker he was able to talk you into buying something else. The reason is not important so long as you are able objectively to examine what went wrong and make a mental effort not to repeat your folly. This is a much better approach than going through a self-recrimination exercise, pointing out how much money you would have made by doing such and such. Reviewing your progress in that way does not teach you anything, and, moreover, it doesn't change the past. In short, it is a waste of mental energy. What has happened has happened, and all you can do is try to learn from the experience and use it as a base on which to build profits for the future.

Another alternative is to go back to the point at which you made the mistake and ask yourself what your options were at the time. Then mentally go through those possibilities, working them through to their possible outcomes. When you have discovered two or three scenarios with positive outcomes, remember them for the next time you are faced with a similar market condition.

This review process should be written down, for it is very easy to forget or to distort what actually went on at the time.

The second part of the review process critiques the plan and the rules themselves. It is a good idea to do this when you are not reflecting on a previous transaction or campaign because it is unreasonable to critique your performance and the plan at the same time. If you feel, with good reason, that the plan and or your objectives need to be changed, then by all means go ahead. Perhaps market conditions or your financial position have changed; perhaps you discover that your tolerance for risk taking is greater or less than you had originally envisaged. Alternatively, you may have just been exposed to a new kind of investment or trading philosophy that you have researched and feel comfortable with. There are many reasons why you might want to change the plan. Be warned against flippant and thoughtless changes, because they will do more harm than good. Treat your plan rather like the U.S. Constitution. It is a solid document, which can be amended only through an arduous process as times and conditions change.

14

Classic
Trading Rules

*If you are intelligent the market will teach
you caution and fortitude, sharpen your wits,
and reduce your pride. If you are foolish and
refuse to learn a lesson, it will ridicule you,
laugh you to scorn, break you, and toss you on
the rubbish-heap.*

—Frank J. Williams

◆ Ten Rules from Bernard Baruch

Baruch listed these rules in his autobiography *Baruch: My Own
Story*. Starting as an office boy at the age of 19, Baruch made his
first million by the age of 35. He then went on to be a trusted
counsel for several Presidents. He states that he was skeptical
about the usefulness of advice and was therefore reluctant to lay
down any hard and fast rules. He offered the following as some
points learned from his personal experience that "might be
worth listing for those who are able to muster the necessary self-
discipline." The rules are simple and self-explanatory.*

---

*This excerpt is taken from *Baruch: My Own Story* by Bernard M. Baruch, 1957, New
York: Holt, Rinehart and Winston. Reprinted with permission.

"Being so skeptical about the usefulness of advice, I have been reluctant to lay down any 'rules' or guidelines on how to invest or speculate wisely. Still, there are a number of things I have learned from my own experience which might be worth listing for those who are able to muster the necessary self-discipline:

1. Don't speculate unless you can make it a full-time job.

2. Beware of barbers, beauticians, waiters—of anyone—bringing gifts of 'inside' information or 'tips.'

3. Before you buy a security, find out everything you can about the company, its management and competitors, its earnings and possibilities for growth.

4. Don't try to buy at the bottom and sell at the top. This can't be done—except by liars.

5. Learn how to take your losses quickly and cleanly. Don't expect to be right all the time. If you have made a mistake, cut your losses as quickly as possible.

6. Don't buy too many different securities. Better have only a few investments which can be watched.

7. Make a periodic reappraisal of all your investments to see whether changing developments have altered their prospects.

8. Study your tax position to know when you can sell to greatest advantage.

9. Always keep a good part of your capital in a cash reserve. Never invest all your funds.

10. Don't try to be a jack of all investments. Stick to the field you know best."

◆ Eleven Rules from Robert Meier

Bob Meier has spent many years writing about and trading futures. He is a personal friend and has given me much encouragement in writing this book. He offers several simple but important rules. Number 10, "Never trade with serious personal problems," is extremely sound. In this day of fast moving technology and high stress, the potential for personal problems is much greater than it ever was. It is impossible to maintain a sense of objectivity when you are down emotionally. Far better in the long run not to trade at all until you can regain a sense of psychological well-being; confident objective decisions are then easier to make.*

The following rules are by Robert H. Meier:

1. Ask yourself what you really want. Many traders loose money because subconsciously their goal is entertainment, not profits. If you are serious about becoming a successful speculator, carefully examine your trading to eliminate destructive compulsiveness such as constantly calling your broker when there is no legitimate reason, and putting on trades "just to be in the market."

2. Assume personal trade responsibility for all actions. A defining trait of top performing traders is their willingness to assume personal responsibility for *all* trading decisions. People who habitually blame their broker, the market itself, bad order fills, or insider manipulation for losses, are never successful.

3. Keep it simple and consistent. Most speculators follow too many indicators and listen to so many different opinions that they are overwhelmed into action. Few people realize that many of the greatest traders of all time never rely on more than two or three core indicators and never listen to the opinions of others.

4. Have realistic expectations. When expectations are too high, it results in overtrading underfinanced positions, and very high levels of greed and fear—making objective decision-making impossible.

5. Learn to wait. Most of the time for most speculators, it is best to be out of the markets, unless you are in an option selling (writing) program. Generally, the part-time speculator will only encounter six to ten clear-cut major opportunities a year. These

---

*Robert H. Meier & Associates, Inc., 335 College Avenue, P.O. Box 667, DeKalb, IL 60115 (815) 758-3808. Robert Meier is a widely published commodity broker, associated with the Rosenthal Collins Group, Fox Investments Division, in Chicago, Illinois. Reprinted with permission.

are the type of trades the savvy professionals train themselves to wait for.

6. Clearly understand the Risk/Reward Ratio. The consensus is that trades with a one to three or one to four Risk/Reward Ratio are sufficient, but this is not true unless you are a floor trader in the pit. There are trades with Risk/Reward Ratios as attractive as one to ten that periodically present themselves to those willing to exercise the ongoing market monitoring discipline required. That is what professionals do.

7. Always check the big picture. Before making any trade, check it against weekly and monthly as well as daily range charts. Frequently, this extra step will identify major longer-term zones of support and resistance that are not apparent on daily charts and that substantially change the perceived Risk/Reward Ratio. Point & Figure charts are particularly valuable in identifying breakouts from big congestion/accumulation formations.

8. Always under-trade. It is easy to forget just how powerful the leverage is in futures and options. It is not uncommon to find speculators holding positions two or three times larger than is justified by their account size. By consciously under-trading, that is taking positions much smaller than you might be able to, you will gradually learn to hold back until you find the real money-making opportunities and stay with major trends.

9. Define your broker relationship. A full-service commodity broker can be a valuable ally, but should not be pushed into the position of making your final decisions. Never tell a broker "do what you think best and call me later."

10. Never trade with serious personal problems. Ignoring this rule is a prescription for disaster. The clarity of thought and emotional control required even for part-time speculator is so great that it is impossible to handle along with serious personal problems. Likewise, trading should not be attempted during periods of ill health, even including a bad head cold.

11. Ignore the news media. The true goals of the national news media are to shock, agitate, entertain, and editorialize a socialist agenda—not provide usable information. Many of the

finest traders avoid all contact with public news, knowing how profoundly it can undermine a trading plan. The more important trading profits are to you, the less you can afford to follow the "news."

◆ Seventeen Rules from S. A. Nelson

S.A. Nelson wrote around the turn of the century. Some of his rules relate to concepts that are different from today's; trading in "10 share lots" for example. Nevertheless, human nature remains more or less constant, so the general undertone of these rules is as valid in the current environment as it ever was.*

1. Bull markets and bear markets run four and five years at a time. Determine by the average prices, which one is under way.

2. Determine the stock or stocks to trade in. They should be railroad stocks, dividend payers, not too low, nor too high, fairly active, and for the bull side below their value; for the bear side above their value. Values are determined roughly by the earnings available for dividends.

3. Observe the position of your stock with relation to recent fluctuations. In a bull market, the time to begin to buy is when a stock has had four or five points decline from the last previous top. In a bear market, the time to begin to sell is when such a stock has had three or four points rally from the bottom.

4. Stick to the stock bought until a fair profit or until there is good reason for deciding that the first estimate of value was wrong. Remember than an active stock will generally rally from $3/8$ per cent. to $5/8$ per cent. of the amount of its decline under adverse conditions and more than that under favorable conditions.

5. Have money enough to see a decline through without becoming uneasy or over-burdened. $2,500 ought to take care of a

---

*This excerpt is taken from *The A B C of Stock Speculation* by S. A. Nelson, 1964, Wells: Fraser Publishing Company. (First published 1903; copyright S. A. Nelson.) Reprinted with permission.

ten-share scale every point down—that is to say, supposing the first lot to be bought five points down from the top, $2,500 ought to carry the scale until the natural recovery from the low point brings the lot out with a profit on the average cost. It will not do to expect a profit on every lot, but only on the average. In a bull market it is better to always work on the bull side; in a bear market, on the bear side. There are usually more rallies in a bear market than there are relapses in a bull market.

6. Do not let success in making money in ten-share lots create a belief that a bolder policy will be wiser and begin to trade in 100-share lots with inadequate capital. A few hundred-share losses will wipe out a good many ten-share profits.

7. There is not usually much difficulty in dealing in ten-share lots on the short side. If one broker does not wish to do it, another probably will, especially for a customer who amply protects his account and who seems to understand what he is doing.

A close student of speculation in all its forms as conducted on the exchanges of this country has arrived at the following conclusions, which, he says, in application to speculation are "universal laws." He divides his conclusions into two groups, laws absolute and laws conditional.

Laws absolute. *Never overtrade.* To take an interest larger than the capital justifies is to invite disaster. With such an interest, a fluctuation in the market unnerves the operator, and his judgment becomes worthless.

1. Never "double-up"; that is, never completely and at once reverse a position. Being "long," for instance, do not "sell out" and go as much "short." This may occasionally succeed, but is very hazardous, for should the market begin again to advance, the mind reverts to its original opinion and the speculator "covers up" and "goes long" again. Should this last change be wrong, complete demoralization ensues. The change in the original position should have been made moderately, cautiously, thus keeping the judgment clear and preserving the balance of mind.

2. "Run quick" or not at all; that is to say, act promptly at the first approach of danger, but failing to do this until others see the danger hold on or close out part of the "interest."

3. *Another rule is,* when doubtful *reduce the amount of the interest;* for either the mind is not satisfied with the position taken, or the interest is too large for safety. One man told another that he could not sleep on account of his position in the market; his friend judiciously and laconically replied: "Sell down to a sleeping point."

Rules conditional. These rules are subject to modification, according to the circumstances, individuality and temperament of the speculator.

1. *It is better to "average up" than to "average down."* This opinion is contrary to the one commonly held and acted upon; it being the practice to buy and on a decline buy more. This reduces the average. Probably four times out of five this method will result in striking a reaction in the market that will prevent loss, but the fifth time, meeting with a permanently declining market, the operator loses his head and closes out, making a heavy loss—a loss so great as to bring complete demoralization often ruin.

But "buying up" is the reverse of the method just explained; that is to say, buying at first moderately and as the market advances adding slowly and cautiously to the "line." This is a way of speculating that requires great care and watchfulness, for the market will often (probably four times out of five) react to the point of "average." *Here lies the danger. Failure to close out at the point of average destroys the safety of the whole operation.* Occasionally (probably four times out of five) a permanently advancing market is met with and a big profit secured. In such an operation the original risk is small, the danger at no time great, and when successful the profit is large. This method should only be employed when an important advance or decline is expected, and with a moderate capital can be undertaken with comparative safety.

2. To *"buy down"* requires a long purse and a strong nerve, and ruin often overtakes those who have both nerve and money. The stronger the nerve the more probability of staying too long. There is, however, a class of successful operators who "buy down" and hold on. They deal in relatively small amounts. Entering the market prudently with the determination of holding on for a long period, they are not disturbed by its fluctuations. They are men of good judgment, who buy in times of depression to hold for a general revival of business—an investing rather than a speculating class.

3. In all ordinary circumstances my advice would be to buy at once an amount that is within the proper limits of capital, etc., "selling out" at a loss or profit, according to judgment. *The rule is to stop losses and let profits run.* If small profits are taken, then small losses should be taken. Not to have the courage to accept a loss and to be too eager to take a profit, is fatal. It is the ruin of many.

4. Public opinion is not to be ignored. A strong speculative current is for the time being overwhelming, and should be closely watched. The rule is, to act cautiously with public opinion, against it, boldly. To so go with the market even when the basis is a good one, is dangerous. It may at any time turn and rend you. Every speculator knows the danger of too much "company." It is equally necessary to exercise caution in going against the market. This caution should be continued to the point of wavering—of loss of confidence—when the market should be boldly encountered to the full extent of strength, nerve and capital. The market has a pulse, on which the hand of the operator should be placed as that of the physician on the wrist of the patient. This pulse-beat must be the guide when and how to act.

5. *Quiet, weak markets are good markets to sell.* They ordinarily develop into declining markets. *But when a market has gone through the stages of quiet and weak to active and declining, then on to semi-panic or panic, it should be bought freely.* When, vice versa, a quiet and firm market develops into activity and strength, then into excitement, it should be sold with great confidence.

6. In forming an opinion of the market the element of chance ought not to be omitted. There is a doctrine of chances—Napoleon, in his campaign, allowed a margin for chances—for the accidents that come in to destroy or modify the best calculation. Calculation must measure the incalculable. In the "reproof of chance lies the true proof of men." *It is better to act on general than special information* (it is not so *misleading*), vis.: *the state of the country, the condition of the crops, manufactures, etc. Statistics are valuable, but they must be kept subordinate to a comprehensive view of the whole situation.* Those who confine themselves too closely to statistics are poor guides. "There is nothing," said Canning, "so fallacious as facts except figures." *"When in doubt do nothing." Don't enter the market on half conviction; wait till the convictions are full matured.*

7. I have written to little purpose unless I have left the impression that the fundamental principle that lies at the base of all speculation is this: *Act so as to keep the mind clear, its judgment trustworthy.* A reserve force should therefore be maintained and kept for supreme moments, when the full strength of the whole man should be put on the stroke delivered.

◆ Thirty-Two Rules from Peter Wyckoff

Peter Wyckoff was a well-known Wall Street research analyst of the 1960s. In his book, he lists a number of rules at the end of each chapter.* Those presented here are just a few of the most useful ones. Rule 15 concerning the conversion of weak points into strong ones is particularly compelling and unusual. Anyone wishing to establish a personal set of rules would be well advised to consider the 32 listed here, especially as they emphasize the need to combine technical and fundamental analysis.

1. Speculation demands cool judgment, self-reliance, courage, pliability and prudence.

---

*This list is taken from *The Psychology of Stock Market Timing* by Peter Wyckoff, 1968 (fifth printing), Englewood Cliffs, NJ: Prentice-Hall. Reprinted with permission.

2. A person's planned buying policy should always dovetail closely with a predetermined selling policy.

3. When in doubt about what to do in the market, do nothing. Nothing can destroy the cool temperament of a man like unsystematic speculation.

4. Look after the losses and the profits will take care of themselves.

5. If you wait too long to buy, until every uncertainty is removed and every doubt is lifted at the bottom of a market cycle, you may keep on waiting . . . and waiting.

6. The worst losses in the market come from uninformed people buying greatly overvalued stocks.

7. Whenever hope becomes a chief factor in determining a market position, sell out promptly.

8. Never buy or sell merely on the basis of background statistics. Technical market considerations and psychology must also be taken into account.

9. Don't believe everything a corporate official says about his company's stock.

10. Check over all the facts carefully yourself and view them conjunctively with other known market factors.

11. Never speculate with the money you need to live. If you can't *afford* a possible loss, stay out of the market.

12. One way to win in the market is to avoid doing what most others are doing.

13. When opinions in Wall Street are too unanimous—BEWARE! The market is famous for doing the unexpected.

14. Never cancel a Stop, or lower it, as the stock nears a trading point in a fast sliding market.

15. Try to analyze your weak points and convert them into strong ones.

16. Forget the idea that speculation depends entirely upon luck, and guard against blind faith in the suggestions of other men.

17. Eliminate trust in any system you do not understand, but still believe in the basic idea of the system.

18. You should consult other market aids besides charts.

19. Never be sentimental about a stock.

20. Before investing in a stock, look into its history.

21. You should be impervious to external forces and have no preconceived opinions to be a successful tape reader. Only the price changes appearing on the tape with attendant trading volume will tell you what to do and when to do it.

22. Always try to look and plan ahead, rather than considering just the last sales bobbing in front of you. The printed prices you see may have already largely discounted the news as it generally is known.

23. Tape reading is no exact science. You cannot form any definite rules, because all markets differ. Therefore, you must work out your own operational methods.

24. Be pliable at all times, but don't overtrade. Plan each campaign carefully, and never blame the tape for any error *you* may make.

25. You should be able to differentiate between what has been, what is now and what the future will be in planning a trading program.

26. Before taking a position, determine exactly where the stock you are watching, or the general market, stands. A study of price, breadth, activity, time and volume will be helpful in this respect.

27. Whatever is hard to do in the market is generally the right thing; and whatever is easy is usually the wrong thing to do.

28. Take an occasional mental inventory to find out exactly where you stand.

29. Do not press yourself! "Speculitis" is malignant!

30. When buying a stock, you should consider how far down it might carry in the event your judgment about it is wrong.

31. Try to avoid holding postmortem examinations of the "might have beens" in the market.

32. Buy the stocks of companies that have shown gradually increasing earnings in industries making articles that people cannot well do without.

◆ *Twenty-Eight Rules from W. D. Gann*

W. D. Gann wrote a great deal about the markets. These rules were taken from his book *How to Make Profits in Commodities,* first published in 1942.* Gann had an active trading career but was not particularly successful. His work has become a lot more popular since the 1980s than when he was alive. In the book's foreword, he stated, "Trading in commodities is not a gambling business . . . but a practical, safe business when conducted on business principles." His rules are aimed at traders. I particularly like Rule 11, "Accumulate a surplus . . . ." One of the most common mistakes made by traders is not knowing when to quit. If you put some profits to one side, this guarantees that you will walk away from the table with at least something, however many mistakes you might make elsewhere.

In order to make a success trading in the commodity market, the trader must have definite rules and follow them. The rules given below are based upon my personal experience and anyone who follows them will make a success.

1. Amount of capital to use: Divide your capital into 10 equal parts and never risk more than one-tenth of your capital on any one trade.

2. Use *stop loss orders.* Always protect a trade when you make it with a *stop loss order* 1 to 3 cents, never more than 5 cents away, cotton 20 to 40, never more than 60 points away.

3. Never overtrade. This would be violating your capital rules.

---

*These rules are taken from *How to Make Profits Trading in Commodities* by W. D. Gann, 1976, Pomeroy: Lambert-Gann Publishing Co. (Original copyright 1942 by Edward Lambert.) Reprinted with permission.

4. Never let a profit run into a loss. After you once have a profit of 3 cents or more, raise your *stop loss order* so that you will have no loss of capital. For cotton when the profits are 60 points or more place *stop* where there will be no loss.

5. Do not buck the trend. Never buy or sell if you are not sure of the trend according to your charts and rules.

6. When in doubt, get out, and don't get in when in doubt.

7. Trade only in active markets. Keep out of slow, dead ones.

8. Equal distribution of risk. Trade in 2 or 3 different commodities, if possible. Avoid tying up all your capital in any one commodity.

9. Never limit your orders or fix a buying or selling price. Trade at the market.

10. Don't close your trades without a good reason. Follow up with a *stop loss order* to protect your profits.

11. Accumulate a surplus. After you have made a series of successful trades, put some money into a surplus account to be used only in emergency or in times of panic.

12. Never buy or sell just to get a scalping profit.

13. Never average a loss. This is one of the worst mistakes a trader can make.

14. Never get out of the market just because you have lost patience or get into the market because you are anxious from waiting.

15. Avoid taking small profits and big losses.

16. Never cancel a *stop loss order* after you have placed it at the time you make a trade.

17. Avoid getting in and out of the market too often.

18. Be just as willing to sell short as you are to buy. Let your object be to keep with the trend and make money.

19. Never buy just because the price of a commodity is low or sell short just because the price is high.

20. Be careful about pyramiding at the wrong time. Wait until the commodity is very active and has crossed Resistance Levels before buying more and until it has broken out of the zone of distribution before selling more.

21. Select the commodities that show strong uptrend to pyramid on the buying side and the ones that show definite downtrend to sell short.

22. Never hedge.If you are long of one commodity and it starts to go down, do not sell another commodity short to hedge it. Get out at the market; take your loss and wait for another opportunity.

23. Never change your position in the market without a good reason. When you make a trade, let it be for some good reason or according to some definite rule; then do not get out without a definite indication of a change in trend.

24. Avoid increasing your trading after a long period of success or a period of profitable trades.

25. Don't guess when the market is top. Let the market prove it is top. Don't guess when the market is bottom. Let the market prove it is bottom. By following definite rules, you can do this.

26. Do not follow another man's advice unless you know that he knows more than you do.

27. Reduce trading after first loss; never increase.

28. Avoid getting in wrong and out wrong; getting in right and out wrong; this is making double mistakes.

When you decide to make a trade be sure that you are not violating any of these 28 rules which are vital and important to your success. When you close a trade with a loss, go over these rules and see which rule you have violated; then do not make the same mistake the second time. Experience and investigation will convince you of the value of these rules, and observation and study will lead you to a correct and practical theory for successful Trading in Commodities.

◆ *Rules from Frank J. Williams*

Frank Williams book, originally published in 1930, contains numerous rules. One important area he seems to emphasize is sound money management through such suggestions as "Pay all bills before speculating," "The broker who demands a large margin is your friend," and "Don't take fliers." He reminds us of an important point that we all tend to forget: "The market moves up slowly, but comes down fast." It is another way of warning us to take precautions against the unexpected.*

Pay all bills before speculating.

Don't speculate with another person's money.

Don't neglect your business to speculate.

If the market makes you irritable or interferes with sleep, you are wrong.

Don't use in the market money that you need for other purposes.

Don't go "joint account" with a friend—play a lone hand.

Don't give a broker "discretionary powers." If you can't run your own account, leave the market alone.

The broker who demands a large margin is your friend. Only a bucket-shop wants you to trade on a slender margin.

Don't buy more stock than you can safely carry. Over-trading means forced selling and losses.

Get accurate information. Demand facts, not opinions.

Don't take advice from uninformed people—they know no more than you about the market.

---

*This excerpt is taken from *If You Must Speculate Learn the Rules* by Frank J. Williams, 1981 (second printing), Burlington, VT: Fraser Publishing Company. (First published 1930.) Reprinted with permission.

Such advice as "I think well of it" or "It is a cinch" means nothing.

Use only a part of your capital in speculation.

Don't buy "cats and dogs" (unseasoned stocks).

Buy good standard stocks that have stood the test of time.

Remember that good stocks always come back—unknown stocks may disappear.

Don't buy in a hurry—there is plenty of time to buy good stocks.

Investigate each stock thoroughly before you buy.

Remember that it is easier to buy than to sell. The salability of a stock is very important.

The market moves up slowly, but goes down fast.

Be prepared to buy your stock outright if necessary. If you can't do this, you are taking chances.

Buy in a selling market—when nobody wants stock.

Sell in a buying market—when everybody wants stock.

The market is most dangerous when it looks best; it is most inviting when it looks worst.

Don't get too active. Many trades many losses.

Long-pull trades are most profitable.

Don't try to outguess the market.

Look out for the buying fever; it is a dangerous disease.

Don't try to pick the top and the bottom of the market.

Don't dream in the stock-market; have some idea just how far your stock can go.

Remember that the majority of traders are always buying at the top and selling at the bottom.

Don't worry over the profits you might have made.

Don't spend your paper profits—they might turn into losses.

Watch the news. Remember that the market actually is a barometer of business and credit.

Don't buy fads or novelties—be sure the company you are becoming a partner in makes something everybody wants.

Don't finance new inventions unless you are wealthy.

Ask who manages the company whose stock you want to buy.

Don't follow pool operations. The pools are out to get you.

Don't listen to or give tips. Good tips are scarce and they take a long time to materialize.

Don't take flyers.

Don't treat your losses lightly; they are serious. You are losing actual currency.

When you win, don't get reckless; put your winnings in the bank for a while.

Don't talk about the market—you will attract too much idle gossip.

Sniff at inside information; it is usually bunk. The big people don't talk about their operations.

Don't speculate unless you have plenty of time to think about it.

Fortunes are not easily made in Wall Street. Some professionals give their lives to the market and die poor.

There is such a thing as luck, but it does not hold all the time.

Don't pyramid.

Don't average unless you are sure you know your stock.

Don't buy more stock than you can afford, just to look big. If you are a ten-share man, don't be ashamed of it.

Beware of a stock that is given an abundance of publicity.

Use your mistakes as object-lessons—the person who makes the same mistake twice deserves no sympathy.

Don't open an account at the broker's just to oblige a friend. Charity and speculation don't mix.

Remember that many people believe they can find better use for your money than you can yourself.

Leave short selling to experienced professionals.

If you must sell short, pick a widely held stock or you may get caught in a corner.

Money made easily in the market is never valued—easy come, easy go.

Don't blame the Stock Exchange for your own mistakes.

Don't shape your financial policy on what your barber advises—hundreds of experts are waiting to give you exact information.

Don't let emotion or prejudice warp your judgment. Base your operations on facts.

◆ *Ten Rules from H. J. Wolf*

H. J. Wolf's two-volume book *Studies in Stock Speculation* was originally published in 1926. In the introduction to the 1966 edition Jim Fraser, the book's publisher, reminds us, "Success means adapting Wall Street knowledge to one's individual needs and emotional make-up." He was no doubt influenced in making this statement by some of Wolf's rules, which are strongly oriented to the maintenance of trading discipline through money management controls.*

1. Do Not Overtrade. Maintain a margin of not less than 10 points on stocks quoted under $50 a share, not less than 20 points on stocks quoted from $50 to $100 a share, and 20% on stocks selling above $100 a share.

2. Limit Losses. Place stops at technical danger points on all trades, and if the location of the danger point is uncertain use a 2-point or 2-point stop, or await a better opportunity.

3. Follow the Trend. Do not buck the trend, and do not hedge. Be either long or short, but not both at the same time.

4. Favor Active Issues. Do not tie up funds in obscure or inactive stocks, and avoid thin-market issues except in long-pull operations.

5. Buy during Weakness. Buy only after reactions confirming higher support.

6. Sell during Strength. Close out on unusual advances at first sign of hesitation; and sell short only after evidence of distribution with lower support followed by lower top.

7. Distribute Risk. Do not concentrate in one issue, but trade in equal lots of several different issues, aloof which are definitely attractive. Avoid spreading over too many different issues.

8. Protect Profits. Never let a 3-point profit run into a loss, and never accept a reaction of over 5 points unless the favorable trend of the stock has been definitely established.

9. Avoid Uncertainty. When the trend is in doubt, stay out. Avoid a trader's market when the ultimate trend is uncertain unless the trade can be protected by a small stop and justifies the risk.

---

*These rules are excerpted from *Studies in Stock Speculation, Volume II*, by H. J. Wolf, 1985, Burlington, VT: Fraser Publishing Company. (First published 1926 by Ticker Publishing Company, New York.) Reprinted with permission.

10. Discount Fundamental Outlook. Never ignore fundamental conditions, and always favor the trade wherein fundamental and technical conditions cooperate. Avoid a trade wherein fundamental and technical conditions are opposed, except in cases of imminent liquidation, or overextended short interest.

◆ *Eight Rules from T. T. Hoyne*

Thomas Hoyne's book on speculation was first published in 1922. The main thrust of his rules tells us to think for ourselves, which is by no means a bad idea.*

1. Speculation is an art. The first principle of every art is to have at the outset a clear conception of the end aimed at.

2. The second great general rule for successful speculation is, Never enter upon any speculation without clearly conceiving precisely the amount of profit that is sought and exactly the amount of loss that will be submitted to in the effort to secure that profit.

3. Every speculator must think for himself.

4. A person must at all times strive to maintain the correct point of view towards the market in which he is trading. This contemplates the effect of the market on himself and other speculators; and their effect upon it.

5. A speculator should first determine never to do anything at all with a haste that precludes forethought.

6. As the first aim of every speculator should be to hold himself free from all crowd influence, he should not, because of greed, at the very outset make his speculation so large in proportion to his available capital that a comparatively small fluctuation against him puts him into a group of speculators psychologically

---

*This excerpt is taken from *Speculation: Its Sound Principles and Rules for Its Practice* by Thomas Temple Hoyne, 1988, Burlington, VT: Fraser Publishing Co., a division of Fraser Management Associates, Inc. (Original copyright 1922 by Thomas Temple Hoyne.) Reprinted with permission.

on the verge of fear and on the point of being swept into crowd action.

7. Never should you accept as authoritative any explanation from any other person for a past action of the market. Think out that action for yourself.

8. A speculator must think for himself, and must do his thinking rigidly in accordance with the method of reasoning he has laid down.

◆ Nineteen Rules from Victor Sperandeo

These rules are taken from Victor Sperandeo's excellent book *Trader Vic—Methods of a Wall Street Master.** His claim to fame is a successful trading career spanning more than 23 years. The rules are designed principally for short-term traders although many of them could be profitably adopted by people with a longer time horizon. Number 17 is unusual: "Never trade if your success depends on a good execution." This reminds us that if a trade has such a small potential, it should not be done at all. I particularly like number 19, "Know and follow the Rules." After all, what is the point of having rules if you don't use them?

Rule Number 1: Trade with a plan and stick to it.

Rule Number 2: Trade with the trend. "The trend is your friend!"

Rule Number 3: Use stop loss orders whenever practical.

Rule Number 4: When in doubt, get out!

Rule Number 5: Be patient. Never overtrade.

Rule Number 6: Let your profits run; cut your losses short.

---

*These rules appeared in *Trader Vic—Methods of a Wall Street Master* by Victor Sperandeo, with T. Sullivan Brown, 1991, New York: John Wiley & Sons. Reprinted with permission.

Rule Number 7: Never let a profit run into a loss. (Or always take a free position if you can.)

Rule Number 8: Buy weakness and sell strength. Be just as willing to sell as you are to buy.

Rule Number 9: Be an investor in the early stages of bull markets. Be a speculator in the latter stages of bull markets and in bear markets.

Rule Number 10: Never average a loss—don't add to a losing position.

Rule Number 11: Never buy just because the price is low. Never sell just because the price is high.

Rule Number 12: Trade only in liquid markets.

Rule Number 13: Never initiate a position in a fast market.

Rule Number 14: Don't trade on the basis of "tips." In other words, "trade with the trend, not your friend." Also, no matter how strongly you feel about a stock or other market, don't offer unsolicited tips or advice.

Rule Number 15: Always analyze your mistakes.

Rule Number 16: Beware of "Takeunders."

Rule Number 17: Never trade if your success depends on a good execution.

Rule Number 18: Always keep your own records of trades.

Rule Number 19: Know and follow the Rules!

Bibliography

Angly, Edward. (1988). *Oh Yeah?* [Compiled from newspapers and public records.] Burlington, VT: Fraser. (Originally published in 1931 by the Viking Press.)

Barach, Roland. (1988). *MINDTRAPS: Mastering the Inner World of Investing.* Homewood: Dow Jones-Irwin.

Baruch, Bernard M. (1957) *Baruch: My Own Story.* New York: Holt, Rinehart and Winston.

Crane, Burton. (1959, 7th printing). *The Sophisticated Investor.* New York: Simon & Schuster.

Douglas, Mark. (1990). *The Disciplined Trader.* New York: New York Institute of Finance, a division of Simon & Schuster.

Dreman, David. (1977). *Psychology and the Stock Market: Investment Strategy beyond Random Walk.* New York: AMACOM.

Dreman, David. (1979). *Contrarian Investment Strategy.* New York: Random House.

Drew, G. A. (1941, 2nd ed.). *New Methods for Profit in the Stock Market.* Boston: Metcalf Press.

Fraser, James L. (1967). *10 Ways To Become Rich.* Wells, England: Fraser.

Fraser, James L. (1978, 2nd printing). *10 Rules For Investing.* Burlington, VT: Fraser.

Gann, W. D. (1976). *How to Make Profits Trading in Commodities.* Pomeroy: Lambert-Gann. (Original copyright 1942 by Edward Lambert.)

Gibson, Thomas. (1965). *The Facts about Speculation.* Burlington, VT: Fraser. (First published 1923 by Thomas Gibson, New York.)

Harper, Henry Howard. (1984, 3rd printing). *The Psychology of Speculation: The Human Element in Stock Market Transactions.* Burlington, VT: Fraser. (First published 1926 by Henry Howard Harper, Boston.)

Hoyne, Thomas Temple. (1988). *Speculation: Its Sound Principles and Rules for Its Practice.* Burlington, VT: Fraser, a division of Fraser Management Associates, Inc. (Original copyright 1922 by Thomas Temple Hoyne.)

Le Bon, Gustave. (1982, 2nd ed.). *The Crowd: A Study of the Popular Mind.* Atlanta, GA: Cherokee.

Lefevre, Edwin. (1980). *Reminiscences of a Stock Operator.* Burlington, VT: Books of Wall Street, a division of Fraser Management Associates. (First published 1923 by George H. Doran, New York.)

Livermore, Jesse L. (1940). *How to Trade in Stocks.* New York: Duell, Sloan & Pearce.

Loeb, Gerald M. (1988). *The Battle for Investment Survival.* Burlington: Fraser Publishing Company. (Originally published by Simon & Schuster, New York.)

Neill, Humphrey B. (1959, reprint ed.). *Tape Reading And Market Tactics.* Saxtons River: Neill Letters of Contrary Opinion. (Original edition published 1931 by B. C. Forbes, New York.)

Neill, Humphrey B. (1975). *The Ruminator.* Caldwell: Caxton Printers.

Neill, Humphrey B. (1980, 4th ed.). *The Art of Contrary Thinking.* Caldwell: Caxton Printers.

Nelson, S. A. (1964). *The A B C of Stock Speculation.* Burlington, VT: Fraser. (First published 1903, copyright S. A. Nelson.)

Pring, Martin J. (1991). *Technical Analysis Explained.* New York: McGraw-Hill.

Schabacker, R. W. (1934). *Stock Market Profits.* New York: B. C. Forbes.

Schwager, Jack D. (1989). *Market Wizards: Interviews with Top Traders.* New York: New York Institute of Finance, a division of Simon & Schuster.

Selden, G. C. (1986, 4th printing). *Psychology of the Stock Market.* Burlington, VT: Fraser. (First published 1912 by Ticker, New York.)

Sokoloff, Kiril. (1978). *The Thinking Investor's Guide to the Stock Market.* New York: McGraw-Hill.

Sperandeo, Victor with Brown, T. Sullivan. (1991). *Trader Vic—Methods of a Wall Street Master.* New York: John Wiley & Sons.

Tharp, Van (1990). *Investment Psychology Guides.* Cary, NC: Investment Psychology Consulting.

Thurlow, Bradbury K. (1981). *Rediscovering the Wheel: Contrary Thinking and Investment Strategy.* Burlington, VT: Fraser.

Train, John (1980). *The Money Masters.* New York: Harper & Row.

Williams, Frank J. (1981, 2nd printing). *If You Must Speculate Learn the Rules.* Burlington, VT: Fraser. (First published 1930.)

Wolf, H. J. (1984, 3rd printing). *Studies in Stock Speculation.* Burlington, VT: Fraser. (First published 1924 by Ticker, New York.)

Wolf, H. J. (1985, 3rd printing). *Studies in Stock Speculation, Volume II.* Burlington: Fraser. (First published 1926 by Ticker, New York.)

Wyckoff, Peter. (1968, 5th printing). *The Psychology of Stock Market Timing.* Englewood Cliffs, NJ: Prentice-Hall.

Wyckoff, Richard D. (1924). *How I Trade and Invest in Stocks and Bonds.* New York: The Magazine of Wall Street.

Wyckoff, Richard D. (1984). *Jesse Livermore's Methods of Trading in Stocks.* Brightwaters: Windsor Books.

Index

Special Introductory Offer:

A three-month subscription for $45.00 of the Pring Market Review for readers of this book (coupon must be enclosed).

Name_____

Company Name_____

Address_____

City_____State and ZIP_____

Telephone_____

❑MC ❑ Visa ❑ Amex ❑Check Enclosed

Card No. _____

Expiration Date_____

Signature_____

In U.S. Funds Only!

Comments or Specific Interest:

_____
_____
_____

Return to:
International Institute for Economic Research
P.O. Box 329
Washington Depot, CT 06794
203-868-7772   Fax 203-868-2683